at home

in the 17th century

edited by
Sara van Dijk

authors
Maartje Brattinga
Alexander Dencher
Femke Diercks
Sara van Dijk
Suzanne van Leeuwen
Marijn Stolk

with the collaboration of
Martijn de Rooij

RIJKS MUSEUM

foreword

What was daily life like in the seventeenth century? That flourishing period of Dutch art and architecture sometimes still feels remarkably close by. In many cities the façades still stand tall, even now forming the backdrop to everyday life for the people who live and work there. And a hushed interior by Johannes Vermeer or Pieter de Hooch in the Rijksmuseum offers viewers the illusion of stepping inside the serene atmosphere of a seventeenth-century house. The doll's houses also on display in the museum, which invite the gaze to wander from cellar to attic, make the seventeenth-century world even more tangible.

But Dutch cities have changed, painters adapted reality as they saw fit, and dolls' houses present an idealised picture of a wealthy household. All of this fuels our curiosity about the reality behind these iconic works of art. What did a day in a seventeenth-century household really look like? To answer that question, this book and the exhibition of the same name focus on people and the objects they gathered in their homes.

The Rijksmuseum's collection of applied arts offers a fantastic point of departure. Ever since the nineteenth century, the museum has been collecting highlights of the decorative arts, including furniture, ceramics, metalworks and textiles, and it employs curators specialising in all these areas. At the same time, the division into these subcategories has led to separate study of each material type and drawn attention away from the context in which all these objects were used. Furthermore, the focus has traditionally been on the artistic merit of an object's design and the skill of its execution – and thus on art objects. But when we turn our attention to daily life, we wish to know about more than just the most beautiful chair and most fashionable bed. We become curious about the pots and pans, the brooms, and the children's toys – all the ordinary types of objects that so often pass through our hands. And that is not to mention everything that has vanished: the food, the smells, the sounds, and above all the people who accumulated and used all those objects.

For this exhibition, our group of curators therefore worked with an archaeologist and an anthropologist. They also co-organised a symposium series,
in productive partnership with the NWO project Freedom of the Streets
led by Danielle van den Heuvel, professor of early modern economic and
social history at Utrecht University, and with the Leiden University Centre
for the Arts in Society (LUCAS). Furthermore, we are exceptionally de-
lighted to be continuing our association with the Victoria and Albert
Museum, in the form of a Strategic Partnership Programme.

Our special thanks go to Marijke Aalders, who showed
great interest in this project and made this publication possible through
her generous contribution. The appointment of an archaeologist was made
possible by the Fonds Dirk Jan van Orden and the Lucy en Bas van der
Vlist Fonds, both by way of the Rijksmuseum Fonds. We also wish to thank
our private donors for their financial contribution to additional research
on the Sonck family's cesspit, which has revealed to us not only what
cookware they used but also what they made in it – a unique achievement
in archaeological research. Furthermore, we are immensely grateful to all
the individuals and organisations who contributed to the exhibition *At
Home in the 17th Century* and to this book by lending objects and providing
images. The exhibition was also made possible in part by the Rijksmuseum
Vrienden, the Stichting Zabawas, the Stichting Thurkowfonds, and, through
the Rijksmueum Fonds, by the Fonds Dirk Jan van Orden, the Lucy en
Bas van der Vlist Fonds, the Sara Geertruida Aalders-Huender Fonds, the
Fonds Sascha Ladenius and a private donor.

This book offers a fresh look at the seventeenth century,
opening the door to everyday life within the home, its occupants, and their
interactions with the things around them. Designed by Irma Boom and
Frederik Pesch, its intimate format invites readers to get to know them up
close and personal. The result is a unique glimpse beyond the front door
– into a world that is sometimes surprisingly familiar, but often radically
different.

Taco Dibbits
General Director, Rijksmuseum

people and possessions

Sara van Dijk

The Amsterdam merchant Isaac Pool was at his wits' end. He was at home when the storm struck between seven and eight in the evening of 1 August 1674, with thunder and lightning, hail and gale-force blasts the likes of which he had never seen before. More than a thousand tiles blew off his roof, all the windows at the back of the house lay smashed to smithereens and the rain poured in. For a moment he thought the whole building would collapse, and he and his wife Maghtelt van Gherwen had fled to the cellar. Their house, De Pool in IJgracht (now Prins Hendrikkade), survived, but the damage was enormous. He wrote in his diary: 'Many beds wet, my wife's clothes in the closet ruined and everything else in such a wretched state that you could hardly look at it all without crying.'[1] It is a rare insight into the emotions of a seventeenth-century Dutchman. But there was a great deal at stake: Isaac's family, his house and his possessions – in short, his home.

Isaac had had his house, which also served as a wine warehouse, built himself. He bragged in his diary that Stadtholder Willem III had briefly stopped in front of it when he was passing with a large retinue in 1672 and had taken off his hat and said: 'This could serve as a castle and dwelling.'[2] As a merchant, Isaac had the wind behind him, and he was not the only one. The Republic of the Seven United Netherlands traded with places all over the world and, what is more, made every effort to secure and retain trading monopolies overseas. The towns on the coast, in the west of the Netherlands, profited the most from this. They expanded in rapid tempo and maintained close connections with one another. Seventy per cent of the population lived in towns in the area roughly corresponding with what is now the Randstad, the urban conglomeration of Amsterdam, Utrecht, The Hague and Rotterdam.[3] In addition, there were many important urban centres in the rest of the country. The Northern Netherlands was the most urbanized region in Europe and the inhabitants were relatively prosperous, with the result that many people could afford to spend time and money on their homes.[4] From Zwolle to Middelburg and from Hoorn to Den Bosch, using locally produced household goods as well as wares from far afield, they turned their houses into comfortable places where a large part of their daily lives played out.

Main characters

A vast quantity of household goods from the seventeenth century has been preserved. The rooms and depositories of Dutch museums are packed with cabinets, chairs and dinnerware. In most cases, however, we no longer know from which houses these things came, let alone who used them. And even when we do know, the items do not always receive full attention. For example, the Rijksmuseum holds the silverware of the wealthy Amsterdam widow Agneta Deutz, on loan from the *hofje* (almshouse) she founded, including a ewer and basin, four candlesticks and a spice box (see **figs. 70–72**). These luxury items have mainly been studied in isolation, based on their style or the place where they were produced.[5] In this publication we explore the connections between these kinds of unique ensembles and the people behind the objects. Who were they, why did they have these things in their homes and what did they do with them?[6] Agneta herself would never have regarded her silver, which consisted of heirlooms and gifts, with an art historian's eye. For her, they were cherished possessions which, while not forming a stylistic unity, merited a place on the dining table.

Besides Agneta Deutz, several other people, about whom we know a great deal from the property or records (or, ideally, both) they left behind, play a central role in this book, including the Zeeland family Boudaen Courten. This rich family of merchants and regents inhabited Het Grote Huis (The Great House) in Middelburg. We are well informed about Johan Boudaen Courten's trading activities and his early years thanks to his letters and the family book that his father Pieter kept.[7] After Johan's death in 1716, a probate inventory was drawn up which lists a set of furniture that was gifted partly to the Rijksmuseum and partly to the Royal Zeeland Scientific Society together with the family portraits (see **figs. 116, 167–170**). It is not only unusual that these items of furniture and portraits have been preserved, but also that we know exactly where they were located in the original house and who the occupants were.

The focus in this book on the people who used the objects led us as a matter of course to the upper middle class and the elite. For, like Deutz and Boudaen Courten, they were prosperous families who willed their property and documented their lives. Details about the lower middle class and the poorest strata of the urban population tend not to be recorded by their own class, but by members of this elite. Inventories, which were mostly drawn up after death for the distribution of the estate, do give some idea of the (at times humble) possessions of this group, but, in the absence of biographical details and objects that have come down to us, they hardly come to life.[8] However, middle-class exceptions can be found, such as the Leiden baker couple Arent van Oostwaert and his wife Catharina van Keijserswaert. They became world famous thanks to their local artist Jan Steen, who painted their double portrait in 1658 (see **fig. 110**). According to the inventory compiled after Arent's death in 1695, the painting had hung in the kitchen. He had by then been a widower for twenty years, but the extra beds throughout the house, including a small wooden cot, recalled the time when the house was filled with family members.[9]

The posthumous inventory of Josina Schade van Westrum, widow of the Den Bosch pensionary (chief functionary and legal adviser) Otto Copes, is of a very different order. Her property likewise attests to a busy family life (she bore fifteen children, six of whom reached adulthood), but it also testifies to her sophisticated lifestyle, with specific rooms in her house set aside for receptions and staff. Among the many surviving inventories, this one stands out on account of the precision with which the clerk carried out his work. Even the food and drinks supplies in the cellar, which are seldom listed, are meticulously recorded.[10]

The notebooks of wealthy women, such as Sara L'Empereur from Leiden and Maria van Nesse from Alkmaar, form another important source on life in such grand houses. Sara's account book covers the years 1660–1663. She lived with her husband Marcus du Tour and their children Justina, Constantijn, David and Susanna in Rapenburg 67 in Leiden. This was a practical choice, for Marcus was the executor of the estate of Sara's cousin Johannes Thysius, who had died at an early age. This Leiden lawyer left a large collection of scholarly and scientific books that were intended for a new library that had still to be built: the present-day Biblioteca Thysiana on the same canal. The couple could therefore easily supervise the building works.[11] Sara's household purchases varied from a costly set of tapestries to repairs to pots and pans, and give some impression of their busy family life, including the many journeys by tow barge that Marcus, who held a senior position at the stadtholder's court, made to The Hague fig. 1. When they moved to that town in 1661, no fewer than four boats were needed to transport the contents of their house.[12]

The two *memorieboeken* (notebooks) of the unmarried Maria from the periods 1623–1639 and 1639–1646 could not be more detailed. Not only did she keep a record of what she spent, she also recorded household tips and recipes, incidents within her family and difficulties with her staff.[13] We seldom have such an intimate insight into the day-to-day concerns of women in the seventeenth century.

Harsh reality

The diary of Isaac Pool shows that, despite the economic prosperity, life in the Dutch Republic was not always easy, even for the wealthy. The weather alone was a regular cause of distress. Europe was going through a minor ice age in the seventeenth century, and the winters were mostly extremely cold. During the night of 14–15 March 1674, the cold was so severe that the urine in the chamber pot beside Isaac's bed froze solid, even though he kept the fires well stoked.[14] And he was wealthy, with several fireplaces in the house and money to buy peat. He also had the connections that enabled him to have new roof tiles delivered within days of the aforementioned summer storm. For poverty-stricken people in cramped, draughty accommodation, such extreme forces of nature were much harder to endure. What is more, the young nation had been entangled in a bloody struggle with Spain until 1648, while, subsequently, wars regularly raged with England and France – or else threatened to. On top of all this, the population was habitually ravaged by epidemics of the plague and smallpox.

All this adversity had repercussions for everyday life, not least for the composition of the household. Ideally, a family would consist of a working father at its head, a stay-at-home mother and a number of children, and possibly a maid. In reality, all kinds of variations existed in

Sara L'Empereur recorded her weekly expenses in her account book. The left page mentions her husband's trip from The Hague and a hat for her son Constantijn; the right page includes provisions such as lemons, oysters, and turnips

the towns. Married couples, with or without children, accounted for just over half of households.[15] Contagious diseases and a lack of medical knowledge meant death was never far away, added to which childbirth, and in particular delivery, presented extra risks for women.

The schoolmaster David Beck was one of the many widowers who had lost their wives in childbirth. He was born and raised in Cologne, but like many of his family members – all convinced Calvinists – he left for the Dutch Republic on religious grounds, settling in Hoogstraat in The Hague in 1617. Within a year he married Roeltje van Belle, who lived nearby, and the couple had three children: Adriaen, Sara and Roeltje. The last child was named after her mother, who died just a week after her birth, in December 1623. David had to hire a wet nurse to take care of the baby, and he was also responsible for looking after his younger brother and sister, Abraham and Odilia, who lived in with him.[16] We are well-informed about David's situation because he kept a diary to give to his children later. The entries for the year 1624 have survived, as have those for the period 1627–1628, when he lived in Arnhem. He had applied for a well-paid job at a French school there and was employed by the city council in 1625. The position even came with its own house, which he sublet as an extra source of income. He and his son Adriaen moved into a room with a landlady who provided meals – a practical solution for a single father. Sara and Roeltje did not accompany him. They were lodged with the families of David's brothers Steven and Hendrick, respectively.

Despite high maternal mortality rates, there was a surplus of women in the towns of the province of Holland. These towns acted as a magnet to single women from the lower classes within and outside the Dutch Republic, many of whom came from rural or war-torn areas and had a better chance of making a living for themselves here, as maids or street vendors, for instance. Moreover, of the many men who joined the army or signed up with the East or West India Companies, only a third returned. A great many women were therefore left widows or on their own for prolonged periods when their husbands were away. Others never even married.[17] The bed warmer which, according to the inscription, women

2 The inscription on this brass warming pan from 1602, for use in bed, explains that it was intended specifically for women who 'have no husband to warm their feet'

This engraved goblet comes from Margaretha van Berensteyn and Zacheus de Jager's refuse pit. The family arms are difficult to identify, but the pair of crowned doves on two pierced hearts reveals that this was a wedding glass

without a husband could use to warm their feet, must have been intended for one of the better-placed ladies of this group fig. 2. The object would certainly have lived up to its rather cheeky promise in the winter when its owner carefully filled it with glowing embers from the hearth and moved it back and forth between the sheets to warm them before going to bed.

The prodigiously wealthy Catholic Maria van Nesse lived alone all her life, apart from her various live-in maids. She chose to do so from religious conviction. In her latter years in particular, she spent less and less on her own needs and ever more on those of the *schuilkerk* (clandestine church) to which she belonged.[18] For although the Dutch Republic was renowned for its religious freedom, there were limits to its tolerance. The separation of Church and state was not yet a fact, and those who were not members of the Dutch Reformed Church could certainly not always openly bear witness to their faith. Besides Roman Catholics, Remonstrants, Lutherans and Baptists were also dependent on house churches for shorter or longer periods of time.

A small minority of the urban population consisted of divorced men and women. Although it was unusual to officially separate, both divorces and legal separations occurred.[19] Thanks to the many deeds that Margaretha van Berensteyn from Enkhuizen had drawn up by her notary, we are allowed an insight into her floundering marriage to the physician Zacheus de Jager. The couple perpetually quarrelled, on one occasion resulting in physical violence when he pushed her to the ground, and he regularly called her names: 'You werewolf, you nuisance, you lying slattern.' In 1649 she left him for good, taking with her the entire contents of their house. The splinters of an engraved wedding glass, found in their waste pit, seem to stand symbolically for their broken marriage fig. 3.[20]

World view

Even though many people were single in the Dutch Republic, matrimony remained the norm. Socially, religiously and juridically, marriage gave both men and women a natural place in society. The family was seen to mirror a greater cosmic order: just as Christ ruled over the Church and a monarch his land, so a father and mother ruled over their household.[21] This idea went back to the Greek philosopher Aristotle, who believed that the whole of the cosmos was organized hierarchically. God was superior to man, man to animal. This subdivision could be further refined, so that, for example, the elite were superior to the lower classes and men to women. Everything had a fixed and unalterable place – in the household, too. The statesman and poet Jacob Cats, the bestselling author of his age, stressed in his *Houwelick* (Marriage, 1625) that the family formed the cornerstone of society. Without wedlock there would be no offspring to populate the towns, no new statesmen to govern the country and no new members of the Church.[22] As a result, parents had a huge responsibility to bring up their children to be good citizens who would in turn fulfil their roles in society.

Sometimes these ideas quite literally found form at home, and not just in the bookcase, where Cats was well represented. The portrait of Josina Schade van Westrum with five of her children depicts her as a personification of the Household **fig. 4**. With one hand at the helm, she points her offspring to the steep path to the Temple of Honour and Virtue, ignoring Bacchus, Venus and Cupid, who represent the sins of wine, love and temptation. The painting hung prominently above the fireplace in the *zaal* (main reception room), the most representative room in their home.[23] A salient detail is that her husband Otto was arrested in his younger years, when he was a student in Groningen, for firing a gun at a member of the *schutterij* (civic guard) when he was drunk. Reality does not always match up to the ideal.[24]

The confluence of Christian and classical ideas may seem contradictory to our eyes, but this is not how they were perceived by the seventeenth-century burgher: gods and heroes from classical antiquity could serve perfectly well as a model for Protestant values. This is because the approach is based on analogy. Whereas our reasoning is inclined to be founded on cause and effect, in the seventeenth century it was common to base arguments on comparison.[25] A father was superior to his family just as Christ was superior to his Church, and figures from classical mythology could portray contemporary vices and virtues.

Christian and ancient virtues are combined in this portrait of Josina Schade of Westrum and five of her children, painted by Theodoor van Thulden in 1651

This principle was developed a good deal further. Despite major break-throughs in the field of medicine, the age-old humoral theory continued to prevail for virtually the entire century. This was a system in which every-thing – including the human body – was classified according to the four elements: earth, water, air and fire. Physicians differentiated between four bodily fluids (*humores*), each with their own properties, which were linked to the four elements: black bile (cold and dry like earth), phlegm (cold and moist like water), blood (hot and moist like air) and yellow bile (hot and dry like fire). In a healthy body, the fluids were in balance; disturbance of this balance resulted in illness. However, everyone had an excess of one of the four fluids and the accompanying temperament (melancholic, phlegmatic, sanguine or choleric). Since everything around us – from the seasons to the positions of the moon – was linked to one of the four properties, every-thing had an impact on the human constitution. In the popular medical handbooks *Schat der gesontheyt* (Treasury of Health, 1636) and *Schat der ongesontheyt* (Treasury of Ill-health, 1642), written by the Dordrecht phy-sician Johan van Beverwijck, concrete advice could always be found, from dietary recommendations to how to keep out draughts and harmful vapours.

The house itself also served as a metaphor. It was not merely the smallest building block in society; it also mirrored the whole of the cosmos. This is beautifully illustrated by Petronella de la Court's doll's house, a showpiece that was intended not as a child's toy but to represent the ideal household **fig. 5**. In the art room, the ceiling is papered with a hand-coloured print depicting the four elements and the four points of the compass **fig. 8**. That of the hallway also portrays the four points of the com-pass, which in turn are linked to the four seasons, displayed as ivory figurines on top of the wainscoting **fig. 129**. The seasons appear in other rooms as well: spring and autumn again on the ceilings of, respectively, the lying-in chamber with its new life and the nursery with a sick child. Summer is represented by the flowering garden (which has its own 'room' in the doll's house) and winter by the kitchen, where a maid is baking waffles – a typical December treat.[26] In this way the house symbolizes the rhythm of the year, the course of human life and the world as a whole.

Behind the front door

The choice of furnishings for the interior of the home depended strongly on a person's outlook on life. Sometimes this was immediately visible, as in the seventeenth-century predilection for series of the four elements or the many biblical scenes that crop up on all manner of household goods. Not only did the decorations reflect the occupants' views – the way they used their belongings did as well. A folding screen protecting a mother and her newborn child from draught, baking pans for making apples puff and thereby compensating for the cold and moist properties of the fruit, clean linen smocks as an alternative to washing the body with warm water – these are but a small selection of examples from the material culture of the seventeenth century, which is inextricably bound up with the thinking of the period.

Genre paintings and the three late seventeenth-century doll's houses that have been preserved appear to offer us a direct insight into that world **figs. 5–7**. Here we see all these objects in use, and yet they do not tell the complete story. Many painters preferred to parade their virtuosity with carefully constructed compositions full of vista perspectives, tiled marble floors and lofty chimneybreasts rather than a real interior. The households of the lower socio-economic classes were frequently depicted in a stereotypical manner, whereas the doll's house presented an ideal image of the houses of the elite.[27]

The way things were used is, then, central to this book. To gain an even better understanding of the lives of seventeenth-century people and their personal possessions, we have 'sifted' through their waste. A whole range of discarded objects can be found in cesspits, from children's toys to cookware. It is these everyday objects that nobody cares about once they are no longer of use that tell us most about ordinary, day-to-day worries and concerns. The more expensive articles, such as gold rings, engraved glasses and silver boxes, on the other hand, tend to be linked with major life events, such as engagements, marriages, births or deaths. They were generally not in daily use but had a fixed place in the house and in the hearts of the occupants. Because of their significance, and very often also

5 Petronella de la Court's doll's house, made between 1668 and 1690, is the earliest surviving Dutch object of its kind. This masterwork includes every type of room, from servants' quarters to the most impressive reception areas

Petronella Dunois's doll's house, like others in the 17th century, was not a child's toy. Petronella was about to marry by the time it was completed in 1676

7   Petronella Oortman's doll's house is unique in the great precision with which all the objects were crafted. All the materials and proportions are correct; even the napkins were woven to scale

because of their value as works of art, it is these objects that have most been preserved in museum collections and therefore constitute a separate category in this book.

It is hard to ascertain the emotional bond that people had with their possessions. In the seventeenth century it was not customary to commit your innermost feelings to paper, although there are exceptions. The diaries of David Beck constitute a rare source on daily life in the Dutch Republic, and, like Isaac Pool, he occasionally allows a glimpse of the emotional significance of his property. Late in the afternoon on 12 July 1624 in The Hague, he started to compile 'an inventory … of all our furniture, resources, goods, clothes, books and jewels, as many as at the time of R[oeltje's] death'. Generally speaking, this was the job of a notary, but David compiled it himself. When he had finished, he played his violin for an hour, on his own in the dark.[28] In his new house in Arnhem, her portrait hung by his bed and he kept a locked chest containing her things, which he rearranged from time to time.[29] Even though she was no longer alive, Roeltje moved house with him.

David's diaries also clearly show that his house was lived in. He occasionally bought new things and tidied up when he was expecting visitors. A house is not a static whole, as inventories sometimes seem to suggest. People and their possessions are always on the move. This goes for every household, but equally to the century as a whole. Thinking and tastes were subject to change, and an interior from the end of the century looked quite unlike one at the beginning. But every person was different and made their own choices in their homes, depending on their social class, religious convictions and origins. It is through their everyday activities – personal care, housekeeping and work – as well as the major events in their lives, such as births, marriage and death, that we get to know the different people behind the front doors and how they shaped their lives.

8 The art room ceiling (fig. 5, middle storey, on the right) is papered with engravings of personifications of the four points of the compass and four elements

house

Femke Diercks

Even if we could transport ourselves to early modern Leiden, Amsterdam or Dordrecht, we could not take a tour of the typical seventeenth-century home, simply because no such thing existed. Homes, households and circumstances were too diverse for that. Domestic life in a small, packed basement dwelling looked completely different from life in a large canal house. Furthermore, the demands made on a dwelling changed in the course of the century, especially among the elite. As such, a house built in 1610 had a different layout and style from one built in 1680. In any case, not everyone's home conformed to the latest fashion, as most were not renovated or rebuilt by every new owner.

A house's location had a powerful influence on the lives of its occupants. Their city and neighbourhood formed essential parts of their network but also set limits on their social mobility. Rather than providing a survey of seventeenth-century architecture or social history, this chapter explores some particular characteristics of cities and houses that can improve our understanding of the lives of their occupants.[1]

Cities

The Dutch Republic was one of the most urbanized parts of Europe, with more people living in cities than outside them.[2] The flourishing cities in the west were a particular draw for newcomers. Most immigrants came from within Europe, but others arrived via extensive mercantile networks from as far away as Africa, Asia and the Americas, often under various forms of physical or economic coercion – even though slavery was prohibited within the borders of the Republic. In the east and south of the country, regions that were much more directly impacted by the wars ravaging the Republic, many cities had garrisons stationed inside their walls. These could temporarily as much as double the population, turning people's lives upside down, for instance because soldiers were quartered in private homes.[3] Almost all the cities in the Northern Netherlands, despite occasional urban expansion, had populations that grew faster than their surface area; people therefore came to live and work in increasingly close proximity to each other.

The city was surrounded by a wall with multiple gates. These were not only important in wartime; they also established the city's daily rhythm. During the day, they were open and the streets bustled with life. In the evening, however, the bells rang to announce the gates' closure, and people had to hurry so as not to find themselves on the wrong side. Business activity ceased and people returned to their own neighbourhoods, leaving the nocturnal streets to the *nachtwachten*, or night patrols.[4]

The city gates were not the only barriers to participation in city life. Admission to the city in a legal and social sense – the status of *poorter*, or citizen – was closed to many people, especially poor immigrants. Citizenship determined what occupations you could practise; it was required not only for joining guilds and the holding public office, but also for setting up your own business. Furthermore, *poorters*, unlike ordinary city-dwellers, had access to all sorts of city services, such as poor relief. If your father was a *poorter*, you automatically became one too; Christian (or sometimes only Reformed) newcomers with sufficient means could purchase this status and ensure its transmission to future generations. Jewish immigrants were often excluded; some cities allowed them to become *poorters*, but not to pass the status on to their spouses or children.[5]

Within the city walls, social and economic inequality was tremendous; most of the Republic's 250 wealthiest families lived in cities, while as much as a quarter of the urban population could barely eke out a living.[6] These households were just one cold winter, lost job or bout of illness away from dependence on poor relief. The various social classes were de-scribed through the metaphor of the body: the elite, or regent class, were the head that governed, and the middle class and commoners were the human body and limbs that obeyed.[7] The middle class included both 'wealthy merchants of high standing' and small craftsmen and shopkeepers, while the commoner class consisted of day labourers and the poor, who were often lumped together.[8] A clear distinction was made, however, between the 'honest poor' on the one hand and vagrants and beggars on the other; the latter were seen as having the capacity to work but refusing, and were judged harshly for it.[9]

In most cities, the wealthiest residents made their homes in the main streets and along the canals. The middle class could be found in the side streets that ran between these main thoroughfares. The poorer you were, the more hidden away your home – perhaps in a narrow alley wedged in between two streets, or a small, makeshift wooden hovel against the city wall.[10] The city plan thus reflected the social order, but that did not mean that there was no contact between the classes.[11] Rich and poor shared the same neighbourhoods and came into regular contact with each other on the streets.

Communities

The neighbourhood where you had your home generally exerted a profound influence over your daily life. Neighbourhoods were not the loosely defined areas they are today, but rather well-organized associations. These included wardens, funds and official regulations specifying the residents' rights and duties **fig. 9**. A typical neighbourhood consisted of several streets and their cross-streets or a section of a canal, usually encompassing no more than a hundred households **fig. 10**. The neighbourhood reduced the vast city to a manageable scale, within which neighbours kept a close eye on each other, providing mutual support but also exercising strong social control.[12] Neighbours were among the first guests you welcomed into your home after your marriage; they assisted in times of bereavement and formed a dependable social constant in life.

Most neighbourhoods were fairly diverse in both income and religion, although newcomers often encountered considerable prejudice and suspicion.[13] In the Leiden neighbourhood of Noord Koeëind, between Oude Vest and Haarlemmerstraat, the neighbourhood wardens described the emergence of a 'multitude and diversity of persons, conditions, and temperaments among neighbours' as a cause of social unrest.[14] In response, the most recent migrants, who were often the poorest, frequently established their own informal networks outside the control of the neighbourhoods they lived in. For example, Francisca, one of the most prominent women in Amsterdam's small Black community, took in sailors and other men as lodgers in her modest basement dwelling on Jodenbreestraat. She would pair them off with women from the community who worked, or had worked, as servants.[15]

Like neighbourhood associations, religious congregations had a strong influence on households, stretching well beyond the front door. In the Dutch Reformed Church, churchwardens would mediate in disputes or marital conflicts.[16] For the Reformed, the rules promulgated by the municipal authorities, the neighbourhood association and the congregation were in line with each other. In contrast, Jews, Catholics and Mennonites could run into situations where the rules of their synagogue or church conflicted with those of the civil authorities.[17] For example, all religious groups were required by the municipal authorities to register marriages, but some failed to comply because the marriage ceremony that mattered to them was the one that took place within their own religious community.

The elite attached at least as much importance as other social classes to where you attended church, where you lived and with whom you associated, yet the neighbourhood associations and guilds so central to middle-class life had much less influence on members of the elite. Instead, elite households focused primarily on maintaining good social relations with a broader group of family members, neighbours and business contacts from the same social class, collectively known as 'friends'.[18] We come across these friends as signatories and executors of wills, as guardians for underage orphans and as advocates of business interests. The elite, even more than other classes, had their own subtle methods of maintaining social equilibrium, including niceties such as social calls, invitations to parties and dinners, and correspondence.

Gift-giving was another such method, as illustrated by a glass received as a present by the Leiden widow Margaretha Flamen. After her husband's death, Margaretha was supported by his relatives. When she remarried, her first father-in-law – the cloth merchant and glass engraver Willem van Heemskerk – presented her with an engraved glass symbolizing her enduring bond with the family **fig. 12**.[19]

9, 10 Various Leiden neighbourhoods had their own distinctive symbols and coats of arms, which were used on official documents and in depictions of the neighbourhood, as we can see in the Gravesteen neighbourhood regulations (above) and the painting of Paltsgraafschap van de Rijn (below)

11 You could open this entire front door, or just the upper part, so you could chat with a passer-by without any children or pets slipping outside

12 Willem van Heemskerk engraved this glass with the words 'Liefde bind volkomen' ('Love binds entirely') in ornate lettering. Under the base he inscribed the wedding date of Margaretha Flamen and her second husband Lucas de Rijp, as well as his own signature and age

Honour

Whatever class you belonged to, mutual solidarity was of great social importance, and when necessary it was enforced by official rules, as illustrated by the regulations of religious congregations and neighbourhood associations. For example, arguments between neighbours in Leiden were settled by compelling the disputing parties to exchange 'friendly words' with each other.[20] An undeserved insult had to be publicly retracted to repair the damage to the victim's reputation.[21] In the seventeenth century, the impact of losing face and social shame – and the urgency of protecting the honour of one's family, neighbourhood or city – were keenly felt. This was understandable, since suffering dishonour could threaten one's position within the social order. The conduct of each member of the household – the husband and wife, their children and their servants (if any) – was a direct reflection on them all. Everyone, from the master of the house to the maidservant, therefore worked to keep up the good reputation of the household. What this involved depended on one's gender. While men's honour and reputation was linked primarily to their professional identity, women's honour was connected almost exclusively to sexual morality.

Accordingly, many written and unwritten rules were aimed at preserving one's 'good name'. What this usually amounted to in practice was that people kept a fairly strict eye on one another's conduct and whether it adhered to the relevant norms. Showing that you observed society's rules was crucial – even more so than protecting your personal privacy. The door was often literally wide open **fig. 11**. In the middle and lower classes, keeping too much of your household life out of sight of the neighbours was even regarded as suspicious. Historians have described this as a 'culture of visibility'.[22]

The elite had, if anything, an even keener sense of honour, but they expressed it in slightly different ways. For them, the essential status markers were the aforementioned social network and specific forms of conspicuous consumption. As the seventeenth century progressed, the elite increasingly distanced themselves from the middle class. This was visible even in the architecture of their houses. The front door no longer opened directly on to the street but was at the top of a flight of steps. In other words, the entrance was literally raised above the level of the common people, and what took place behind those closed doors was none of your business, unless you were invited in.

The powerful interconnectedness of honour, the neighbourhood and the household became manifest in times of escalating tension between urban social classes. Riots broke out in Amsterdam in 1696 over the introduction of a new tax on funerals, with the commoners rising up against the regents in an event that became known as the Aansprekersoproer (Undertakers' Riot). The new law stated that those who could not afford to pay the tax would have their funerals organized by the city. Accordingly, they could no longer choose who would carry the coffin or officially deliver the news of the death (*aanspreken*). This turned what should have been a final tribute to the deceased into incontrovertible proof of poverty, bringing shame upon the family.[23]

On 30 January 1696, a furious crowd marched in protest from the city hall through the streets to the residence of Burgomaster Jacob Boreel on Herengracht **fig. 13**. Upon arrival, the insurgents smashed Boreel's windows. After a young demonstrator was stabbed to death by the captain of the *schutterij* (civic guard), the unrest intensified. A group of protesters pulled a lamppost out of the ground, rammed down the burgomaster's front door and smashed almost all his possessions to bits. Boreel himself had been taken to a safe place by neighbours, but his mirrors, paintings and porcelain were all destroyed and thrown into the street or canal.[24] The mob moved on to another two houses before the former burgomaster Jacob Hinlopen was able to calm their outrage.

The angry protesters rebelled against the law on funerals because they felt deeply dishonoured by it. Their actions looked like chaotic looting on the surface, but in fact they arose from distinct social conditions. The rioters' fury was directed not at the city hall, where the uprising began, but at the private houses of the burgomasters, whom they held personally responsible. By smashing their windows, defacing their house fronts – symbols of their social status – and destroying their pos-

13 This print depicting the looting of Burgomaster Boreel's house during the Aansprekersoproer (Undertakers' Riot) of 1696 was made approximately ten years later, on the basis of eyewitness accounts, and was included in 18th-century books on Amsterdam's history

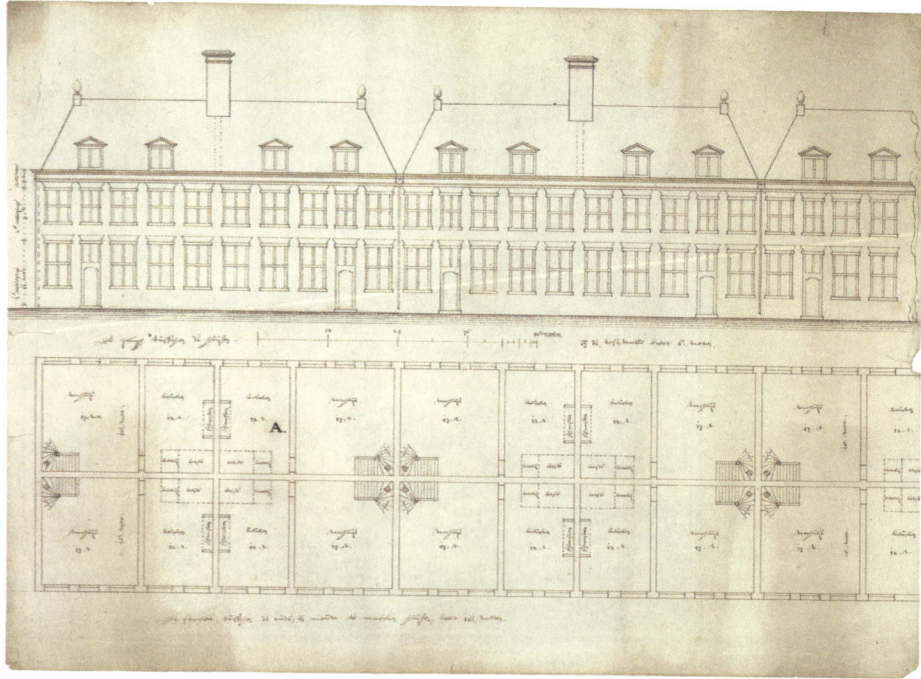

14 This unexecuted design for homes for weavers strongly resembles the dwellings built in Waardgracht in Leiden: each home was to have a *voorhuis* (front room) large enough for a loom and a kitchen with a box bed and a *bottelarij* ('buttery' or pantry)

sessions, the demonstrators struck at the burgomasters in their safe havens, their homes.[25] For whether you were rich or poor, your house was a necessity of life.

Cramped quarters

Fundamentally, a home must protect its occupants from the elements and serve as a place to sleep, eat and work. Many city-dwellers in the Dutch Republic had homes that barely met these basic needs, living in cramped one- or two-room dwellings and consequently spending much of their time on the streets.[26] The focal point of such a home was the fireplace, which gave light and heat and was also used for cooking. A housing project commissioned on Leiden's east side in 1659, which was intended for workers in the growing textile industry, offers an impression of this type of dwelling. The smallest houses had a floor area of approximately 25 square metres, with two rooms plus an uninsulated attic and no outdoor space **fig. 14**.[27] Most one- or two-room dwellings were not designed properly by an architect, however, but were situated in damp cellars, the upper storeys of the houses of wealthier city-dwellers, dark alleys or wooden shacks outside the city walls.[28]

The poor were sometimes eligible for free housing provided by wealthy private individuals (*hofjes*, or almshouses) or by the city authorities, such as monastic cells converted into tiny apartments in Broerenklooster, a former monastery in Zwolle **fig. 15**.[29] This support enabled the beneficiaries to live independently. Others lacked the capacity to do so because of physical or mental disabilities. If they had no family members who could care for them, they were accommodated in institutions run by the city or Church, such as leper houses, mental hospitals and homes for elderly men or women; such institutions were small communities, in which residents were often kept under strict supervision, and they served as alternative homes for those who needed them. Residence there was sometimes temporary and sometimes for life; Annetje Visser, a woman with microcephaly who lived in the Leprozenhuis (Leper House) in Amsterdam, died there in 1698 at the age of 98 **fig. 16**.[30]

15   Stairs in the courtyard of the Broerenklooster in Zwolle provided access to small dwellings in former monastic cells, which were placed at the disposal of the poor. The ground floor was clearly also used for other purposes

Annetie met het klein hooftiege
naamst Annetie Visser Yebooren
1600 Gestorven 698 Priego alhit
Sonder Zer veelen Godt die Syt
gij moet niet Steelen

16 Portrait of Annetje Visser, known as 'Annetje with the small head', made after her death in 1698.
According to the inscription, she cried 'incessantly with zeal "God has said thou shalt not steal"'

17 The estate inventory of Tomes Hendricks of Zwolle, drawn up by the Stadsarmenkamer (city poor relief service) on 14 October 1673, shows that aside from a bed and bedding, some clothes, and a few cooking utensils, he possessed virtually nothing

Despite this institutionalized care and the broader network of poor relief, the living conditions of many poor people were wretched, especially in the western cities, where population growth was highest. Many buildings there were divided by their owners into several small units that could be rented separately. 'That's right, four households in a house sometimes – that is to say, in the front, the back, the cellars, … it beggars belief,' Amsterdam chronicler Tobias van Domselaer wrote about Jonkerstraat and Ridderstraat.[31] These streets, which would eventually be demolished as part of the city's twentieth-century urban renewal programme, were situated just behind the Montelbaanstoren, in an area that was home to many seventeenth-century immigrants employed in shipping or at the nearby shipyards.

We have an exceptionally detailed image of living conditions in such houses in the city of Zwolle. After visits to the poor relief recipients there, city officials wrote vivid descriptions of the grinding poverty they had witnessed. For example, they remarked of the home of Hendrickien, a resident of Edincks Hof, that 'a blind horse could not have done any damage in that house'.[32] In other words, Hendrickien's little room was almost empty, and what little she did possess was practically worthless. Most poor city-dwellers had accumulated a little more than Hendrickien, but not much. The reports by the Zwolle officials paint a picture of dark, musty rooms with no fresh air, in which many people had to live together in very close quarters. It is important to acknowledge the difference in class between these officials and the people they were describing; we see Hendrickien's home only through their eyes, and not through her own.

The homes of the poor were sparsely furnished with old objects, whether rented or not – generally a few chairs and a mattress with bedding but without a bedstead; larger pieces of furniture, such as a table to sit at or a cabinet for secure storage, were often absent **fig. 17**. Moreover, almost everything they possessed was broken, or as the officials termed it, in poor condition.[33] People in this situation had no choice but to fix the legs of their chairs again and again, to continue using cooking pots with large cracks, and to patch up old clothes until they literally fell apart from wear. Therefore, some types of object that were then very common have not been preserved. The most widely used type of seating, a simple *driestal* (three-legged stool), is now familiar solely from pictures figs. 107, 124.

Middle-class homes

People who were better off unsurprisingly tended to have larger homes; more importantly, however, they had separate rooms for specific everyday activities such as cooking and working. Houses with a more or less standardized layout – a *voorhuis* (front room or area), a *binnenkamer* (inner room), a kitchen in the courtyard, an upper storey and an attic – were especially popular among the seventeenth-century urban middle class fig. 18.

In the eastern provinces and rural areas, where population growth was not as rapid, the typical house was a *dwarshuis*, oriented parallel to the street.[34] This method of building required more space but let more light into the rooms. In the more urbanized west of the country, the most common type of house was the *langhuis*. Built perpendicular to the street on a long, narrow plot, it used the available ground more efficiently.[35] But both house types had more or less the same basic layout. The specifications drawn up in 1634 for the renovation of Het Blauwe Lam, a house on Nieuwezijds Voorburgwal in Amsterdam, provide a clear picture of how the various rooms were to be constructed and arranged.[36]

The voorhuis

Stepping through the front door, you immediately entered a well-lit space: the front room of the house, or *voorhuis*. This formed the transition between the street and the innermost part of the house. It was often furnished as a kind of reception area, with a single cupboard and a row of chairs or a built-in bench, and with prints or paintings adorning the walls.[37] The *voorhuis* was unheated, but a wooden platform called a *zoldertje* protected those who sat on it from the worst cold from the stone floor and also provided better access to daylight from high windows fig. 19. In the specifications for Het Blauwe Lam, the *voorhuis* had a petit granit floor and a bench with a hinged seat under the window.

18   The interior layout of this house on Anjeliersgracht (now Westerstraat 130) in Amsterdam offers a clear impression of a middle-class home, with a *voorhuis* with a small *comptoir*, a *binnenkamer* with a hearth and a box bed, and a corridor leading to the kitchen, with the garden in the back

19   Even though this portrait was obviously staged, it offers an impression of what went on in surgeon Jacob Hercules's *voorhuis* (front room). His work included shaving and bloodletting. His wife Anna Jans is sitting on a *zoldertje*, a raised platform, while their children Frans and Francijntje play beside her

Huis Bonck in Hoorn has one of the few surviving 17th-century *hangkamers*. This is a type of mezzanine suspended from the ceiling of the *voorhuis*, which often served as a *comptoir* (office)

This box bed, built into panelling for a home in Dordrecht, was placed near the hearth as usual to make optimal use of the heat. The oak panels are decorated with geometric patterns and ebony details. The cradle in the photograph was made in a very similar style

Tradespeople often used the *voorhuis* as a shop or a workplace.[38] Merchants' larger houses also had a *comptoir* in the front, a room furnished as an office so that there was no need to bring business associates into the rest of the house. The *comptoir* could be off to one side or in a *hangkamer*, a wooden structure suspended from the rafters **fig. 20**. Het Blauwe Lam was also designed with a *hangkamer*, which was furnished with a table and two benches, as well as a special hatch designed to let in heat from the side room below.

The binnenkamer

The majority of life took place in the *binnenkamer* – the heart of the home, where the family slept, ate, played and prayed. A fire burned in the hearth almost all day long, which kept the temperature pleasant. The specifications for Het Blauwe Lam state that the room was to have wood panelling into which both the hearth and a box bed would be incorporated. This type of panelling – in wood ranging from simply painted deal to expensive oak inlaid with ebony – gave the *binnenkamer* a unified appearance **fig. 21** and kept out rising damp from the stone walls. The box bed in Het Blauwe Lam was in the usual position, close to the warmth of the hearth, and had storage space built into the foot. Beds, sofa beds and box beds could also be present in other rooms of the house, since separate bedrooms were not yet standard. For privacy while sleeping or engaging in other activities in bed, one could draw the curtains, as Jacob Cats emphatically recommended: 'and neither punish nor caress your wife/ where someone else will hear, or see the sight/ bed curtains must/ be firmly shut'.[39]

The kitchen

The first activity to be assigned a room of its own was cooking. It was moved out of the *binnenkamer*, in full view of everyone in the house, into an extension in the courtyard or a separate outbuilding in the garden. Cellars dug below the house were also used for this purpose, although ventilation was often a problem there.[40] A separate kitchen provided more space not only for cooking but also for rest and recreation in the *binnen-*

kamer; furthermore, food odours no longer lingered there all day. But this type of kitchen did require sufficient funds to keep an additional hearth burning. To make matters worse, some cities levied tax based on the number of fireplaces in the house.

Het Blauwe Lam was designed with a two-storey annex in the garden, accessible via a half-open gallery. On the upper level was an elegantly furnished room where the residents could receive guests, while downstairs was the actual kitchen (*kookkeuken*): a basement room with furnishings including a box bed and an oak mantelpiece, a peat chest under the window and a state-of-the-art sink. It was specified that the placement of the chimney in the *kookkeuken* should not lead to any smoke or odours that would form an inconvenience in the reception room upstairs. The kitchen walls were to be covered with earthenware tiles from top to bottom. Such tiles enhanced a room's atmosphere and were easy to keep clean – an important feature in a peat-fuelled kitchen, where surfaces could rapidly become covered with soot.

The corridor

One part of the house is easy to overlook but was crucial for regulating the flow of traffic: namely, the corridor. A door or doorway in the back of the *voorhuis* led to the corridor, which traversed the entire length of the rear of the house, all the way to the garden. The rooms off this corridor – usually the *binnenkamer* and the kitchen – could be closed off with doors, allowing better management of the flow of air through the house: draughts and damp were seen as extremely unhealthy. The designers of some dwellings even sacrificed part of the *voorhuis* to create a small vestibule or enclosed entryway to keep out draughts. The corridor also offered a certain degree of privacy, as housemaids and journeymen did not have to pass through the *binnenkamer* on their way to the kitchen.

Het Blauwe Lam had a niche placed in the wall of the corridor with a lead holder for a ewer and basin, so that members of the household and guests could wash their hands before meals. The plans also included hooks for hanging up a coatrack.

The first floor and attic

A spiral staircase in the corridor or *voorhuis* led to the first floor, which contained more sparsely furnished rooms for both sleeping and daytime activities. The hearths in these rooms would have been lit much less often; extra heating was a luxury. The floor of this level lay directly on top of the wooden rafters below, forming the ceiling of the ground level. Although floors of this kind were efficient to build, they must have creaked and groaned when you stamped too hard on them. Finally, the attic was used to store peat and any materials needed for the shop or workplace below.

Sanitary facilities

The room missing from the seventeenth-century house was the bathroom. It was not customary to take baths in this period; people washed their faces and bodies, combed their hair and cleaned their teeth in spare moments in the general-purpose rooms of the house.[41] When nature called, most houses had not only chamber pots in various rooms for emergencies and cold nights **fig. 30**, but also a privy (outdoor toilet) in the garden. It was connected to a cesspit or sewer that emptied into the nearest canal. In the specifications for Het Blauwe Lam, the privy is covered with white and green tiles. The door, the doorframe and even the toilet seat were included in the commission.[42]

Urban palaces

The urban elite preferred to build their houses in the centre of town, along the main thoroughfares. Although members of this group tended to cluster together, urban extensions intended primarily for them, such as the Vierde Uitleg (fourth expansion) of the Amsterdam canals, were a rarity.[43] Similar plans for Utrecht were never carried out.

Building a new house in the teeming city centre had its drawbacks. Most plots were narrow and deep, suitable for middle-class houses. But these were unsatisfactory to the urban elite, who merged two plots, or sometimes even three, to make space for more and larger rooms, in keeping with their social prestige **fig. 22**. Such houses were also 'made

In this drawing, the painter and inventor Jan van der Heyden not only illustrates the use of the fire hose that he invented but also offers a fascinating cross-section of an urban palace and all its contents, going up in flames

23 The unusual shape of this house at Rapenburg 48 in Leiden resulted from the decision to build a coach house. From the second half of the 17th century onwards, coaches were the ultimate in luxury transport

with extremely opulent decorations in the interior, resembling royal palaces more than merchants' houses', as Melchior Fokkens wrote about the canal houses along Amsterdam's Keizersgracht.[44]

This preference for 'palaces' was shared both by people with 'new money', such as the well-heeled Leiden textile dealer Wouter van Halewijn and his son Benjamin, and by established upper-class families such as the former burgomaster of Dordrecht Abraham van Beveren and his wife Elisabeth Ruysch.[45] Both had to wait for years to acquire three adjacent buildings and the required permits – on Rapenburg in Leiden and in Wijnstraat in Dordrecht, respectively – before they could finally begin building their urban palaces. But even the largest plots in the city centre were surrounded by buildings, compelling them to adapt their wishes to the force of circumstance. Wouter and Benjamin added a new wing in the back of Rapenburg 48 – an already impressive house – that ran behind the adjoining houses at 42, 44 and 46.[46] This allowed them to build a passage all the way to Pieterskerkhof, the street behind Rapenburg, where they placed their coach house. The house looks like one large block from the front, but in the rear it turns by necessity into a thin structure winding along one side of the large garden **fig. 23**.[47]

Unlike middle-class families, who generally had carpenters build or alter their homes, the elite hired renowned architects. Well-known designers such as Philips Vingboons, Pieter Post and Arent van 's-Gravensande created not only public buildings but also private urban palaces. This brought the Dutch classicist style, which was already in use for public buildings and symbolized the order and regularity of city government, to the homes of regents.[48] In Dordrecht, Abraham van Beveren even went so far as to employ several architects. He first hired the Leiden city architect Van 's-Gravensande, perhaps in combination with his lesser-known brother Pieter Noorwits from The Hague. But he was evidently unsatisfied with this first design, because he had Pieter Post make new drawings and then awarded him the commission **fig. 24**.[49] Post designed not only the house front and floor plan but also many interior decorations, such as mantlepieces, doors, and door and window frames. As a member of Holland's provincial executive (the Gecommitteerde Raden), Abraham spent a great deal of time in The Hague and left his wife Elisabeth in charge of the building works, with assistance from her father.[50] It was not unusual for women to take on such tasks when their husbands were away from home for extended periods.[51]

Post's floor plan for the building now known as De Onbeschaamde (The Shameless One) clearly illustrates how this type of large house departed from the standards for middle-class dwellings fig. 25. Such houses did, of course, maintain a separation between the two essential activities of cooking and working, but they also contained a growing number of specially furnished rooms for social functions.

The zaal

The most important additional part of the house was the *zaal* (reception room). 'In all Residential Buildings that aspire to be something, *zalen* are prevalent and useful … [They] serve for receiving people, for important visits, and as accommodation,' wrote the Amsterdam bookseller Willem Goeree in 1681 in a popular booklet on house building.[52] In De Onbeschaamde, the *zaal* was large enough to hold a Leiden textile worker's entire home. With three high windows overlooking the garden, the *zaal* was bright and spacious and could, just as Goeree advised, 'set itself apart from dark, miserable little Rooms'. Goeree's recommendations speak to the social ambitions of his readers; by his standards, the owner of a house with a large, well-lit *zaal* was much more distinguished than someone who had to receive his guests in the stuffy *binnenkamer* (inner room) of a middle-class house.

Since the *zaal* was used for various occasions, it was rather sparsely furnished. In contrast, no expense was spared on decorating the room. Wall hangings such as tapestries, rich fabrics, gilt leather, paintings and painted wallpaper created a sense of unity and luxury. Such reception rooms traditionally had a state bed (grand, canopied bed with elaborate hangings) on display. These were not used for sleeping; rather, their costly textiles, which harmonized with the rest of the interior, lent the room an

Pieter Post's design for the façade of the house at Wijnstraat 123 in Dordrecht, includes classical elements such as Corinthian pilasters, festoons, and a naked putto in the pediment, from which the house took its 19th-century nickname of De Onbeschaamde (The Shameless One)

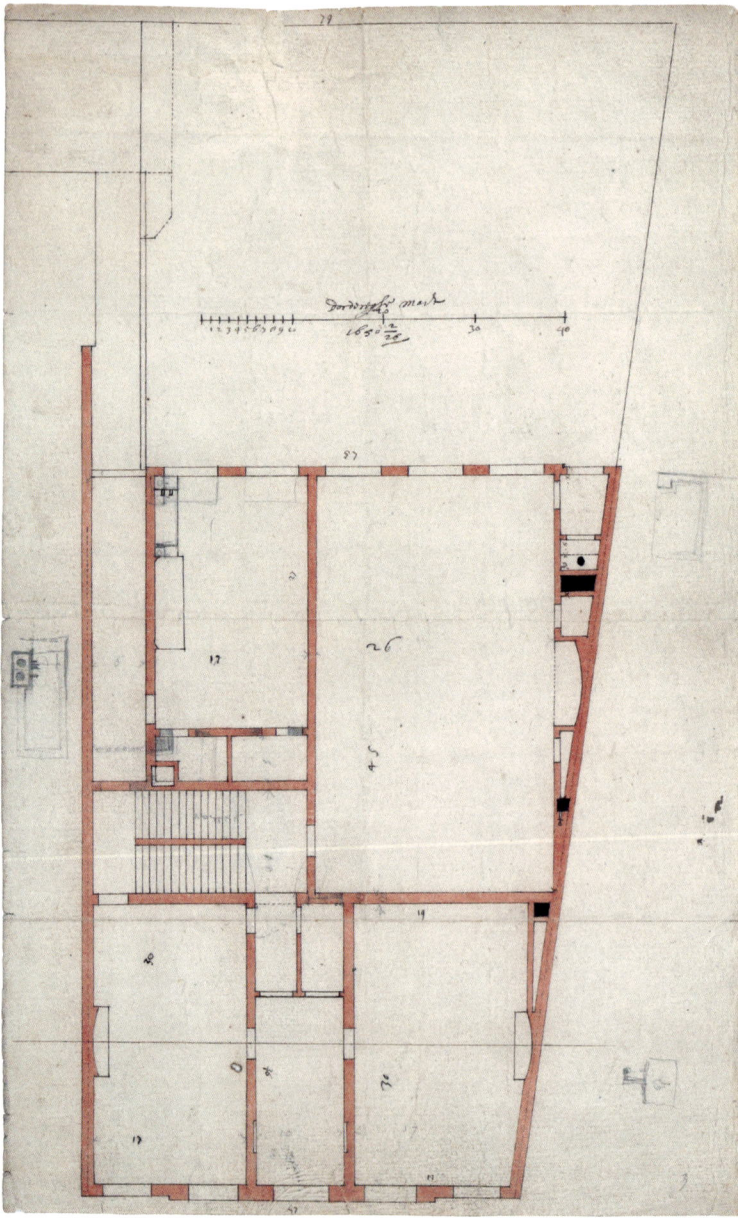

25 Ground plan of De Onbeschaamde. The corridor with the staircase led to the spacious *zaal* (reception room). The wall with the fireplace was designed by Post to conceal the trapezoidal shape of the plot of land and make the room rectangular

aura of distinction. Not until late in the seventeenth century did these beds slowly vanish from the *zaal*. Aside from the state bed, the *zaal*'s most eye-catching feature was the hearth, to which architects devoted a great deal of thought **fig. 26**. For De Onbeschaamde, Pieter Post made detailed drawings of the mantelpiece and planned to be personally involved in ordering the marble, which had to come from a quarry near Liège.[53]

The occupants did not spend time in the *zaal* every day. Most houses also had a more intimate family room, where the majority of daily life was situated. In De Onbeschaamde, this was the *pronkkeuken* (best kitchen) next to the *zaal*. With its two built-in pantries, it was somewhat reminiscent of a middle-class *binnenkamer*.

Separate dining rooms were uncommon in the urban palaces of the elite until well into the seventeenth century. Zeeland was one of the provinces where this trend, which came to the Dutch Republic from Flanders, first took root.[54] In other cities, the *zaal* remained in use for major receptions, with tabletops placed on trestles when necessary – for example, during the wedding banquet of Leonora Huydecoper and Jan Hinlopen in 1657 at her father's house at Singel 548 in Amsterdam. During this celebration, spread over three days, the *zaal* and antechamber were furnished with enough large tables for all 86 guests **fig. 27**.[55]

Service areas
In many urban palaces, the service areas – which included kitchens, pantries and laundry rooms – were in the basement or attic. Over time, more staff activities took place out of sight of the household. The servants' sleeping quarters, which were often in the attic, were expected to be situated as far away as possible from those of the principal residents. 'The Servant's Bedroom and those of the Maids should be kept as distant from the others as fire from flammable things,' Goeree wrote, showing a disdain for household staff that illustrates the growing distance between social classes in the domestic setting.[56] In middle-class houses, this kind of distance between the family and the servants was unattainable, because they all lived in much closer quarters.

This fireplace comes from the *zaal* (reception room) in Joan Huydecoper's urban palace, Singel 548 in Amsterdam, which was also furnished with Delft tapestries depicting landscapes and a state bed. The fireplace itself may have had a blue finish

26

This portrait by Gabriël Metsu shows the family of Leonora Huydecoper and Jan Hinlopen in an imaginary interior. Their wedding banquet took place in the *zaal* (reception room) of her parents' home

27

The entrance hall

An urban palace did not have a crowded *voorhuis*. It was a place not for work but for genteel living – or at least, it was meant to give that impression. An elevated doorstep, or stoop, raised the entrance above the hubbub of the street. Family coats of arms, mottos and mirror monograms replaced middle-class signboards on the house front. Once through the front door, a visitor would enter the cool serenity of the entrance hall, which was often adorned with painted or sculpted personifications and plenty of marble. To go any further into the house, you needed an invitation. This was quite a different experience for visitors than arriving in the bustling *voorhuis* of a middle-class home.

The comptoir or library

The *comptoir* – located in or next to the *voorhuis* in middle-class homes, a clear indication that it was intended for business – increasingly took on a different role among the elite. Although this room had generally been the nerve centre of whatever enterprise had made the owner and their family rich, business was gradually compelled to make way for a more refined way of life. *Comptoirs* devoted to practical matters were gradually replaced by studies in which books and collections of curiosities occupied a central place, where the gentleman of the house could entertain friends and other interested guests.[57]

Living

A house was more than the backdrop against which life unfolded. Its size and location reflected the class and neighbourhood to which a person belonged. From impoverished one-room dwellings along the city wall to extravagant urban palaces in the city centre, in any house the layout and furnishings of the rooms influenced what you did there and how. If a house had a separate kitchen, then the woman of the house would spend less time in the *binnenkamer*. If there was a writing desk in one of the rooms on the upper floor, then you would spend more time there, writing letters or doing the accounts, than if there was only a bed. Those prosperous enough to keep more than one hearth lit could make serious use of more of the rooms in the house in the winter than those families who had to huddle around their one fireplace together for a little light and warmth.

Rooms and the objects in them held a significance that went beyond their everyday functions. An extra chair in the *voorhuis* or *binnenkamer* was an implicit sign of hospitality. A biblical scene on a linen cupboard was intended not only for visitors but above all for the woman who opened the cupboard every day, as a reminder of her faith and her role in the household (see **fig. 96**). Gifts presented as tokens of friendship were cherished, and whenever the recipients saw them, they could pause to reflect on their ties to the people in their lives. It was the interaction between rooms, objects and people, as well as the neighbourhood in which the house stood, that defined life in the home.

body

Suzanne van Leeuwen

In 1648, the Leiden legal scholar and book collector Johannes Thysius bought a 'silver beard brush' and made a note of it in his account book, in which he kept track of all his personal and household purchases.[1] His list of expenses included a variety of other 'kitchenware and items for daily use', including an 'ebony brush with silver, a shaving basin' fig. 28 and 'tweezers'.[2] He must have spent quite a bit of time in front of the mirror at home, making sure he looked his best. In the only surviving portrait of him, his face is clean-shaven except for a thin moustache, and his lush hair pours down over his shoulders fig. 29. Even though, as we have just seen, Johannes had his own grooming accessories at home, his account book also tells us that he visited a barber regularly, paying six and a half guilders for '½ year of shaving' in 1652.[3]

Notes about personal grooming, such as Johannes's, offer intriguing glimpses of what were regarded as customary and desirable attitudes towards personal hygiene, illness, treatment and recovery. Diverse perspectives on what was healthy or unhealthy for the human body found expression in all sorts of body-related objects, such as clothes, medicine, toiletries and accessories. These objects offer us a very close look not only at seventeenth-century Dutch lives but also at the most intimate parts of the home: the rooms used for sleeping and the privy (toilet). Concern with one's health and appearance was woven deep into the fabric of everyday life, from waking in the morning to retiring to bed in the evening.

Bright and early

Just after rising in the morning, it was important to go 'to the room' right away to relieve yourself. Or at least, such was the advice given by Dordrecht doctor Johan van Beverwijck in his popular book *Schat der gesontheyt* (Treasury of Health, 1636).[4] He believed that delaying a visit to the toilet could make the 'filth' dry up and lead to constipation. Most households had at least one chamber pot available for urgent needs fig. 30. Bowel movements generally took place in the privy – once a day for 'restrained individuals', according to Van Beverwijck, 'and twice for those who eat a bit too much' fig. 31.[5]

MYNIAER IS OM

28 The semi-circular gap in the rim made it possible to hold this shaving bassin close to the throat to catch hair and shaving cream. The bowl is practically a billboard for shaving equipment, with its images of combs, scissors, ointments, and bottles

Around 1658, this portrait was painted of Johannes Thysius in the latest fashion, with long, curly hair (possibly a wig) and a thin moustache. He wears an informal, wadded housecoat in a Japanese style

29

After you did your business, it was time for some primping to make yourself presentable: 'As soon as a person stands up, he will comb his hair, rinse his mouth, clean his teeth and tongue, wash his ears and nose, rinse his eyes and his entire face with cold water, and [massage] the body, especially the arms and legs.'[6] As this description suggests, it was not unusual to wash only the face, and with cold water at that. A typical and widely accepted theory at the time, based on the concept of the four 'humours', was that immersing the body in warm water was dangerous: it was said to open the skin's pores, making it easy for germs to invade the body and for essential bodily fluids to escape.[7]

Linen underwear was regarded as ideal for absorbing dirt and bodily fluids; accordingly, most people were more inclined to wash their undergarments than to wash themselves.[8] This explains why the most essential piece of clothing during this period, worn by both men and women, was a linen smock **fig. 32**.[9] How often you could change your smock depended on how many you owned as well as on how often you did laundry. In 1680, an Amsterdam woman wrote that although her parents washed their linens only a few times a year, they had such a large supply that the family members were able to change into a clean smock regularly: 'My mother was a very hygienic woman … [we never wore] the same smock longer than a full week in winter, or half a week in summer.'[10]

The Leiden baker Arent van Oostwaert had sixteen smocks, according to a probate inventory drawn up after his death.[11] He wore those smocks not only as underclothes but also as part of his work outfit in the hot, dusty bakery, as can be seen in a double portrait of him and his wife Catharina van Keijserswaert (see **fig. 110**). She is wearing a bodice with the low boat neck that was in fashion around 1650. Beneath the bodice, many women wore a corset, then known as a pair of stays, with a linen smock underneath it **fig. 33**. The stays shaped and supported the waist, bust and back, literally tying them into place.

This undergarment was worn from a young age. For example, Maria van Nesse of Alkmaar mentions in her notebook that she is having stays made not only for herself but also for Sijfert, the one-year-old daughter

30 The proverb on this red earthenware chamber pot, 'tijt soete lief koomdt te bedt' ('time sweet love come to bed'), relates not only to a proverb about harmony between spouses but also to the place where this object was used, near the conjugal bed

In Petronella Dunois's doll's house, the 'smallest room' is behind the kitchen. On the tiled privy is a wooden board with a hole; in a real privy, the porcelain lid reduced the stench from the cesspit below

This men's smock, made of linen, is marked with the initials GSB (as yet unidentified) and the numeral 1. When the smock was washed outside the home, this mark ensured that it could be returned to the rightful owner

32

These stays and busk are reinforced with vertical bands of whalebone (baleen) and can be laced shut. The separate sleeves are tied on with silk ribbons at the armholes

33

of a housemaid in her circle of acquaintances.[12] The preference was for not only adults but also children to be well dressed. This is also illustrated by a beautifully preserved late seventeenth-century cream silk jacket for a baby **fig. 34**. The embroidered garment is lined on the inside to keep the infant warm.

As a gift, girls sometimes received a bodkin: a flat needle that made it easier to lace a corset.[13] It could be made of silver or of brass and was sometimes inscribed with a name or initials and date **fig. 35**.[14] Portraits made between 1610 and 1640 sometimes show bodkins in use as hair ornaments **fig. 36**.[15] This had the advantage that the needle was always within reach, although it did have to be placed in the hair securely. In 1643, the aforementioned Maria van Nesse wrote that she was having a 'new silver needle' made because the one she had received from her sister Adriana in 1630 had fallen out of her hair.[16]

Spotless white collars, made of starched linen and lace, completed the ensemble and were worn by men, women and children alike. These form some of the most eye-catching elements of seventeenth-century dress in portraits.[17] Early in the century, they developed into true fashion accessories.[18] Ruffs, pleated collars that appeared lightweight, often involved a good deal of fabric **fig. 37**. To keep them upright when worn around the neck, they were held up by a special wire frame known in Dutch as *portefraas* and in English by the French term *supportasse* **fig. 38**.[19] Maria van Nesse was evidently among those who liked to wear a ruff: in 1646 she removed the ribbon from her supportasse for repair, even though flat lace collars had been coming into style since approximately 1625 and the ruff and supportasse were gradually vanishing from the fashion scene. The older generation went on having their portraits painted in ruffs until fairly late in the 1660s.[20]

At the mirror

Some people had a fully equipped vanity table so that they could always look sharp. Recipe books, herbals (botanical treatises) and *secreetboeken* (literally, 'books of secrets') also described numerous means of beautifying

34 This baby jacket is decorated front and back with yellow silk floral motifs. The opening runs all the way down, so that the infant's hands can slip easily into the sleeves

35, 36   The bodkin with the inscription *SARA* has a blue cut-glass pendant.
Such needles could be worn in the hair as an ornament, as the print shows

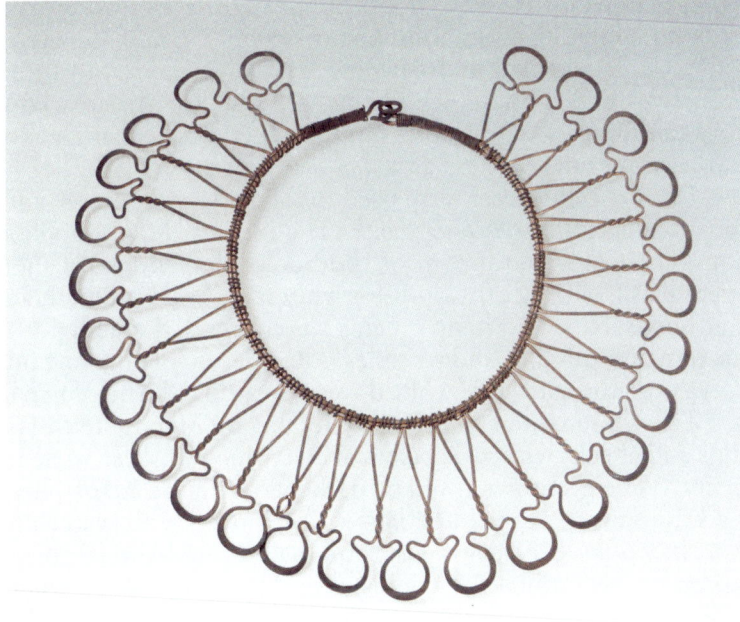

37, 38 The ruff is marked with the letters 'CY' in red silk, and consists of a linen collar to which has been sewn a long strip, nearly 20 metres, of very finely pleated linen batiste. The supportasse is made of silver-plated copper. That looked impressive from behind, where it was just visible beneath the collar

oneself. There were recipes for making your hair grow, dying it or curling it, for cleaning and whitening your teeth, and for removing unwanted hair or spots from your face. In combination with extant toiletries from the period, these books offer an impression of the daily rituals of self-care, which involved a great deal of cutting, combing, dyeing, tooth-picking, shaving and applying of lotions.

From the mid-seventeenth century onwards, it was customary among the upper classes to commission silver, or even gilt silver, toiletry sets consisting of matching, identically decorated objects, sometimes personalized with the family crest.[21] For example, Sara L'Empereur had a silver toiletry set with a mirror, a comb box, a number of candlesticks and two washing sets, as we learn from her 1685 will. Gesina Haagswolt, who lived in Leeuwarden, was the probable owner of a luxury six-piece toiletry set comprising a mirror with doors, a rectangular clothes brush, a round brush with a handle, a pincushion and a comb case, all covered with red silk velvet and adorned with lace made of silver and gold thread **fig. 39**. Toiletry sets such as these would have provided the basic accoutrements of the wealthy lady's vanity table, supplemented with creams and ointments in earthenware pots or glass flasks **fig. 40**.

Ointments were used for all sorts of cosmetic and medical purposes. *Het natuurlyk tover-boek* (The Natural Magic Book, 1684) by Simon Witgeest (pseudonym of the bookseller and publisher Willem Goeree) lists a variety of recipes for whitening skin and teeth and dyeing hair at home. Face and hand creams were intended chiefly for removing spots, freckles, pimples and wrinkles.[22] Recipes involving lime juice, white lead, eggs and the entrails of white doves were said to be helpful in lightening skin.[23] The whiteness of the skin could also be highlighted by colouring the lips and cheeks with red cochineal dye, which was also used as pigment for paint.[24] The eyebrows could be darkened with the aid of a heated clove and a little saliva.[25] Unwanted hair was removed with water mixed with fifty or sixty pulverized eggshells.[26] And pain could be relieved with a salve based on alabaster, like the one used by Maria van Nesse when she had hurt her leg.[27]

This vanity set consists of a book mirror, pincushion, two brushes, a comb bag, and a cloth for the table. The mirror could be placed upright on the table or hung on the wall. Pins were used to hold clothing together

39

For cleaning and whitening teeth, all manner of caustic and scouring substances were recommended, including lime juice, alum and powdered porcelain.[28] Chewing pieces of porcelain was also said to keep the teeth firmly in place.[29] But for centuries, the most important form of dental care had been using a toothpick between the teeth. Smooth, pointed objects such as birds' claws, chicken bones, goose quills and straw were well suited to this purpose, but toothpicks could also be made of wood, ivory, bronze, copper, or even gold or silver.[30] Toothpicks fashioned from precious metals were worn as jewellery in the early seventeenth century **fig. 41**.

Hair was rarely washed with soap, but other steps were taken to ensure a respectable appearance. Baldness and hair loss were combatted with a range of oils and salves, including some based on honey, but these recipes are unlikely to have been very effective.[31] Indeed, in the summer of 1634, Maria van Nesse had a hairpiece made with curly hair to protect her head from the cold.[32]

It was also not unusual to bleach or dye the hair on one's head.[33] For example, Witgeest writes that the 'peasant women of Waterland' (not far north of Amsterdam) bleached their hair blonde with soapy water containing extra lye. Red and grey hair ('undistinguished hair') could be dyed black with a solution of 'strong water' (nitric acid), silver and sal ammoniac. This mixture had to be carefully prevented from touching the scalp, otherwise it would make the hair fall out.[34]

For daily hair care, the comb, and particularly the lice comb, was traditionally the most important item.[35] A comb was used not only for styling the hair but also for keeping it clean; it removed dirt and lice and redistributed the natural hair oils more evenly.[36] Every household, regardless of social class or income, had a comb. Luxury varieties were made of tortoiseshell or elephant ivory, but unadorned, wooden combs were the most widespread type **fig. 42**.[37]

While combing their hair, both men and women protected their clothes with a type of short linen or cotton cape called a *kamdoek* (literally, 'combing cloth'; **fig. 43**). In the first quarter of the seventeenth century, this practical garment became an increasingly important part of

40a-i   These small jars of ointment, made of red earthenware, are found in excavations in large numbers. In fact, they have been described as the 'disposable plastic of the 17th century'

41, 42 This bronze pendant in the shape of a mermaid, an archaeological find, has a toothpick on the right and a spoon on the left for cleaning the ears. The wooden lice comb, which remained unchanged in design for centuries, was used to remove tangles, lice, and dirt from one's hair

women's domestic attire and was eventually worn outside the home as well. This was still mainly done for practical purposes: the kamdoek protected the clothes underneath it, which were made of expensive, non-washable materials such as silk and wool.[38]

In the early decades of the seventeenth century, women's hair was often hidden under a cap with a bonnet (*huif*) worn over it, both at home and in the outside world.[39] But displaying one's hair became increasingly normal, at least in public. Perhaps this explains why curly hair became more fashionable in the Northern Netherlands (and, in fact, throughout Europe) from around 1630 onwards – to judge by the many ringlets and other curls found in portraits. In Leonora Huydecoper's family portrait, she has a combination of hair combed straight back and lovely ringlets (see **fig. 27**). Agatha van Neck and her three eldest daughters also have curls in abundance (see **fig. 55**). For those 'with their hair hanging straight down like a pound of candles', Witgeest offered several remedies.[40] One was to soak each individual lock in a pot of boiling water for two hours; it was claimed that when dried, the hair would form long-lasting curls. And for curly hair 'like someone from Brazil', you could treat your hair with a hot iron comb. Witgeest describes a method specifically for ringlets: before bed, the hair is treated with gum arabic dissolved in water and then curled up using tobacco pipes or slips of paper. Left in this state under a nightcap all night, then combed out in the morning and sprinkled with a little powder, the curls will last all day.[41]

Healthy and sound

Of course, we all know that beauty is only skin deep. Van Beverwijck believed that in the time God grants us, the really important thing is to master the 'art of healthy living'.[42] According to humoral theory, health and equilibrium in the human body depended not only on the four bodily fluids known as humours, but also on the 'non-natural' factors that still form the foundation of a healthy lifestyle today: mental health, air, good things to eat and drink, exercise and relaxation, adequate sleep, and the retention and discharge of fluids such as sweat and menstrual blood.[43] 'Air'

43 This *kamdoek* ('combing cloth'), a short cape made of linen batiste and bobbin lace, kept the garments underneath clean and was also a fashionable accessory

This colourful enamelled pomander can be opened to reveal six compartments filled with different spices: mace, *slach* (a mixture of ambergris, musk, and civet), rose petals, cinnamon, clove, and angelica

44

referred to the natural environment in general: the nature and quality of the air and water, the climate, the changing of the seasons, and the land on which people lived.[44] Special care was taken to avoid miasmas, or 'bad air' (*mala aria*), which were said to enter the body by way of the skin or breath and cause illnesses such as the bubonic plague.[45]

On 14 September 1624, David Beck, a schoolmaster in The Hague, wrote in his diary that he felt sick in his 'brains, heart, and body' and was preparing for a 'Christian demise'.[46] In the preceding weeks he had lost a number of acquaintances to the plague and had attended funerals in Delft for people who had succumbed to that 'Gift of God' or 'hasty disease'.[47] Now it was his turn, he thought. But he turned out to have no more than an upset stomach, and after some retching and belching he felt much better.

Infectious diseases and other health problems were commonplace, and the people of the Dutch Republic tried all manner of techniques to ward them off, treat them and cure them. In the fight against the bubonic plague, the priority was to make sure that you and your relatives would not be infected. That was not easy, because what truly caused the plague to spread remained unknown. Alongside copious prayer, people implemented a variety of preventive measures intended to protect their bodies and homes.[48] In these efforts, fragrances played a crucial role. To dispel miasmas and protect their skin by perfuming the air around them, both men and women wore accessories that gave off scents.[49] For example, Johannes Thysius bought two pairs of 'perfumed gloves' in 1648, one with black lace and the other with gold and silk lace.[50] Maria van Nesse, deciding to take no risks, protected herself from the plague in various ways. One was to use a pomander, a spherical ornament filled with fragrant herbs and spices, either in the form of a kind of pellet of aromatic gum or with separate compartments for each of the spices fig. 44. Pomanders frequently took the form of a decorative openwork pendant to be worn on a chain around the neck or waist.[51] Besides her pomander, Maria had a 'silver pill for the plague' (a small plague amulet), which she wore on an old chain.[52] In 1624 and 1636 – notorious plague years in Alkmaar – she also bought cakes marketed as preventing this illness and sent for consecrated white bread rolls from Utrecht.[53] She distributed these rolls to friends, acquaintances and relatives.

Fragrant herbs and spices were not only worn on the body but also used to disinfect the house. A 'clean and pure' house was deemed just as essential as personal hygiene. According to an anonymous pamphlet from 1655, the most important thing was to open only the northern and eastern windows of one's house; since the plague was borne by 'noxious western and southern air', those windows had to stay closed.[54] Another possible measure was to scatter aromatic substances in the fire or burn scented lozenges.[55] *Den schat der armen* (The Treasury of the Poor, 1626) contains recipes for protecting the home from the plague, for instance by tossing a mixture of crushed bay leaf, rosemary, myrrh, cinnamon, incense, thyme, nutmeg and rue onto the hot coals in the hearth every morning and evening.[56]

Despite the many remedies on the market, illnesses and other medical complaints were unavoidable. On 8 August 1642, Catharina Fourmenois (see **fig. 169g**), who lived in Zeeland, gave birth to her thirteenth and last child, a son named Hendrick. In the surviving family chronicle, her husband Pieter Boudaen Courten writes that, several weeks after the delivery, Catharina's bladder began to bother her, and 'making water' (urination) became painful. The pain grew worse and worse. It was not until 15 December 1646, more than four years later, after a multitude of unsuccessful recommendations and treatments, that the Zierikzee city doctor, Willem Boenaert, diagnosed her with a large bladder stone. In a final attempt to 'soften' the stone and make it crumble, the oil of 'sweet almonds' was administered into her bladder twice a day through a catheter, but it made no difference. Surgery was the only remaining option, and on 4 January 1647 Catharina asked her husband to 'have it removed, in the name of God'.[57]

The surgical removal of a bladder stone was one of the most frequently performed operations in the seventeenth century. It was a painful, risky procedure and often a last resort when the stone could not

45   Catharina Fourmenois's bladder stone was removed with special
      forceps through an incision (via the anus or uterus) in 1647

be made small enough to pass naturally.[58] Unfortunately, it was often unsuccessful, and some patients who survived the surgery were incontinent for the rest of their lives.[59]

In this instance, Catharina was in good hands. Willem Boenaert was not just any physician but a specialized surgeon and 'cutter for the stone', and the inventory of his medical library shows that he had a good grounding in this field.[60] After a quick trip to Vlissingen to pick up special forceps, he operated on Catharina in her home on 8 January.[61] Soon after the operation, she was advised to eat soup and the meat of young fowl and drink as little as possible.[62] After two weeks she developed a fever, but by early April she was strong enough to return to church for the first time. The operation had been successful, and Catharina still had more than eighteen years of life ahead. The remarkably large bladder stone, a full 5 centimetres in size, has remained in the possession of her descendants for centuries, as a memento of this unusual occurrence **fig. 45**.[63]

Bedroom secrets

Some families have passed down written records describing a household's most intimate moments. Joan Huydecoper Jr, the burgomaster of Amsterdam, jotted down the letter 'c' (for coitus) in his diary for each day he had sexual intercourse with his wife, Sophia Coymans.[64] On rare occasions, there was more than one 'c' on a single day, and in 1659 he even calculated his monthly and annual coitus figures.[65] His notes show that the couple's sexual relations continued during Sophia's pregnancies, all the way up to two weeks before delivery. While moralists like Jacob Cats declared that the purpose of intercourse should always be procreation, Joan's notes show that people sometimes had sex for other reasons.[66] Furthermore, physicians did not necessarily advise against couples 'lying together'. They noted that couples should be careful not to imperil the unborn foetus with 'too much ploughing of the field' but believed that frequent kissing and love-making could lead to an easier delivery.[67] In fact, they encouraged men to 'discharge their natural seed' regularly to remain 'fresh' and maintain their health.[68]

Van Beverwijck believed that the healthiest time of day for intercourse was the morning, when food had been fully digested and the spirit refreshed. But, he wrote, the most pleasurable time was in the evening, and some people took this as a reason to have a large midday meal and a light supper.[69] Van Beverwijck regarded winter and spring as the best seasons for sexual contact; summer was too hot, and autumn brought various illnesses. Unfortunately, Joan did not record the times of day in his diary, but the annual figures show that he and Sophia enjoyed an intimate 'embrace' regularly in the summer of 1659.[70] It was a blustery, rain-swept summer – all the more reason to huddle indoors together.[71]

In 1695, Isabella de Moederloose, a pastor's widow in Zeeland, published a remarkable piece of writing: a frank account of the most intimate details of her married life. Around 1690 Isabella had married the Reformed clergyman Laurentius Hoogentoren, an older widower with two teenage children, who had already known Isabella as their governess. Laurentius died not long afterwards, and he and Isabella had no children of their own, but her memoir makes it clear that the couple had every reason to be satisfied with their love life. They teased each other with off-colour jokes, praised each other's looks, and squabbled about their age difference and sexual desires. For example, Laurentius tried to persuade Isabella to perform fellatio, to her disgust. When the pastor was uninterested in sex, he would tell Isabella, 'I'm cold.'[72] He may have been referring to the tenet of the humoral theory that sex was 'not only damaging, but often fatal' to 'cold and dry people' – in other words, to the elderly.[73]

After Laurentius died, rumours made the rounds of their village of Heinkenszand and the nearby city of Goes about why Isabella had never become pregnant. In a conversation with a cousin, Isabella was very clear about the reason: the pastor had never 'given seed' to her. She complained several times in her book about his practice of 'first arousing nature and then throwing away the seed'.[74] This was a clear case of coitus interruptus, and may explain why the couple never conceived a child. It was probably a conscious choice on Laurentius's part, so that his modest estate would not have to be divided between more than two children.[75]

This form of contraception, and the periodic abstinence advised by the Church, were not the only seventeenth-century methods of family planning. Van Beverwijck describes a variety of plants and herbs for 'cleansing the womb', including two recipes for the 'expulsion of male seed'. For instance, water lily root was said to 'benumb the testicular seed', and rue, if 'placed below', could extinguish the 'Excitement and the Seed'.[76] The doctor used the terms 'from above and below' and 'injected' when describing how women were to self-administer these mixtures. He probably had in mind an instrument known as a vaginal syringe or douche.[77] This would be used to introduce cleansing or contraceptive herbal preparations vaginally, a form of birth control that remained in use well into the twentieth century. The painter Jan Steen depicted syringes in a number of his sexually charged scenes of 'doctors' visits'. These are usually described as enema syringes, for introducing medicine into the digestive system, but they are possibly vaginal syringes. The message of these paintings is, after all, that the woman lying in bed could not be cured with medicine, but only by her husband or lover.[78]

In 1997, the excavation of a cesspit in Zwolle city centre uncovered two 17th-century wooden objects that may be identifiable as early vaginal syringes. One of the items, made of four separate boxwood parts, has the explicit shape of the male sexual organ **fig. 46**.[79] The hollow interior would have been filled with a fluid that could be ejected into the vagina by pressing the plunger. Looking at the shape of this syringe found in Zwolle, we might wonder whether it had not only a practical but also an erotic purpose. The use of artificial phalluses, made of smooth materials such as glass and ivory, was certainly not unfamiliar to women. In the mid-seventeenth century, the French erotic novel *L'Escole des filles* (known in English as *The School of Venus*), which described sexual acts, was translated into Dutch under the title of *De schoole voor de jonge dochters* (The School for Young Daughters). An English edition from 1680 includes illustrations of the acts, and its frontispiece depicts three young ladies at a dildo stall. Further research is needed, however, to place the use of the two Zwolle syringes in context.[80]

Although the vaginal syringe was mainly intended for vaginal douches with herbal preparations, it was not unheard of for this phallic object to be used for erotic purposes. This one, made of boxwood, was found in a cesspit in Zwolle

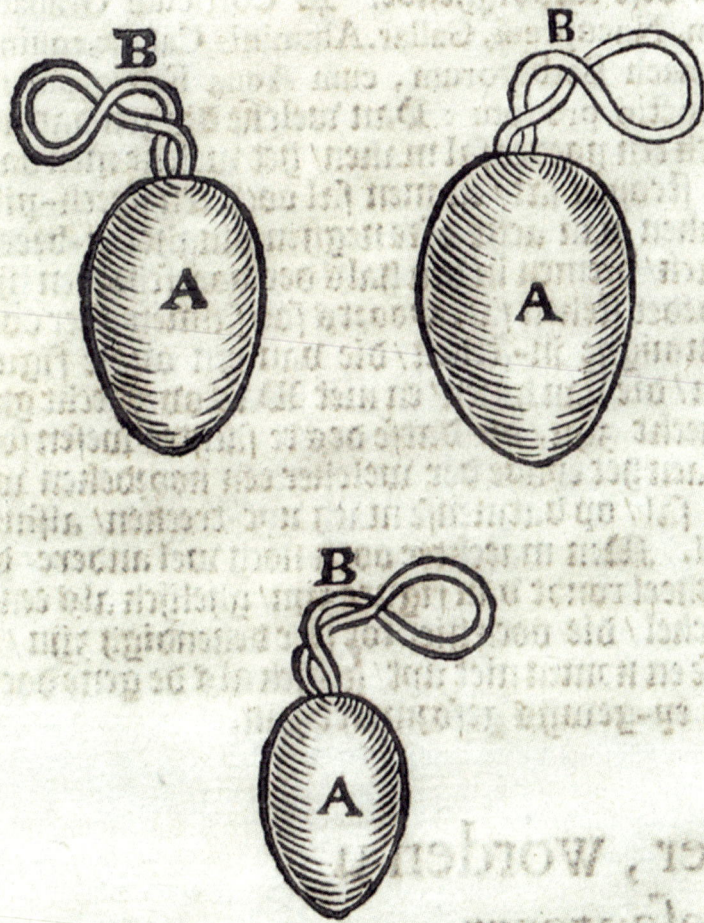

Cotton or woollen suppositories, soaked in herbal preparations, could be used either as pessaries or to treat medical complaints

Along with her sex life, Isabella de Moederloose also discussed an even rarer subject in her seventeenth-century life writings: menstruation and the discomfort it caused to women. This was prompted by her request to her husband for them to sleep in separate beds when she was menstruating. She feared that Laurentius would be disgusted by the 'stench' and no longer want to be with her, and so offered to come to him afterwards 'like a new bride or fresh rose', 'with clean clothes on and properly cleansed'.[81] According to Isabella, her husband was utterly opposed. 'They would call us Jewish,' he replied, and he joined her in bed despite the supposed smell, saying, 'I'm sure to get used to it.'[82] The pastor was referring to the Jewish tradition in which the menstruating woman, the *niddah*, sleeps in a separate bed from her husband for her twelve 'impure' days. Only after a symbolic cleansing in the *mikveh*, the ritual bath, do traditional Jewish women have sexual contact with their husbands again.[83]

Isabella's comment about 'clean clothes' suggests that her nightclothes, probably a linen slip and possibly linen underpants, became dirty.[84] Medical works tell us that, in addition, it was not unusual to insert cotton or woollen 'pessaries' or 'suppositories' into the vagina **fig. 47**; these were often soaked in herbal preparations to treat medical conditions, but women may also have used them to absorb menstrual blood and as a form of contraception.[85]

Although theories about the purpose of menstruation varied, medical experts agreed that it was essential to women's health.[86] According to the theory of humours, it was the only way for women to rid themselves of accumulated bodily fluids.[87] Van Beverwijck observed that this 'discharge' took place monthly, usually between the ages of about fourteen and around forty-nine or fifty.[88] Reaching the age of fertility was in any case an important event. There were even two saints, Lucy and Catherine, who offered aid and protection to young Catholic women in connection with menstruation, fertility and pregnancy. So it may not be entirely coincidental that when Ael van Juckema in Friesland was around sixteen years old, she received a silver reliquary from her father depicting these two saints among others **fig. 48**.[89]

Irregular menstrual periods were seen as an illness, and books of medical advice contained recipes and treatments for two contrasting purposes: promoting monthly menstrual flow and putting a stop to it.[90] One substance thought to encourage menstruation was aloe vera. This plant's medicinal and cosmetic properties were well known in the seventeenth century.[91] In 1644, Maria van Nesse wrote in her *memorieboek* (notebook) that she had bought eight stivers worth of washed aloe from the pharmacist Willem Stope, from which he had made 36 pills. Maria had been taking such pills for some time to 'cleanse and relieve her stomach', but this time the pills were intended for her needleworker Dieurtge, to provoke menstruation. A year later, Maria gave her maid's sister Aeltge aloe vera pills rolled 'in liquorice', also intended to make her menstruate (or perhaps resume menstruating).[92]

Along with these pills, Maria also took gentian root for her stomach trouble,[93] often just before going to bed. She probably hoped she would start the next day with a 'soft bowel movement'.[94] Van Beverwijck emphasized the critical importance of sleep to good digestion and for dispelling fatigue and refreshing the mind and spirit. He recommended sleeping on one's side, with the arms and knees slightly bent.[95] The best time for sleeping was at night (after all, a person is not an owl), and preferably one or two hours after the evening meal; seven or eight hours of sleep was sufficient, depending on the body's 'natural warmth'.[96] By nature, children had more than enough body heat, while adults grew colder with the years and therefore needed less sleep.[97] Elisabeth Strouven, a nun in Maastricht, went to bed at nine in the evening during Lent, after coming home from church at seven or eight o'clock, eating a piece of bread, and praying. But she rose at four in the morning to pray in silence for an hour.[98] In his Arnhem diaries from 1627–1628, David Beck took almost daily note of his sleeping and waking times. He usually retired between ten and twelve at night; by sunrise he was up again, preparing for a new day.[99]

When we read what people like David Beck and Maria van Nesse wrote about their personal lives in the seventeenth century, it is surprising how many words are devoted to the care of their inner bodies,

This silver box, which Ael van Juckema received when she was about sixteen, is gilded on the inside and originally contained a relic. The lid shows the coats of arms of her paternal and maternal grandparents

48

and to the health and illness of the writers themselves and their families. Visiting or being visited by a doctor, surviving an operation, taking medicine for ailments large and small, and fearing the plague were all subjects seen as meriting discussion in writing, alongside records of births and deaths. The many ways people tried to maintain or recover their health represented hope in an uncertain world and formed an integral part of daily home life. From the privy to the vanity table with its toiletries, from the clean linen smocks in the chest of drawers to a fragrant pomander: all these objects and practices combined to form the foundation of a healthy, presentable body and a pure spirit.

mealtime

Sara van Dijk

Panic broke out in the Van Nesse household one morning in the middle of June 1640. Maria had just broached a new barrel of *bière de mars* in the cellar; no more than four glasses had been tapped when it suddenly started to roll. It smashed open, emptying its entire contents. The cellar floor had to be mopped in great haste, for there were other provisions that had to be kept dry. But Maria's main concern was where she could get hold of a new barrel. Produced in early spring, *bière de mars* had a high alcohol content and lasted longer, unlike beer brewed in the summer. Her regular supplier, the De Ruijten brewery, could not help her. Fortunately, her odd-job man, the cabinetmaker Jan Kornelisse, tipped her off that the Boompje brewery still had half a barrel.[1] The incident shows just how seasonal and labour-intensive cooking was in the seventeenth century. Whether managing supplies or laying the table, cooking the daily fare or serving a festive meal, the mistress of the house had her work cut out for her.

Keeping stock
A well-to-do household such as Maria's had a large quantity of foodstuffs at its disposal. The storeroom in Petronella de la Court's doll's house gives a good insight into this. Seven tiny wooden barrels bear the inscriptions 'Rice', 'Hulled Barley', 'Barley', 'Green Peas' and 'Wheat Flour'. There are also two meat-curing barrels, a vinegar barrel, an egg rack and two bundles of dried fish.[2]

Maintaining such a large stock was no mean feat, as we learn from the rare sources of three wealthy women: the *memorieboek* (notebook) of the unmarried Maria van Nesse from Alkmaar, the highly detailed inventory of the widow Josina Schade van Westrum from Den Bosch and the account book of Sara L'Empereur, wife and mother of four surviving children in Leiden.[3] We are seldom allowed so intimate a peek into the lives and everyday concerns of housewives in the seventeenth century. Although a large number of inventories, such as Josina's, have been preserved, drawn up after death for the purposes of distributing inheritance, hers is more detailed than most, and we are even afforded an insight into her food supplies, which were generally not mentioned.

All year round these women were busy laying in non-perishable goods, such as flour, rice, spices and dried fruit, and preserving fresh produce, including dairy foods, vegetables, fruit, meat and fish fig. 49. Sara paints a vivid picture of the annual rhythm of her life in the monthly to-do lists she jotted down at the back of her account book: May was the month to stock up on butter. Walnuts had to be candied before St John's Day (24 June). From then until Christmas the salmon was no good, she noted. In September, beans had to be preserved, followed towards the end of the month by the pickling of lettuce and cucumbers and marmalade making. At the end of October, it was time for laying in apples, turnips and carrots.[4]

November was the butchering month, and many women were preoccupied with processing the meat. In November 1640, Maria van Nesse noted down the recipe for *beulingen* (soft sausages) as these were made at the hospital in Alkmaar, with cloves, pepper, juniper berries and a handful of salt. A few days later, she stuffed her own sausages, replacing the juniper berries with mace; she then boiled them in water with barley. Three years later, in the same month, she purchased half an ox that her brother had had slaughtered. She salted the meat, which like cheese was popular on bread, and gave the priest a portion.[5] The butchering season was an excellent moment to present meat and meat dishes to family and acquaintances, not just because it was too much for one household but also as a friendly gesture.

Ensuring all these foodstuffs did not perish could be challenging. Supplies were preferably not left lying around in the kitchen, in the vicinity of the fire, but kept in the cellar or in a *spinde* (food cupboard). The doors of a rare early seventeenth-century example are executed in a waffle pattern with small holes for ventilation fig. 50. Inside it has two shelves for food and drinks. Despite careful preservation, decay was always lurking around the corner. Maria noted two recipes to 'make butter that is rancid sweet again', although that did not prevent her from having to go to the trouble of purchasing fresh butter from two different farmers through a third party when the old butter had gone off in 1645.[6]

Along with woven baskets, metal buckets were often used for bringing home purchases, especially fish. This lavish specimen has a lid decorated with a coat of arms and flowering vines

This food cupboard with ventilation grilles, dating from approximately 1610 to 1630, is made of deal or spruce wood but painted as if it were oak, and its pilasters resemble the decoration of luxurious linen cupboards

The cellar of Petronella Oortman's doll's house is hidden in a drawer of the cabinet. This area is used for storage of wine, beer, cookware, and cleaning products

51

Josina had a food storage cellar, where, besides the five opened casks of butter, a flour barrel and jars of capers and fat, beer and wine were also stored. The inventory lists 'a wooden beer or wine rack in the wine cellar'.[7] This was probably not a separate space but a screened-off area. In seventeenth-century doll's houses, the storeroom had a slatted wood partition. The cellar in Petronella Oortman's doll's house, which is ingeniously concealed in a drawer beneath the house, is a good example **fig. 51**; the partition, behind which the drink supplies were kept, has a door with a lock. This enabled the mistress of the house, who held the key, to control who had access. Beer and wine barrels lie on a duckboard, precisely as described in Josina's inventory. On the wall in the doll's house above these is a shelf with holes in it, in which the round-bellied wine bottles could be stored upside down to keep the corks – a seventeenth-century invention – moist. Since the size of wine bottles was not standardized, this was much more practical than a wine rack.[8] In addition to three barrels of beer with a total content of over 500 litres and an opened cask of wine, Josina also kept two bottles of Fronténac, a white Bordeaux wine, in her cellar.

Maria likewise kept her liquor supply safely locked away behind such a slatted partition. On a loose sheet of paper, she kept a tally of how many jugs of wine and beer had already been tapped.[9] For this, special wine jugs were used **fig. 52**, which she regularly had to replace. For beer she used lidded tankards, which could be drunk straight out of **fig. 53**. There is an obstinate belief that people used to drink beer to avoid the polluted water of the canals. But in fact, although beer consumption was high, clean drinking water was available, chiefly by harvesting rainwater in underground basins or through the fresh river water brought in by ship. Moreover, bottled spring water was also on sale.[10] Even the inventory of a humble Zwolle bricklayer who relied on poor relief lists '2 spa water jugs'.[11]

Laying in and managing provisions demanded both commodity knowledge and vigilance. Sara's notes reminding her of the different tasks throughout the year and Maria's worry about obtaining fresh supplies of beer or butter when something had gone wrong clearly show the amount of time and effort involved in this side of the housekeeping – even though

This type of pewter jug was used for serving wine. Thanks to the long spout, the wine could be poured into the glass in a graceful arc

Beer was drunk from lidded tankards. This one has a peg on the inside to indicate the volume of liquid, so that you could keep careful track of how much beer you poured

53

these affluent women had help at home and did not have to earn a living as well. According to the much-read moralist Jacob Cats, a watchful eye was crucial for a good housewife. At market stalls, she had to be able to distinguish beef from game and local from imported fruits, and to recognize when 'a good bargain was a pickpurse'.[12] Such knowledge was not only important for the housekeeping budget but also vital for the preparation of tasty and healthy meals.

On the hearth

No doubt all three women, Maria, Sara and Josina, worked in the kitchen themselves, whether or not assisted by a maid. The 1660 manual *De verstandige huys-houder* (The Wise Housekeeper) recommended that everyone should decide for themselves how the tasks were divided, though hastened to add that, while there were family men who 'understood the art of cooking', it was better that they leave that task to their wives, who could always hire a cook if necessary. Preparing the daily meal was above all a woman's work.[13] This meant great responsibility rested on her shoulders, for she not only had to be able to cook well and keep everything spotlessly clean, more importantly she had to have a good knowledge of her ingredients, as Cats had also already stressed. For if you were not careful, the anonymous author of the housekeeping manual warned, you could pick the wrong herbs from the garden and poison the whole family with a simple green salad.

Besides being tasty, a meal also had to be healthy. Though they were gradually shifting, ideas on this matter in the seventeenth century were still rooted in the ancient humoral theory.[14] In accordance with this, all foodstuffs were divided into categories based on the opposites hot/cold and wet/dry. If your bodily fluids – and hence you yourself – were out of balance, you could remedy this and remain healthy by eating the right food. This was far from an exact science. What was understood as healthy depended on the individual, the season, the preparation method and the combination of ingredients. A cold, moist apple was fine in the hot, dry summer but less suitable in the winter, unless you baked it with spices, giving it a warmer character. You could compensate for the cold, wet properties of lettuce by adding a warming oil and salt to drew out the moisture. This explains the derivation of the word 'salad' from the Italian *insalata*, meaning 'salted'.[15] Our current classification of certain wines as 'dry' also comes from the humoral theory. Wine was warm and, depending on the variety, dry or wet. Warmth was a quality generally preferred above that of cold and wet, and wine came to be regarded as both a drink and a medicine. A large rummer for white wine from 1640 literally tells the consumer that it is good for the stomach with its engraved inscription 'This is a stomachal' – a term that is no longer in use **fig. 54**.[16]

How did women come by this knowledge? Cookery books, written by physicians or famous cooks, were readily available both in Dutch and French, but it is unclear for which readers they were intended. The instructions are summary, and it is telling that the examples that have survived are in such good condition, without the stains or dog-eared pages that you would expect from intensive use in the kitchen.[17] Cats devoted attention to healthy cooking; then there were the highly popular medical manuals *Schat der gesontheyt* (Treasury of Health, 1636) and *Schat der ongesontheyt* (Treasury of Ill-health, 1642) by the Dordrecht physician Johan van Beverwijck, and herbal guides such as the *Cruydeboeck* (Book of Herbs, 1554) by Rembertus Dodonaeus, which were reprinted several times in the seventeenth century. The Frisian aristocrat Andriese Lucia Bronkhorst came across a recipe for a fortifying broth with egg in this kind of literature. It was apparently worth remembering, for she wrote down the instructions on a loose sheet of paper and slipped it into the cover of her account book.[18] Similarly, Sara's notes on what needed to be done and when can also sometimes be traced back to advice books.[19]

There must have been a very lively exchange of tips and recipes. In January 1634 Maria recorded two different recipes for rice pudding one under the other. She had received the first from the cook at the hospital, who put the milk on early in the morning, at seven or eight o'clock, and allowed it to simmer until the afternoon. 'It has to be stirred for an hour,' Maria added. The second had come through her niece, who reported that at her brother's house the rice had first to be washed and

This rummer, 23 centimeters tall, bears the inscription, 'Dit is stomachael' ('This is good for the stomach'). A play dating from 1658 mentions French wines that are 'gesont en stomachael' ('healthy and good for the stomach')

then be boiled on a high heat until it had sufficiently thickened. The proportions were the same in both methods: three-eighths of a pound of rice to about three pints of milk. A few years later, Maria prepared the porridge in her copper pot using three pints of milk and noted that it was only thick enough with three-quarters of a pound of rice.[20] This was not just a useful reminder for her when cooking, but also vital information when working out how much rice she had to have in stock.

Experience with cooking on an open fire and with all the accompanying kitchen utensils was at least as important. In the simplest homes, people lived and cooked in one and the same room, the hearth being the principal source of light and heat. There will not have been room for much more than a kettle and a single earthenware cooking pot. For most people, therefore, a hot meal consisted of furmity (a thick porridge of milk and grain) or pottage (a one-pot meal of legumes or grain and, for those who could afford them, vegetables, meat or fish), supplemented with bread.[21] Endless stirring was vital to prevent burning, as Maria noted. This was an uncomfortable job, standing bent over the hearth. In the second half of the seventeenth century, a new invention came into vogue in the richest households: the potager (brick oven), with a small iron door behind which the fire burned. It still had no flue, but it made cooking a lot less arduous and allowed greater control over the fire.[22] In either case, a housewife or kitchen maid had a command of fire craft, a skill that, behind the barbecue on a hot summer day, we now regard as typically male.

The simple stews stand in sharp contrast to the elaborate meals that Josina was able to serve with her enormous collection of cookware.[23] Her collection of pots and pans in the kitchen alone is impressive. She had saucepans, stewpots made of copper, a large number of copper baking pans, a pan for roasting hare, a tinplate jam-making pan and 'a tinplate pan for baking apples' (a semicircular tin pan, the open right-hand side of which could be turned to face the fire when making puffed apples). She also had iron chafing dishes, which were filled with smouldering peat for simmering dishes. Off the kitchen there was also a 'small kitchen' or scullery with a stand on which all the earthenware was kept, which varied from oil jugs and jugs for heating cream and milk to Delft blue-and-white dishes and plates. No cooking was done in the scullery, but the scullion (kitchen servant) may have done the washing up there.[24] Josina kept the cooking utensils and equipment she used most in a room off the scullery. Here, for instance, stood the turnspit, a spit that was fitted with a winding mechanism that automatically rotated it.

In addition to all the roasts and other refined dishes, Josina served ordinary pottage in pewter pottage dishes of all shapes and sizes: large or small and deep, with or without the family arms. She may well have cooked these stews in the 'large copper kettle, with a repaired base'. This shows that ordinary food was served even in well-to-do households and that functional items were more often repaired than replaced. This applied just as much to Maria and to Sara, the latter of whom had the handle of her skimmer mended and her pots and pans tinned anew to prevent interaction with acidic foods.[25] It was above all the amount of equipment they owned that distinguishes their kitchens from those of the lower classes, and the room they had to create separate spaces for cooking, washing up and storing provisions.

Revealing waste

We only know Josina's cooking utensils on paper, thanks to the extensive inventory of her estate. Archaeologists, however, also retrieve original kitchenware. Many urban households had a wooden or brick cesspit beneath their houses or in their gardens that was used as a latrine or refuse pit for household waste. Sooner or later the remains of every meal ended up here, offering us a wealth of information on seventeenth-century eating habits. A cesspit at the house Ramen 1 in Hoorn, in the province of North Holland, excavated in 2019, turned out to be an exceptionally rich source.

Burgomaster and ambassador Albert Sonck moved here with Cornelia van Segwaert, his second wife, in 1638. They both had one or more children from their first marriages as well as a son, Meindert, who was born in 1626. The house was more than large enough for the blended family, and when Meindert married Agatha van Neck in 1653, the young

Jan Albertsz Rotius portrayed the Sonck family in 1662. Meindert and Agatha are seated amid their children (in order of increasing age from left to right): Albert, Geertruyd, Margaretha, and Cornelia. Baby Lucia and her nurse were added later

55

couple continued to live there. They had nine children in total, some of whom can be seen in a charming family portrait fig. 55.[26] Not only was the house spacious but so was the accompanying refuse pit, and that was rare. Its size meant that it never needed to be emptied. More usually, when cesspits became too full, the contents were scooped out by privy-cleaners. What is more, several households often made use of the same cesspit, and many towns had a collection service for household waste. As a result, archaeologists seldom encounter the waste of a single household.[27] The Sonck family's cesspit is a fantastic exception.[28] The excavation brought to light not only discarded pots and pans but also countless food remains fig. 56. This allows us a unique insight into their kitchen.

    Like Josina, Cornelia and Agatha possessed a large arsenal of cooking utensils. With the exception of a few pewter spoons, they seldom threw metal objects away. When these were broken, they were generally melted down and hence did not end up in the cesspit. The variety of ceramics found in the cesspit, on the other hand, was enormous: cooking pots and jugs for heating milk and other liquids (with three legs to stand them in the hearth), frying pans, saucepans, colanders, drip trays – all robust earthenware fig. 57. Apart from an apple baking pan, these were ordinary pots that could be found in every Dutch kitchen, rich and poor: there was no difference in the quality of the cooking pots and pans, and those in wealthy homes were identical to those of less well-off citizens. It was the quantity of this functional earthenware and what was cooked in it that indicated the family's prosperity.[29]

    Albert Sonck was not only doing well financially, his titles and positions also brought him the right to hunt. Through letters we know he hunted in the Beemster, a polder not long reclaimed from a lake to the south of Hoorn.[30] His spoils were found in the cesspit: grey heron, bean goose, bittern, water rail, snipe and teal. These kinds of water birds were generally roasted, though they could also be used in pies. Such exquisite ingredients were in keeping with Albert's standing, not just because he could show off with them but because they were considered healthy. Like your gender or star sign, according to the humoral theory, your place on

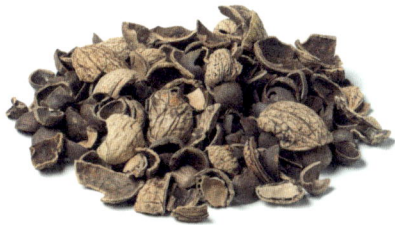

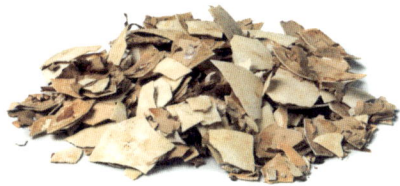

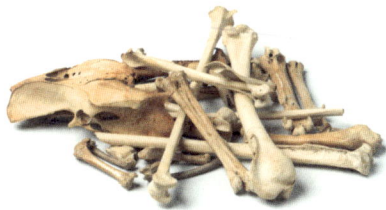

56a–f The Sonck family had a varied diet. From top left to bottom right: nutshells (almond, hazelnut, walnut), eggshells (duck, chicken), fruit pits (cherry, plum, grape, medlar, peach), poultry bones, mussel and oyster shells, and fish remains

57a–l Cookware made of red and white earthenware, from the cesspit of the Sonck family in Hoorn. The legs made the jugs and pots stand stably on the burning peat in the hearth

58   Detail of a kitchen interior by Reynier Covyn, c. 1665–1670. The maid is preparing fish in large pewter dishes. The fish has been scored so that it will cook faster and better absorb the sauce

the social ladder affected your physiological condition. A farmer was best off eating turnips from the land; for gentlemen of high standing, air-bound fowl was more suitable.[31] Other costly kinds of meat from the butcher and the poulterer also appeared on the menu: veal, ham, chicken and duck.

    A great deal of fish remains were also found. The fish the family ate included cod (both fresh and dried), haddock, whiting, herring, plaice, flounder, ray and eel. Most physicians were not very enthusiastic about fish. It was by nature too cold and wet, although you could compensate for that, for instance, by frying the fish at a high temperature. Braising was another way of cooking fish. This was not done in the hearth but between two plates on a chafing dish with red-hot peat, as described in the cookery books of the period. A painting by Reynier Covyn depicts this fig. 58. The kitchen maid has placed a pewter plate with fish on a chafing dish and is pouring sauce over them from a long-handled pan – the exact same type as was discovered from the Sonck household (see fig. 57i). The sauce was usually sweet and sour, with a base of vinegar or verjuice (the sour juice of unripe apples or grapes) and a lot of spices. The warming and drying properties of these ingredients made up for the bad qualities of the fish. Another option was the addition of mustard or nuts, such as walnuts or almonds, which can also be seen in the painting.[32] It can hardly be a coincidence that apple and grape seeds (with traces of pressing) were among the waste in the cesspit, as were black mustard seeds and large quantities of almond skin and walnut shells (see figs. 56a, e). Apart from pepper, cumin and coriander, no other spices were found, possibly because they deteriorated more quickly underground.

    It is more difficult to deduce from the archaeological finds how eating habits changed over time. Even though Meindert's wife Agatha took over the kitchen and everything that went with it from her mother-in-law Cornelia, it is likely that she or her domestic servants had a different approach to seasoning. Meindert's father Albert died in 1658, at a time when something of a revolution was taking place in the culinary domain. In 1651, the French chef François Pierre de la Varenne had published a cookery book in which he promoted a more natural flavour. Instead of sweet and sour and an excess of spices, he proposed sauces based on butter and a moderate use of flavourings. It was the first step towards French cuisine as we know it today. Within as little as two years the cookbook was published in Amsterdam, and it was accompanied by a shift in attitudes to health. Though the humoral theory continued to exercise a profound influence until late in the eighteenth century, very slowly it gave way to a more modern form of science that was founded on observation.[33] Agatha would have used spices to flavour her fish but less excessively than her mother-in-law.

Daily bread

In addition to meat, fish, vegetables and fruit, the Sonck family ate a great deal of bread. This was the main staple in their diet. Van Beverwijck regarded it as a gift of God: after the Fall, Adam had to work for a living and eat bread 'by the sweat of his brow'. The heavy labour of growing and milling wheat, kneading and baking it was at the same time a punishment and a gift, according to the writer.[34] In the country it was customary to bake your own bread, but in the towns most people bought their bread from the baker. There was a wide variety of breads. Besides millet and buckwheat, remains of wheat and rye, the two main ingredients for everyday bread, were found in the Sonck family's cesspit.

In the advice literature of the period, a fairly strict social distinction was made between the latter two grains. Rye was hard to digest and was therefore more suitable for those who did physical work than for 'delicate folk'.[35] Wheat was the healthiest. Although it was warm and moist, according to the humoral theory, this was compensated by adding salt, which extracted moisture from the bread. A mixture of rye and wheat, known as maslin, struck a happy medium.[36] In practice, this advice was not strictly followed; certainly not in Holland, Zeeland and Utrecht, where the rich ate both wheat and rye bread, as did the Soncks. Sara L'Empereur also purchased both kinds of bread every week. In the week of 21 August 1660 she bought fourteen white bread rolls, a white loaf and rusks, a rye loaf and on two occasions a 'professor's loaf' – a name suggesting that this more expensive white bread was more suitable for those who worked with their heads rather than their hands.[37] A standard rye loaf was much larger and heavier than a wheat loaf or wheat baps, which meant that in Sara's family just as much rye as wheat bread was eaten. In the east of the Netherlands, where incomes were lower, the consumption of rye bread was considerably higher.[38]

Not everyone could afford enough bread. Illness, a death or some other calamity could plunge a family into poverty. Moreover, the effects of war were on everyone's lips, at least in the eastern and southern provinces, which lay in the firing line for the main part of the Eighty Years' War against the Spanish. Van Beverwijck explicitly mentioned that rye rusks, which kept well, were suitable not only for seamen and those who did heavy work, but also for 'towns under siege'.[39] In addition, bread prices fluctuated: there were regularly increases of 50 or even over 100 per cent. Estimates vary, but probably a quarter of the population had to resort to poor relief at some point. The organization and precise form the relief took varied from town to town. In addition to the town council, many church communities were active in poor relief. The needy were mostly given bread, butter and peat, and occasionally money. For their bread ration they received a note or a bread coin, which they could exchange at the baker's or the poor relief office (see **fig. 106**).[40] In principle, the poor were given the relatively cheap twelve-pound rye loaf, though in Delft, for example, wholemeal wheat bread was specially available for young children, the sick and the elderly.[41] Wealthy citizens likewise did their bit. Maria van Nesse handed out white bread and pancakes to the poor on feast days, noting proudly on one occasion that she herself had baked pancakes for no less than ten hours at a stretch.[42]

For the poorest, bread would have been the mainstay of their daily fare. The menu of the middle classes was more varied, and bread often formed part of a hot meal.[43] The journal that schoolteacher David Beck kept in The Hague in 1624 corroborates this. He regularly described what he ate, and that was seldom a bread meal. If he ate it at all, he had a reason for doing so. For example, he ate bread and butter on officially recognized days of fasting or prayer, or he skipped supper and made do with a piece of white bread around ten at night.[44] Twice he indulged in a hot white bap at breakfast, a doubly guilty pleasure, for white bread was unanimously frowned upon because it caused constipation, and when warm it was even worse because it resulted in a bloated stomach.[45]

Fine dining

The whole world came together on the seventeenth-century dinner table. The Sonck family ate fowl from the Beemster, olives from Spain or Italy, grain from Poland and pepper from India, served on Delft earthenware, Italian maiolica or Chinese porcelain **fig. 59**. It was not just the provenance of the ingredients and the crockery that brought the outside world into the home. The decorations on the different items on the table showed that the daily meal formed part of a wider world vision that was dominated by the Church and ideas from classical antiquity.

The humoral theory was not an independent healthcare system, indiscriminately adopted from the ancient world. It was part of a way of thinking that declared that everything in the cosmos was governed, and hence connected, by the same ordering principle. Thus, the four humours corresponded with the four elements (earth, water, air and fire), and the four seasons, wind directions and continents: in short, the whole world. Seventeenth-century imagery was full of metaphors of this kind, and everyday activities at times literally brought you face to face with the cosmic order. A woollen tablecloth featuring flowers and, along the four edges, what at first glance appear to be amusing rural scenes, alludes to the four elements **fig. 62**.[46] Children flying kites and blowing bubbles stand for air, casting iron for fire, fishing and sailing for water, and digging for earth. The four scenes also refer to the four stages of human existence, from play until death, whereby the boy's fragile soap bubble already points ahead to the grave that will ultimately be dug. The spade in the soil, the axe in the tree, the flowers that bloom but will eventually wilt: all bring life and death together in a representation of the rich but transitory earthly existence, at the base of which lie the four elements.

59a–g These blue-and-white decorated plates from the Sonck family's cesspit come from several different countries. There are plates from Delft, Italy and China

60a–d The Soncks had waffle beakers for beer (upper left) and a selection of berkemeyers for wine, each made slightly differently. The green glass articles were imported from Germany

61a–d Each diner at the table had their own spoon, which could be used both for serving yourself and for eating. Forks were used only for cutting, and were therefore not found in the cesspit, unlike these tablespoons

This mid-17th-century woollen table carpet is adorned with scattered flowers, and along the borders we find the four elements: air, fire, earth, and water

On this linen damask napkin, six putti represent the seasons: two warm themselves by the fire in the winter, two carry a basket of spring flowers, and two harvest grain in the summer

When setting the table, a heavy woollen cloth like this was overlaid with a gleaming white linen tablecloth, with folds crisp from the linen press, just like the matching hand towels and napkins. The finest were of damask, which, in the right light, revealed the patterns woven into the fabric. Some were personalized with names and family arms and a scene precisely tailored to the size of the napkin and woven into the fabric (see **fig. 94**). Napkins depicting the four seasons were a lot cheaper. They were more coarsely woven and had a repeat pattern, and the napkin was simply cut off at the right length regardless of whether it cut through the middle of a scene. As a result, one napkin might show three putti personifying winter, spring and summer, and the next a different combination **fig. 63**. Representations of the seasons were popular everywhere in the home, from ceiling paintings to silver dishes, with a concentration on and around the dining table, where the connection with the harvest and its impact on the body's constitution were most strongly felt.[47]

The place where the dining table stood depended on the layout of the house. Most of the rooms were multifunctional, used for both living and sleeping. Tables and chairs and china cabinets generally stood in rooms with a box bed. It was not until the second half of the seventeenth century that separate dining rooms or *pronkkeukens* – where meals were taken but no cooking was done – started to become more common in the province of Holland, although they remained exceptions.[48] Meindert may have created a dining room in the house at Ramen 1 after his father passed away in 1658. In one of the rooms from this period, fragments of gold leather have been found, which was a popular wallcovering for a dining room. Along with tapestries, this was the most expensive wallcovering, with the great advantage over woollen tapestries that it did not absorb the smell of food. Thematically the fragments are also a perfect fit. They allude to a quotation from the Roman writer Terence, *sine Cerere et Baccho friget Venus*: without Ceres (food) and Bacchus (wine), Venus (love) grows cold **fig. 64**.[49] At mealtimes the whole family came together. Feeding and good breeding went hand in hand. Children were not only spoon-fed the cosmic order and table manners; religion, too, played an important role at mealtimes.

This gilt leather is decorated with a pattern similar to the Sonck family's: Bacchus and Ceres surrounded by fruit and flowers. It must give off a beautiful glow in a candlelit dining room

Portrait of a family praying before a meal, 1627. The connection between piety and prosperity is evident from the thriving children at the richly laid table in this portrait, with poultry and white rolls on pewter plates, a silver salt cellar, and a dainty porcelain bowl of strawberries (see detail)

Reformed moralists, such as Jacob Cats and Petrus Wittewrongel, recommended saying grace before a meal and giving thanks for it afterwards. This was a popular theme in family portraits, as in the anonymous painting of a family seated round a table in 1627 fig. 65. Vines trail into the room through a window, a direct allusion to Psalm 128, which tells of a good and devout man: 'For thou shalt eat the labor of thine hands; happy shalt thou be, and it shall be well with thee. Thy wife shall be as a fruitful vine by the sides of thine house, thy children like olive plants round about thy table. Behold that thus shall the man be blessed that feareth the Lord.'⁵⁰ The biblical notion that man had to work for a living after expulsion from Paradise was never far away. If grace before the meal was an insufficient reminder, the earthenware crockery with its religious embellishments, such as a dish with the inscription 'Honour God', repeated the message fig. 66. It reaffirmed the beliefs of those at the table, big and small. This applied not just to Protestants; plates with the Madonna and Child were a popular Catholic variant fig. 67.

Catholics differed, however, in their fasting rules, which prescribed weekly fast days (Wednesdays and Fridays) and longer annual fasting periods (from Ash Wednesday to Easter, during Advent and the so-called Ember Weeks: periods of contemplation upon the change of the seasons). Meat and dairy products were banned from the menu then. The Dutch Reformed Church had abandoned these rules, but the government could still proclaim days of prayer and fasting in times of emergency, such as outbreaks of plague or war, whereby citizens were required to eat nothing – or as soberly as possible – that day and to listen to two or three sermons.⁵¹

Amsterdam also had a relatively large Portuguese Jewish community. In their country of origin they had been forced to convert to Christianity, but in the Dutch Republic many had returned to their own religion. The remains of pigs, rabbits, eels and shellfish, which they were not allowed to eat according to the *kashrut*, the Jewish dietary laws, do not therefore appear among their kitchen waste. Kosher coins, on the other hand, which marked the meat of animals that had been ritually slaughtered, were regularly found. A long time was to pass before members of this group

This earthenware dish is painted with the words 'Eert God' ('Honour God'). Protestants emphasised the importance of God's word and typically used words alongside images as decorative elements in the home

As the meal progressed, the scene of the Madonna and child on this painted earthenware dish would gradually emerge

68a–g Portuguese migrants often brought their own earthenware cooking vessels and drinking cups (*púcaros*), so that they could prepare familiar dishes

purchased custom-made Jewish tableware, such as Passover Seder plates with Hebrew inscriptions: we do not come across these until the eighteenth century.[52] The first generation of this group of migrants was still using Portuguese cooking earthenware, which was quite different in form from Dutch cookware figs. 68c, e–g.[53] They also had special unglazed cups, *púcaros*, from Lisbon figs. 68a, b, d. The water you drank from these smelled of clay, or, as a contemporary so beautifully described it, of 'steamy, sun-scorched soil after a rain shower'.[54] It was literally the taste of home.

Silver tableware

While sources such as inventories and doll's houses show a good cross-section of seventeenth-century tableware, original sets have seldom been preserved, and it is no longer possible to lay a table exactly as it would have looked in someone's home. It is therefore most extraordinary that a large number of the objects from the rich widow Agneta Deutz's house should still be together. Agneta married Gerard Meerman from Delft in 1651, and after his death she married the Delft Burgomaster Zacharias van Beresteyn, who also died only five years after their marriage. She then returned to her parental home, De Ster (The Star), on Keizersgracht in Amsterdam. Since she lived at logger-heads with her only son, Jan Meerman, she decided to give him his legitimate share of the inheritance and to invest the rest of her fortune in founding a *hofje* – a group of almshouses built around a courtyard – for older, unmarried women.[55] Agneta bequeathed part of her estate to the Deutzenhofje, the complex named after her, to furnish the trustees' room, including all her '*tapisserie*-upholstered chairs' and, in a slightly later version of her will, her 'silver spice box … together with a chased ewer and basin and the four chased silver candlesticks'.[56] In addition, the trustees were allowed to make a personal selection of the things they needed for their annual dinner. Thanks to an inventory from 1700, we know that they chose a floral table carpet, a tapestry table-covering that matched the chairs, table linen, silver tableware (including salt cellars, a mustard pot and cutlery), a small porcelain oil jug and teaware. With the exception of part of the silver on loan to the Rijksmuseum, most of these objects are still at their original location fig. 69.

The regents' room in the Deutzenhofje, a complex of almshouses in Prinsengracht in Amsterdam. The writing desk in the corner on the left, the table with the flowered carpet, the matching chairs, and the portrait of Agneta Deutz over the mantelpiece all come from her estate

This basin and ewer, which belonged to Agneta Deutz and her first husband, Gerard Meerman, were made by Andries Grill, a silversmith in The Hague, in 1649

71a–d These four silver candlesticks in the auricular style belonged to Agneta Deutz. Johannes Grill made the first of these in Amsterdam in 1652, and Willem Brugman made the other three in Delft that same year

Silver spice box that belonged to Agneta Deutz, originally made for her parents-in-law Frans Meerman and Maria Ysbrandsdr de Bije. It contains a number of separate spice containers with sliding lids

Agneta's silver ewer and basin is a real showpiece **fig. 70**. The water jug and bowl are executed in the auricular style, with abstract decorations reminiscent of skinfolds, shells and sea monsters. The handle of the jug consists of three intertwined fish-like creatures. The bottom of the basin is adorned alternately with raised and wrinkled planes, evoking the rippled surface of water.[57] The choice of water and fish here alludes to the name of the user: the middle section of the basin is engraved with Gerard Meerman's family crest, featuring a merman. The right-hand escutcheon remained blank because the set was made in 1649, before his marriage to Agneta. The decoration is perfectly in keeping with the hand-washing function of the ewer and basin, the water of which was regularly perfumed with rose water.[58] For drying the hands the trustees had over eleven linen towels, which no doubt matched the four tablecloths and 52 napkins, which were similarly from Agneta's estate.[59]

In the year following their marriage, Agneta was given an imposing candlestick by her mother, which was over 30 centimetres high.[60] It had been made in Amsterdam, and that year Agneta had three others made to the same design by a local Delft silversmith **fig. 71**.[61] The spice box, which holds five loose containers for serving the costly spices, is dated 1616 and was an heirloom from Gerard's parental home **fig. 72**. It was customary to sprinkle finished dishes with spices to taste, just as we season with pepper and salt today. Cinnamon was especially popular, but ginger, cloves, mace and nutmeg were also among the flavourings that were added at the table.[62] The lid is engraved with the coat of arms of Gerard's parents, and the box is adorned with festoons of flowers and fruit in a style that matches a sample book for silversmiths from 1600.[63] Agneta's silverware was therefore a collection of gifts, personal purchases and heirlooms that had accumulated over the years and did not form a stylistic unity, but it was sufficiently valuable to justify its ongoing use after her marriage to Zacharias, after his death and after her own passing.

Agneta's decked table must have been a beautiful sight. When a servant poured the scented water out of the silver ewer over Agneta's hands and those of her dining companions, the folds and lobes in the basin came to life. The flickering light of the candles reflected in the silver and revealed bit by bit the scenes in the damask linen. The green or clear glassware and the blue-and-white patterned plates, which she undoubtedly also owned, stood out beautifully against the dazzling white tablecloth, as did the dishes themselves, which everyone seasoned according to their own taste and temperament with the fragrant spices from the silver box. Dinner could now be served.

Hospitality

Most of the tableware of wealthy citizens was made not of silver but of pewter. Maria had her maids scourge the pewter with a dry abrasive until it gleamed like silver.[64] In her kitchen, Josina Schade van Westrum had a special pewter cupboard with glass doors, containing no fewer than 147 items: dozens of both flat and deep dishes, large platters and small plates (the majority bearing the coat of arms of Josina and her husband Otto Copes), and all kinds of smaller tableware, such as salt cellars and oil and vinegar bottles.[65] Such an imposing amount of pewter was not just excessive or ostentatious; for those who could afford it, it was also a sign of another important aspect of seventeenth-century gastronomy: hospitality.

It was perfectly acceptable to stay for 'dinner' (the midday meal) or 'supper' (in the evening), whether by appointment or unannounced. David Beck regularly stopped by the home of his best friend Herman Breckerfeld, his mother-in-law, and other friends and relations for a meal. Of the eighty-odd meals he mentioned in his journal in 1624, three-quarters were dinner or supper with friends or family or with guests in his own home. These were often informal occasions with a simple menu, such as rice pudding, smoked sausage with root vegetables in the winter or salad with an egg in the summer.[66] As Cats advised in his *Houwelick* (Marriage, 1625): 'Even if guests arrive unexpectedly/ Even if your cooking is bad, you don't need to be ashamed;/ Bring out what you have, even if that is salt and bread.'[67]

Aside from such spontaneous visits, in higher social circles we regularly come across more lavish meals and real feasts, which could cost a fortune. Maria prepared a supper for ten family members in 1633, with rabbit, poultry and a pie that she had baked herself in her brother's pan. Since the Middle Ages pies had been the centrepieces at banquets. Simple pies or sweet tarts could be baked at home in a so-called 'Dutch oven': a round copper baking pan on legs that could be stood in the hearth and covered with a recessed lid to hold smouldering peat, so that it was heated from above and below.[68] Maria borrowed hers from her brother and noted in her recipes that the quantities had to be adjusted to the size of the pan. When she was obliged to return it when her brother got married, she had a new one made to exactly the same dimensions.[69]

If you really wanted to splash out, you called in a piemaker or cook. Occasionally these were professional caterers who arranged whole banquets, including the hire of glassware, platters and extra chairs.[70] On 20 November 1660, for instance, Sara L'Empereur recorded a payment to the 'cooke' for a pie with a filling of 150 oysters.[71] Her cousin Johannes Thysius, who spent part of his youth at Sara's parents' home, celebrated the end of his schooldays in grand style. The poulterer delivered a choice of fowl, including four woodcocks and fifty finches; the cook baked roast hare in puff pastry and a lime pie, and roasted or braised the birds. Pewter tableware and rummers were rented for the Moselle wine.[72] A lavish feast such as this was served à la française, in several courses, whereby the platters with a medley of different dishes were elegantly and symmetrically set out. The guests brought along their own cutlery in a handy case (see **fig. 142**). The fork was only used to hold the food in place when cutting, not for eating: you did that with a spoon or with your hands.[73]

Johannes made a point of mentioning the '*bakster*', probably a confectioner who supplied the dessert, sweetmeats such as marzipan, anise sugar, biscuits, macarons and – to counterbalance all the sweetness – capers. Besides biscuits and comfit (sugared spices), an assortment of confiture was served. This might be jam and marmalade as we still know it today, as well as fruit in sugar syrup or candied or crystallized fruits, served in an array of small dishes **fig. 73**. Such a sweets banquet was not just a delicious finale and a visual spectacle, it was also thought to be good for the health. Sugar was available at the apothecary and was said to 'close'

In Petronella Oortman's doll's house, we find an abundance of fresh and candied fruits in porcelain dishes on the kitchen counter, ready to be served

the stomach, although with supplies increasing from the colonies it was already becoming more and more of an indulgence for the upper classes in the seventeenth century.[74]

An elaborate meal involved a similarly elaborate system of etiquette.[75] Besides instructions on how to behave at the table, there were strict rules about reciprocity: if you were a guest, you were obliged to return the invitation, Cats insisted. Naturally, lavish banquets were reserved for a select company, and he was aware that not everyone could afford them. In such cases you could not be expected to return the favour.[76] Above all, guests had to feel welcome. In Cats's view, that did not just depend on pleasant conversation at the dinner table, avoiding politics and controversial subjects, but also on the tableware: 'The wife must attend closely to the food and the kitchen,/ Whether the dishes are well polished and the linen laundered,/ Must show with her deeds and with appearances,/ That the guests are loved and valued friends.'[77] Josina's polished pewter dishes and her equally well-stocked linen cupboard were a sign as much of her cordiality towards her guests as of her status and wellbeing.

Women like Josina, Sara and Maria had a profound knowledge of ingredients, recipes and cookware. They did not use this merely to dish up a tasty meal, but also to stay healthy and to strengthen social ties. A considerable part of their homes and their daily activities were given over to eating and drinking. This applied to all strata of the population: from the elite, who laid on festive banquets in the finest rooms of their houses and who could afford well-stocked storerooms and china cabinets, to the lower social class, whose domestic life was concentrated around the hearth and whose sole possessions consisted of a few textiles and a handful of simple cooking utensils.

house-
keeping

Alexander Dencher

It is January 1660, and the Leiden housewife Sara L'Empereur is updating
her household ledger. She records the costs of the various meals her family
enjoyed during the holidays. She also notes payments to the tailor for her
husband's velvet dressing gown and to the silversmith for buttons, a new
spoon and repairs to tableware. The new year has brought more expenses:
Sara has settled accounts for the peat bill, paid taxes on deliveries of water
and beer, had a broken bed warmer repaired and dealt with numerous
other matters. Halfway down her ledger she notes, 'I forgot this', and
carefully records a payment to the sexton and the prices of purchases
including anise sugar, raisins, woollen fabric and down.[1]

The turn of the year remains a busy time for many of us,
and we still have the same basic needs as Sara and her family: food, clothes,
heat, hygiene and safety. Yet seventeenth-century housekeeping was very
different from today's chores. There were more tasks, and they were more
complex and time-consuming. Household ledgers kept by housewives
such as Sara provide insight into all the work that had to be done around
the house, as do objects like a curfew (fireguard, see **fig. 80**), a linen press
or a napkin.

The ideal housewife

A household consists of the people and domestic animals living under
the same roof. Sara's household at Rapenburg 67 in Leiden **fig. 74**, for
instance, also included her husband Marcus du Tour, four children, two
housemaids and one manservant. Of course, a seventeenth-century household could be larger or smaller than Sara's or have a different composition.
Examples include the households of the unmarried Maria van Nesse and
her maids in Alkmaar, the widows in Amsterdam's Deutzenhofje, and the
schoolteacher David Beck, a widower who lived with his son Adriaen in
the Roer family home in Arnhem. Caring for the home and its occupants
– in short, housekeeping – was almost always the responsibility of the
lady of the house. The famous seventeenth-century Dutch doll's houses,
which were not toys but precious works of art, provide an idealized
representation of households in Sara's day (see **figs. 5–7**). Petronella Dunois,

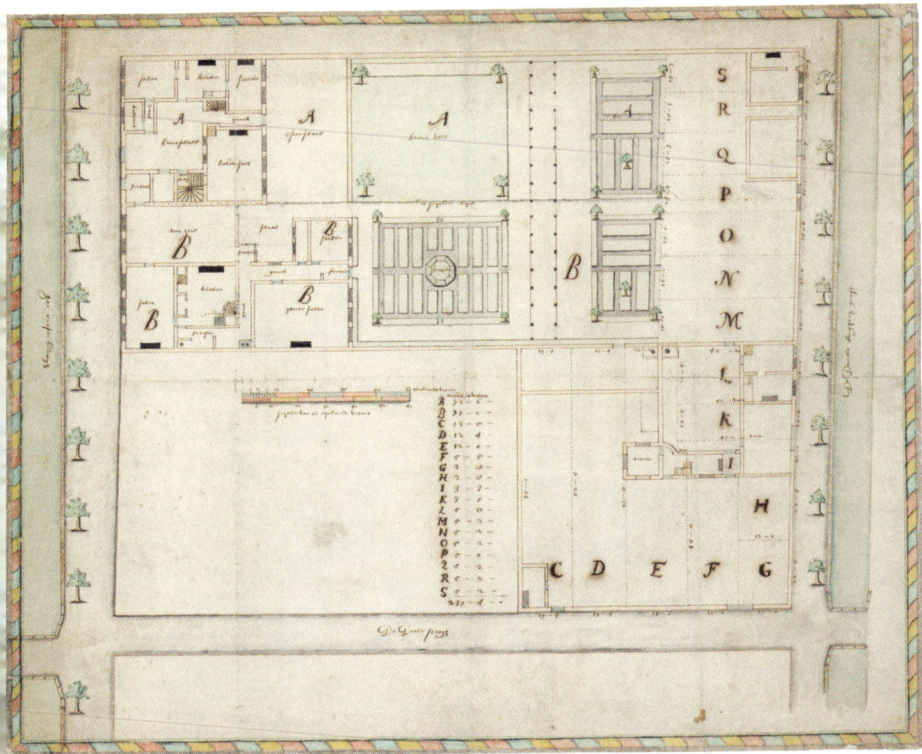

74 Sara L'Empereur's home at Rapenburg 67 in Leiden had a central courtyard. On the ground floor were a closet, a large *zaal* (reception room), a kitchen, and 'tower stairs'. The house also had a large back garden with yards and a bleaching field

A belt with a collection of keys was a practical and symbolic attribute of the housewife. She could also hang other useful housekeeping items from it, such as scissors, a small knife, a cutlery case, or sewing equipment

75

for instance, who also lived on Rapenburg after her marriage in 1677, owned a doll's house that illustrates how a home was meant to be furnished, how the lady of the house treated her guests and how she delegated tasks to her servants.

Notions of the ideal household inspired writers in the Dutch Republic to fill many pages. Their inspirations included both lessons from the Bible and the intellectual heritage of the classical world. Widely read Christian and Jewish authors – such as Jacob Cats, the clergyman Petrus Wittewrongel and Rabbi Menasseh ben Israel – referred to housekeeping by the Greek term *oeconomia*, which can also be translated as administration or management.[2] Their source for this term was the ancient philosopher Aristotle, who likened the running of a house (*oikonomia*) to that of a city (*polis*), postulating that a virtuous and honourable household was a necessary condition for participation in public life.[3] These ideological underpinnings of ideas about housekeeping visibly influenced the interior of the home; many domestic objects were carefully decorated with elements from biblical and mythological stories or from classical architecture figs. 77, 78, 80, 95, 96.

These authors described the running of a household as the responsibility of the man of the house, but in practice it was often his wife who played the leading role, both in performing and in delegating household tasks. Since the sixteenth century, the housewife's status had been elevated by Protestant theologians' growing appreciation of the mother's contribution to child-rearing. Church leaders regarded the mother and father as joint managers of the house – a role that had practical value for most wives, since it won them greater respect from their children and their servants.[4] Alongside the long-standing perception of the father as the *pater familias*, the head of the household, the mother thus came to be seen as the *domina domus*, the mistress of the house. The symbol of this new status was the housewife's belt with her collection of house keys and her small cylindrical cases of sewing equipment and other tools fig. 75. According to Cats, the acquisition of 'a key to the house and all its affairs' marked the transition from bride to wife.[5]

76   Eva Wtewael was portrayed by her father Joachim as a virtuous housewife-to-be with a sewing pillow, a basket of mending, and an open prayer book or Bible on the table (fig. 77)

This draw-leaf table was most likely in Utrecht painter and flax dealer Joachim Wtewael's reception room and can be found in his portrait of his daughter Eva (fig. 76)

77

Almost all households, except for the very poorest, had a cupboard for storing textiles. Joachim Wtewael's family passed this one down from generation to generation

The seventeenth-century image of the ideal housewife was strongly influenced by the biblical Book of Proverbs, which celebrates the good housewife's characteristics and virtues. It describes her value as 'far above rubies' and adds that she is always at work: 'She seeketh wool and flax, and worketh willingly with her hands. … She perceiveth that her merchandise is good; her candle goeth not out by night. … She looketh well to the ways of her household, and eateth not the bread of idleness.'[6] This ode to the housewife was a great inspiration not only to authors like Cats but also to artists such as Joachim Wtewael in Utrecht, who painted an affectionate portrait of his 21-year-old daughter Eva seated at the table **fig. 76**.[7] Although the table is largely concealed by a tablecloth, the visible leg is an exact match for the table from her parental home **fig. 77**. Here she is portrayed with the attributes of a virtuous and prosperous housewife (although she died before she could marry): she has a sewing pillow in her lap, a basket of mending by her feet and an open Bible or prayer book on the table. These objects could be found in every well-to-do household and allude both to the woman's worldly tasks in the home – in particular, taking care of clothes and other textiles – and to her spiritual tasks as a devout wife and mother.

Yet the seventeenth-century ideal of the housewife was unattainable for many women. Sewing and embroidery were not only virtuous activities but important skills from a financial perspective. Along with caring for their homes and families, most women also had to earn a living to survive and lacked the means to hire domestic help. But even when money was not an issue, a housewife could find herself in a difficult position. According to the housemaids of Zacheus de Jager, a physician in Enkhuizen, he found himself in marital trouble because he had made a daughter from his first marriage responsible for running the household, rather than his new wife Margaretha van Berensteyn.[8] She was not given any money for groceries or even allowed to be involved in doing laundry. This led to years of domestic conflict and ultimately divorce. Cats had harsh words for men who did not entrust their spouses with the management of the household, calling them 'busybodies' and 'wife-tormentors'.[9]

On the floor next to this woman is a foot stove, and propped up against the chair is a curfew (or fire-guard). She may have just lit the fire in the hearth. The valance (or chimney cloth) helped to guide the smoke up into the chimney

79

Curfews (or fire-guards) were used to cover the fire in the hearth at night so that it could be rekindled more easily in the morning; they also served to decorate the dark fireplace

Rhythm

Every household started the morning by lighting a fire in the hearth, the main source of warmth and light fig. 79. This was the task of the housewife herself or her servants, if she had any. Before bedtime the evening before, the smouldering fire was covered with a curfew made of brass or glazed earthenware; holes provided ventilation, making it easy to rekindle the fire the following morning.[10] An example from 1637 is decorated with biblical symbolism; the story of the explorers who returned from the Promised Land with bunches of grapes reminded the members of the household to trust in God's justice and providence fig. 80.

The day was divided by the bells of the church or city hall. There were six working days a week and one day of rest, Sunday for Christians and Shabbat for Jews – although this commandment was not always obeyed.[11] In a city like Amsterdam, the beginning and end of the working day coincided with the opening and closing of the city gates, an activity announced by bell-ringing.[12]

Over the course of the century, clocks became more widespread in the home and workplace as a means of telling time.[13] Expensive timepieces such as longcase clocks were often kept in the entrance hall, as can be seen in Petronella de la Court's doll's house (see fig. 5). The striking of the hours would have resonated throughout the dwelling. The dial of one early clock of this longcase variety shows not only the time but also the phase of the moon fig. 81.

In Sara L'Empereur's home the day began at six, and before half past six she would take her young son Constantijn to school.[14] She kept her housemaids Sara and Mary on a strict schedule; they swept and tidied each day before breakfast and then had set tasks for each day of the week. On Mondays they cleaned the *zaal* (reception room) and on Tuesdays the *voorhuis* (front room); on Wednesdays they not only cleaned the dining room but also scrubbed the house; and on Thursdays they cleaned the *achterkamer* (back room). On Friday mornings, they cleaned the stairway and the doors in the corridor. In the afternoon, they scourged the pewter jugs and dishes. On Saturdays they tackled the entire house, including the

81   This longcase clock was a costly showpiece that made it possible to tell the time in the home. Its mechanism was kept in motion by weights on long pendulums, which were out of sight in the tall, narrow case

courtyard. Saturday was generally seen as housecleaning day, and it was then that Maria van Nesse and her sister Adriana had their houses dusted and scrubbed by their live-in housemaids.[15]

The housekeeping schedule depended not only on the hour of the day and the day of the week, but also on the season. Some houses hired additional staff for the annual spring cleaning, as Maria and her sister did in 1645. The Huydecoper family had spring cleaning done not only in their house in Amsterdam but also in their country estate of Goudesteijn. This was a largescale operation, which even served as a reason for cancelling visits.[16]

The garden was also looked after at regular intervals; in the spring and autumn, a gardener tended to the greenery behind Sara L'Empereur's house. During the summer, the chimney sweep did his work, since chimneys were not normally in use at this time of year.[17] In the autumn, preparations began for winter: a stock of fuel was laid in, and food was preserved in brine. When temperatures dropped, the summer bedclothes were replaced with thick woollen curtains to keep out the cold.[18] The poorer classes had less work in the winter than in the summer, and the early dusk shortened the working day. This decrease in income led to greater dependence on local poor relief for necessities such as food, clothing and peat.[19] In contrast, wealthier households purchased extra delicacies during the winter holidays and therefore had greater expenses, as Sara's account book reveals. On 18 December 1660, she recorded deliveries of cabbage, meat and fish, but also a whole turkey, two rabbits, oysters and a pound of pears.[20]

The household budget

In practical terms, the proper functioning of any household depended on its financial means. The wealthy could spend more on food and expensive clothing, as well as on domestic help, peat for heating the home and candles for light. A remark by Constantijn Huygens, the renowned diplomat in The Hague, about the house commissioned by himself and his wife Susanna van Baerle offers a clear impression of seventeenth-century views on money: 'If the possession does not fit the man, it is just like a pair of shoes: too large and you sprain your foot, too small and they pinch you.'[21] The display of wealth had to be in proportion to a household's social status; moderation was an essential part of civic virtue. This humanist perspective on household spending lay at the root of the seventeenth-century approach to house-keeping, regardless of class.

How much the average household could spend is difficult to say, because events such as wars, epidemics and poor harvests impacted both the supply and the price of goods. Yet patterns of expenditure on the most essential goods (food, clothing and fuel) are roughly comparable, in proportional terms, across larger and smaller households.[22] Likewise, both rich and poor did most of their shopping on credit, relying on mutual trust between the customer and the shopkeeper. Honour and creditworthiness were closely related.[23]

The budget was carefully managed by the housewife, who, according to period sources, was often seen as more competent and capable than her husband when it came to organizing and running the household. This is clear from sources such as the archives of city poor relief organi-zations, which treated women as primarily responsible for household finances.[24] Single men often found women to look after them. The school-master David Beck, for example, boarded with the Roer family in Arnhem, where the mistress of the house, Marrijtgen, took care of the housekeeping.[25] In well-to-do circles, a woman might manage more than one household at once; after the death of his wife in 1637, Constantijn Huygens depended on his cousin Catharina Suerius to keep his household running smoothly for 31 years.[26]

One of the housewife's main tasks was to keep the house well stocked. The purchases noted in Sara's ledgers are mainly of groceries including bread, meat, milk, vegetables and fruit, or as she put it, 'this and that for meals'.[27] Cats described going to the market as an important re-sponsibility of the mistress of the house, since it was her husband's money she was spending, and he advised mothers to prepare their daughters for this duty **fig. 133**.[28] Sara kept track of her trips to the market, but she also sometimes sent her housemaid out on errands for her.[29] Having the servants

The contents of the linen cupboard reflected the family's prosperity. The meticulous arrangement of the contents of this miniature cupboard from Petronella Dunois's doll's house illustrates the great care with which textiles were stored

This sewing pillow probably doubled as a vanity mirror. Its precious materials and refined decorations made it a valuable object, undoubtedly cherished by its owner

do the shopping was even more typical among the wealthy women in Amsterdam's Sephardic Jewish community, who often had poorer Ashkenazi girls as servants, specifically as maids or wet nurses.[30]

Purchases of fabric for clothes and household items represented a significant part of the household budget. Rolls of cloth were stored in cupboards, often in large quantities **fig. 82**. When Josina Schade of Westrum died in 1704, she was in possession of around 22 metres of linen and a full 28 to 38 kilograms of yarn and thread. Margaretha van Berensteyn in Enkhuizen had at least 100 metres of fine linen in 1649, as well as large amounts of scarlet, fur, silk damask, satin, a type of silk fabric and English broadcloth.[31] Since textiles were expensive, housewives needed to know how to assess their quality and learn their many uses. Sara L'Empereur described purchasing cloth, ribbons and thread with which the tailor Gert Andriessen made clothes for all the members of her household, including the domestic staff.[32] The high prices of clothing and fabric led many housewives to do their own mending, and decorated sewing equipment was a customary gift for marriageable women from all social strata **figs. 83**.

Heat

Every household had a supply of peat, which had been the main form of fuel in the Dutch Republic since the Middle Ages **fig. 84**.[33] In the winter, local governments distributed additional peat to the poor, often as part of an aid package that also included money, bread and clothing.[34] Some households consumed much more peat than others. Maria van Nesse used about fifty baskets of peat a year, not much more than the residents of the Deutzenhofje (an almshouse complex in Amsterdam), who received forty baskets per person, per year.[35] Maria van Oyen and Cornelis de Jonge van Ellemeet's very affluent household consumed no less than 450 barrels of peat a year on average in their house in The Hague and another 135 in their Rotterdam residence.[36] Buying peat was regarded as men's work, but this was yet another task often undertaken by women. Sara L'Empereur had large amounts of peat delivered to her home twice a year: 106 barrels on 12 June 1660 and 120 on 13 November of the same year.[37]

The hearth had a central place in the house, as the primary source of heat and light, and the members of the household gathered there daily. Probate inventories show that a table and seating were often found near the fireplace.[38] The hearth and chimney were placed against one interior wall, which made it possible to heat two rooms at the same time. Most households had two hearths, but Sara's large house on Rapenburg boasted no fewer than seven.[39] The number of permanent fireplaces was directly related to household wealth, and when necessary the public authorities could institute a tax based on the total number in a single household.[40] The homes of the very poorest families sometimes had no hearth at all; in 1686, the officials responsible for relief of the poor in Zwolle noted that Albertje Houderdouw and her two young children were living in a cellar without a chimney, so the asphyxiating peat fumes could not escape.[41]

When designing homes for wealthier households, architects paid special attention to the hearth (see **fig. 26**). The costliest fireplaces were impressive creations, constructed with imported stone or carved wood, but plaster decorations in the same fashionable styles could also be obtained at more affordable prices.[42] Hearths were often surrounded with glazed earthenware tiles. These ceramic surfaces served a practical purpose, but they also added colour and lustre to an interior **fig. 86**. The back of the hearth was protected by a cast iron fireback, often decorated with political or historical themes **fig. 87**. This plate was heated by the flames and continued to radiate warmth even after the fire had been extinguished.

Valances were typically hung around the fireplace opening to direct the smoke up the flue (see **fig. 79**). These chimney cloths added a splash of colour to the interior and could be made of thick dyed wool or of less expensive linen. At the time of Margaretha van Berensteyn's divorce in 1649, she had as many as six valances; some were costly, made of red, green and blue silk and embellished with tassels and fringes.[43] The blue valance and matching tablecloth in the Amsterdam home of Anna Spiegel and her husband, the Burgomaster Anthony Oetgens van Waveren, form an early example of colour coordination that contributed to the interior's visual unity **fig. 88**.[44]

Woven baskets were useful for storing and transporting goods such as peat. Although they were widely used in all echelons of society, the only remaining examples are in doll's houses

84

In Petronella Dunois's *turfzolder* ('peat attic'), we can see not only baskets of peat but also stacks of foot stoves and even a mousetrap. The attic is a dry place and therefore ideal for storage

Tiles were used not only to decorate hearths and skirting boards, but also to protect walls from heat, dirt, and damp. Furthermore, they were easy to clean

Since the hearth occupied a prominent place in the home, a great deal of effort was put into decorating it. This fireback alludes to the Peace of Münster, which marked the end of the Eighty Years' War

88a, b When the cat's asleep, the mice will play, this valance (chimney cloth) seems to be telling us. The accompanying tablecloth is decorated with other animals, whose meaning is unclear

Oil lamps were commonly used for illumination in dwellings large and small. If the oil was impure, it often smelled bad and gave off fumes

In addition to her seven hearths, Sara also had at least one iron stove, which was most likely in the only room on the ground floor without a fireplace.[45] Since stoves did not rely on a stationary chimney, they could be used to heat any room in the house. The smoke was conducted outside through a long copper pipe. Stoves were imported from Germany and almost always decorated with biblical scenes, cast in relief (see **fig. 113**). They were very valuable, and homeowners frequently brought them along when moving house; Sara's husband had probably purchased theirs along with their residence in 1656.[46]

Foot stoves, chafing dishes and bed warmers, fuelled by hot coals, were useful devices for distributing heat around the house. Foot stoves were inexpensive and often executed in a simple style, as we can see in the doll's houses of Petronella Oortman and Petronella Dunois, where they are stored away in kitchen cupboards or in the attic **fig. 85**.[47] Bed warmers could also be filled with glowing embers and moved back and forth between the mattress and the blankets to heat the bed. In 1653, Sara received a silver bed warmer from her cousin Johannes Thysius – the pinnacle of luxury.[48] And according to the inscription on another bed warmer, made of brass (see **fig. 2**), it was intended for single women who had no husband to keep them warm.

Wool was also essential for warmth, and its insulating properties made it especially comfortable. During harsh winters, city poor relief services provided needier households with much-needed woollen underwear, usually donated.[49] Wool could also be used around the house for bedspreads and curtains; the thick, heavy material kept the cold at bay. In the very wealthiest households, these items – together with other woolen furnishings such as decorative cushions, chimney cloths, upholstered furniture, and tapestries – added colour and texture to the interior.

Light

While heat was a necessity, illumination was normally seen as a luxury. Even candleholders and sconces made of copper, brass or silver were costly. More elaborate chandeliers were an extravagance for the very wealthy.[50]

Johannes Thysius's account book tells us that two candleholders and a pair of wick-trimming scissors, which can be used to make candles last longer and smoke less, were among the most expensive silver household objects that he owned.[51] And when Margaretha van Berensteyn left her husband's home, she took 25 copper candlesticks with her, and not merely because of their practical value.[52]

Beeswax candles were expensive throughout the European market, but in the Dutch Republic you could purchase more affordable tallow candles from the butcher.[53] Many large households stocked up on candles two or three times a year, usually as winter approached and then again in spring when the supply ran low. Maria van Nesse bought an impressive 420 candles in 1624 – some for religious purposes – and distinguished in her household ledger between candles of larger and smaller size.[54] Maria van Oyen's household used thick table candles, night candles and beeswax candles. This last variety was six times as expensive as the other two, which were made of tallow.[55]

Another widely used light source was the oil or tallow lamp, which was inexpensive and resistant to draughts **fig. 89**.[56] Such lamps did have their disadvantages: they gave off smoke and foul odours because of frequent impurities in the fuel. Those who could afford candles probably preferred them; Maria van Oyen's meticulous household records rarely mention lamp oil.[57] Yet lamps were also found in prosperous households. In March 1660, Sara L'Empereur wrote that she had bought five pints of lamp oil.[58] In large houses, oil lamps were probably used mainly by servants; tellingly, the miniature oil lamps in doll's houses were usually kept in the kitchen fireplace.[59]

Cleaning

Heating the house with peat and lighting it with lamp oil generated a great deal of smoke, so soot had to be removed almost daily. Fortunately, a large arsenal of cleaning products was available. Brooms and brushes were indispensable and have often been found in the cesspits of both rich and poor households **figs. 90, 91**.[60] Among the wealthy, such items were typically bought in bulk; on 3 April 1660, Sara L'Empereur purchased thirteen brooms and thirteen *kantboenders* – probably short-haired brushes – just in time for the annual spring cleaning.[61] A week later, she bought half a dozen *heiboenders*, whisk brooms without handles, made of tough heather twigs and especially well suited to scrubbing the kitchen.[62] A *ragebol* – a long-handled brush for dusting hard-to-reach places – was used in Sara's household too. Floorcloths and mops, also essential for cleaning, were made of wool. Many buckets were made of painted wood and had iron or brass handles.[63] Most households probably bought soap in large quantities as well, as did Sara L'Empereur and Maria van Nesse.[64] Maria kept her cleaning supplies in the kitchen, while in doll's houses the dusters and other brushes were generally stored in the same attic room where clothing was dried **fig. 92**.

As the *domina domus*, Maria was in charge of housekeeping and saw to it that cleaning was done properly and that everything necessary was available. She kept precise records of whatever had to be purchased and of the different methods of cleaning household items. She scrubbed ironwork with a mixture of oil and sand, which she removed with an old brush before polishing the iron with hot sand and rags. The same procedure was used for knobs on chairs, with oil and 'blacking' that most likely produced a finish reminiscent of gleaming ebony. Maria's proposed method for cleaning a precious reliquary was to start by scrubbing it with lukewarm soapy water and, if that did not suffice, to rub it with a wet rag and chalk and then dry it with warm cloths.[65]

Sara's aforementioned cleaning schedule appears to have been based on widely accepted conventions. It differs little from another cleaning regimen published in the mid-eighteenth century. The anonymous author of this later document stipulates that the stoop, the *voorhuis* (front room or area) and the corridor should be cleaned every Monday, Tuesday, Thursday and Friday. On Wednesdays the entire house and the stoop should be scrubbed, and on Saturday the entire house should undergo another deep cleaning. While the family was having breakfast, the housemaids could strip the beds, fold the sheets and blankets, fluff the pillows

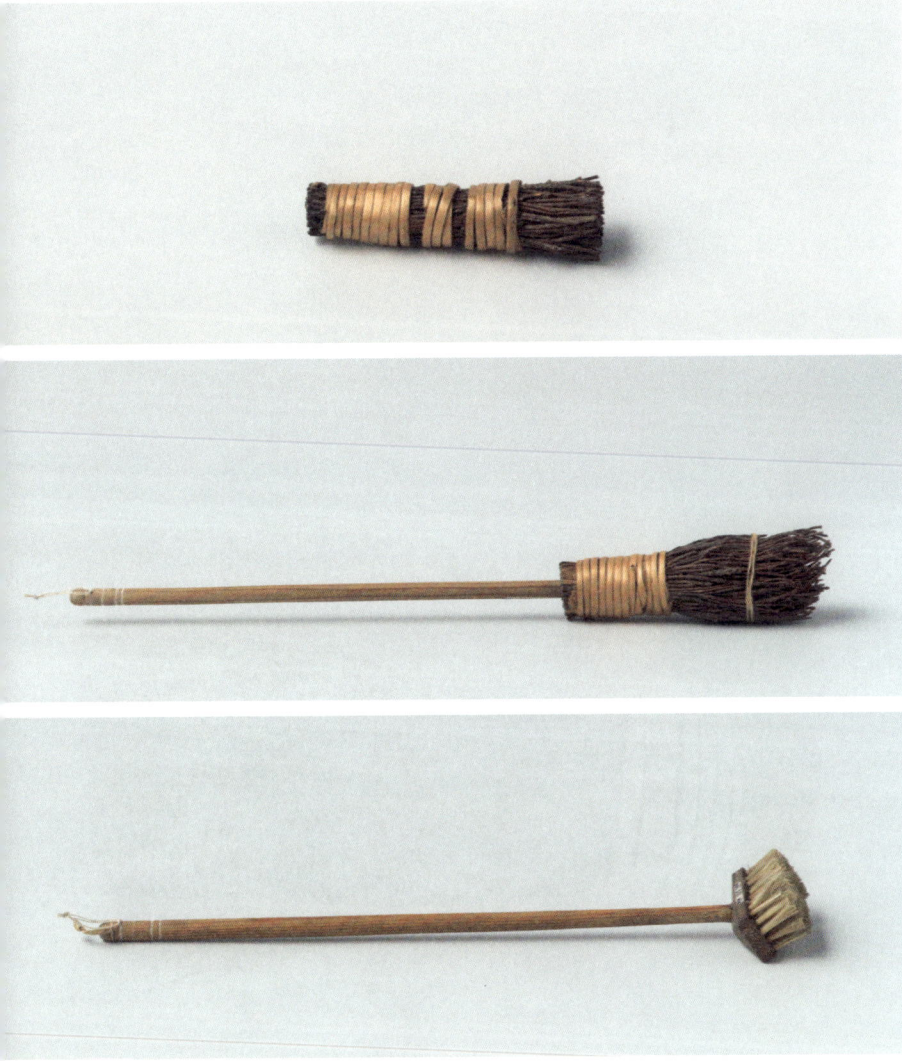

90a–c In doll's houses, we find a range of cleaning implements that correspond to purchases by women such as Sara L'Empereur and Maria van Nesse

Small whisk brooms such as this were used for sweeping and scrubbing in every household. They wore out quickly but were inexpensive and easy to replace

and air them out for at least an hour.[66] Airing out linens and circulating air through rooms properly was essential for the health of the household. Johan van Beverwijck, a physician in Dordrecht, warned his contemporaries of the harmful nature of 'confined air' in unventilated rooms, and emphasized the importance of considering the supply of fresh air when building a house, since it played such a crucial part in preventing 'unhealthy vapours'.[67] Once everything had been aired out and freshened up, the beds could be made and the sheets were smoothed with a bed stick.[68]

The accounts of Dutch cleanliness written by foreign visitors evoke the thorough cleaning regimens practised in homes like Sara's and Maria's. From the early seventeenth century, visitors described the cleanliness of houses in the Republic and told tales of the Dutch housewives' cleaning mania. Historians sometimes relate this phenomenon to the widespread belief that a clean house was the sign of a clean conscience, but there was another important reason for the Dutch preoccupation with domestic cleanliness. Housekeeping manuals underscored the importance of cleaning for health reasons. The kitchen in particular had to be kept clean, so that 'no spiders, flies, or other venomous pests' ended up in the food.[69]

It is important to note that Sara and Maria were among the minority who could afford domestic help for daily cleaning. Only 18 per cent of the population had live-in housemaids; a larger proportion hired help for specific cleaning jobs at specified intervals, or when needed.[70] Households in the Dutch Republic employed fewer domestic workers overall than households in other European countries, but the proportion of servants who were women (maids, cleaners, housekeepers and wet nurses) was much higher.[71] Male servants, such as valets and coachmen, were only employed by the wealthiest households.[72]

Amsterdam's prosperous Sephardic community employed a relatively large number of domestic servants, from diverse backgrounds. Historical documents show that these servants were Christian, Ashkenazi and African in origin; some of the Africans had migrated from Portugal to the Netherlands with their Sephardic employers. In Sephardic households, as elsewhere in the Dutch Republic, it was the man of the house who drew up the contracts for domestic workers, but the housewife who supervised them.[73]

Laundering

After cleaning, one of the most important household tasks was tending to the linens. This was because the cleanliness of table linens, bed linens and undergarments was meant to indicate the *zindelijkheid* (cleanliness, purity, propriety) of the family.[74] Clean linens, like a clean house, were viewed as evidence of successful housekeeping and a virtuous housewife. The extensive laundry list in Petronella de la Court's doll's house offers a glimpse of the quantity and variety of textiles that had to be cleaned **fig. 93**. But the frequency of laundering depended on the household; Maria van Nesse, for instance, had her laundry done once every five weeks by a washerwoman when her own maid had severely injured her thumb.[75] The high numbers of garments we find listed in probate inventories suggest that laundry was done less often than today, partly because it was very demanding, labour-intensive and time-consuming work.

Linen was by far the most widely used fabric in the home. It was ideally suited for undergarments and had a variety of domestic functions – its smoothness, breathability and ability to absorb moisture meant that it could be used to dry both objects and the body.[76] According to one frequently reprinted pamphlet, the inventory of linens in the typical middle-class home consisted of sheets, pillowcases, napkins, towels, handkerchiefs, and smocks to wear to bed.[77] This list is largely consistent with the Leiden baker Arent van Oostwaert's probate inventory. At the time of his death in 1695, he owned no less than one large and six smaller tablecloths, twenty-two bedsheets, twenty pillowcases (plus another twelve in poor condition), fifty napkins, ten towels, fifteen handkerchiefs and sixteen smocks.[78] The importance of linen is also evident from the detailed commentary included in such inventories, which typically include descriptions of the condition, type and quantity of the linen and in some cases even of the woven patterns.

In Petronella de la Court's *kleerzolder* (attic laundry room), we can see everything that was needed to keep clothes and linens clean and free of wrinkles: a mangle board, a linen press, laundry baskets, and irons

On the laundry list in Petronella de la Court's doll's house, the items sent to the laundry were ticked off. This included tablecloths, towels, and napkins, as well as underpants

The seventeenth-century household fabrics that have survived include a relatively large amount of table linen. This was used across all social strata and was not only attractive but also protected the diners' furniture and clothing. Households of modest means could afford linens that were plain and somewhat coarse. These textiles were also used by servants in large households.[79] By contrast, the most expensive table linen was Haarlem damask, which displayed light-and-dark patterns in raking light. A linen damask set included a tablecloth, napkins and a towel. One truly exceptional set was made for Taco van Camminga and Lucia van Grovestins, a couple in Friesland, after their wedding on 4 November 1638 **fig. 94**. Woven into the linen is a popular pattern depicting the mythical poet Orpheus surrounded by animals. The family's coats of arms, normally woven into the edge of the tablecloth, instead take up a prominent position in the middle.[80] Alongside the arms of Taco and Lucia, we also find those of their parents, grandparents and great-grandparents – in other words, they dined with four generations at the table.

Wealthy families owned linen in large quantities. Petronella Dunois from Amsterdam, at the time of her marriage to the Leiden regent Pieter Groenendijk, had twice as many tablecloths and nearly six times as many napkins as Arent the baker.[81] Josina Schade van Westrum, in Den Bosch, had even larger quantities stored in the cupboards on the upper floors of her home: 83 bedsheets, 99 pillowcases, 48 tablecloths, 221 napkins, 95 towels, and 16 cloths and covers for cupboards.[82] These were decorated with woven tiled patterns that are frequently mentioned in probate inventories: 'rose', 'lavender' and 'pavije'.

Laundering such large quantities of linen was exhausting work and probably the first chore that households would outsource as soon as they could afford to do so.[83] Furthermore, the need for soap and for fuel to heat the water made laundering an expensive task.[84] Because textiles were so costly, laundry baskets were usually kept under lock and key (see **fig. 92**),[85] and clothing was marked with red stitching so owners and servants would be able to identify it (see **fig. 32**).

Josina was fortunate enough to have her own washhouse in a practical location at the edge of her garden, equipped with a copper furnace, boilers and three washtubs.[86] The clean water most likely came from a rain barrel, and the used water could be discharged into the Binnendieze waterways. Rain barrels were also used to collect water for consumption and personal hygiene.[87] Van Beverwijck, who had a rain barrel in his courtyard, wrote about the importance of clean water and consequently of making sure that the water in one's barrel had not been polluted by a lead gutter or a dirty roof.[88] In times of scarcity, water had to be purchased from brewers, who sometimes demanded outrageous prices. The architect Simon Stevin therefore argued that each household should have its own basin for collecting and filtering rainwater.[89]

After linens were laundered in clean water, they were bleached a brilliant white. Bleaching often took place locally; Amsterdam was served by Haarlem, but other cities such as Rotterdam, Gouda and Delft had their own bleaching businesses.[90] Bleaching was a time-consuming process: the laundry was soaked, soaped and boiled and then laid on a grassy field while still wet.[91] According to Maria van Nesse, everything had to be washed at least four times before the linens could be laid out in the field.[92] The combination of sun, water and fresh air both restored the white colour to the linen and removed the unpleasant odour of the soap.[93] Then the cloth was laundered again, and if necessary the process was repeated.

Linen could also be bleached on a smaller scale in the home. The women who lived in the Deutzenhofje used their courtyard to bleach linen.[94] Maria and her brother-in-law owned bleaching fields outside Alkmaar, while Sara had a large bleaching field behind her garden (see fig. 74). It was still too small for all the household's laundry, however, so she also paid for bleaching repeatedly throughout the year.[95]

Once the cloth reached the desired shade of white, it was prepared for delivery. The laundry usually arrived back still wet, because the final steps of laundering often took place in the home, as the attic rooms of doll's houses illustrate. There, wet laundry was put through a mangle, hung up to dry, ironed, folded and pressed. The mangle board played an

This tablecloth (detail) and the matching towels and napkins are made of the finest linen then available. Keeping them clean and in good condition was a demanding job and frequently outsourced. This set was woven on commission

important role in this process. This wooden board was smooth on one side and decorated on the other – often with biblical proverbs – and was accompanied by a long, round rolling pin. To remove wrinkles from wet linen, one wrapped the cloth around the rolling pin and then moved the smooth side of the mangle board back and forth over the surface.[96] This was strenuous work, and the inscription on a mangle board from 1665 shows how much pride women took in the results: 'Washed white and folded neatly, it is the ornament of a beautiful woman' **fig. 97**. After the linen was smoothed with the mangle board, it was hung up to dry.

There were various ways of giving the dried white linen a dazzling appearance. Accessories such as caps, collars and cuffs could be treated with starch or gum and then polished with a glass slickstone.[97] Heated irons were used mainly for clothing.[98] Some early irons were made of earthenware, but as the century went on, new types and materials were introduced. The most luxurious were made of copper or brass, and some had iron baseplates.[99] Certain irons, like those in miniature in Petronella Oortman's doll's house, could be filled with charcoal or another type of fuel such as coal or peat **fig. 98**.

Then the crisp linen was folded and placed in a linen press. This process created sharp creases, which signalled to guests that they were dining on clean linen.[100] The decorations alluding to antiquity on linen presses from the first half of the seventeenth century indicate the prominent role they played in a home's interior. An early example with Ionic columns and other classical formal elements is reminiscent of the architecture of that time **fig. 95**. Later in the century, the linen press fell into disuse; at first, it still occupied a prominent place in the *voorhuis*, but in the Amsterdam doll's houses, for instance, we can see that it was moved to the drying attic.

The clean laundry ended up in the cupboard, where it was stored until needed for laying the table or making the bed. A housewife could use homemade herbal sachets – perhaps containing rose or lavender, which were also frequently found as patterns on household textiles – to impart a delightful fragrance to her linen.[101] Since linens were used daily, the linen cupboard occupied a prominent place in the home. It not only served the practical purpose of storage but also had symbolic meaning, representing the household's possessions and thus the housewife's cleanliness and prosperity. The most opulent cupboards were veneered with various types of wood (see **fig. 82**) or made of carved oak, like the one with four doors decorated with biblical scenes of Susanna and the Elders **fig. 96**. Whenever the owner opened those doors, she saw the story of the chaste heroine whose faith in God protected her from false accusations of immoral conduct.

Passing down

Linen cupboards held a prominent place in the home and in the household, and their daily use gave these pieces of furniture great personal significance. Sometimes they remained in the same family for many years, like the painter Joachim Wtewael's table – visible in the portrait of his daughter Eva – and his linen cupboard, which were passed down by way of his granddaughter Aletta Pater **figs. 76–78**.

This applied to other furnishings as well. When Sara L'Empereur died in 1685, her eldest daughter Catharina received all the furniture with upholstery that her mother had embroidered over the course of her life.[102] Catharina may well have assisted in this work: handling a needle and thread was one of the most important skills a future housewife could learn from her mother. The transmission of skills such as sewing, cooking and cleaning from one generation to the next was fundamental to the seventeenth-century household. What we know for certain is that Sara's embroidered furniture embodied the special bond between mother and daughter; the pieces are the first objects she mentions in her will, even before her precious diamond ring and silver toiletry set, which she also left to Catharina.

Objects such as the linen cupboard, the heather whisk and the mangle board offer us a closer look at the seventeenth-century household's daily routines. These objects convey the taxing work required inside and around the house, in contrast to idealized genre paintings, which

Although this linen press was intended for relatively small textiles, the classical design elements endow it with a monumental character

96   The doors of this linen cupboard depict biblical scenes of Susanna and the elders.
     Susanna's faith and chastity made her a role model for women, but furniture
     decorated with religious scenes must also have appealed to other family members

97, 98 Using a mangle board was strenuous but rewarding work. It made fabric lustrous and free of wrinkles. Clothes irons like these examples from Petronella Oortman's doll's house were filled with small coals and had matching stands

rarely depict such labour, let alone convey its full reality. Women like Sara L'Empereur and Maria van Nesse, along with whatever household staff they had, made sure that freshly laundered clothing and linens were always available and that the house remained warm and clean. They also knew how to keep their homes well stocked, manage their household finances and identify trustworthy suppliers. The degree of skill and knowledge they needed to keep their households running smoothly was impressive. Today, we would identify such work as a field of expertise: *oeconomia*, or household management.

work

Marijn Stolk

Walking the streets of a seventeenth-century city, you find yourself surrounded by the spectacle of signboards and gable stones bearing the names
of houses. The scent of smoke and freshly baked bread from domestic
hearths and nearby bakers' ovens fills the alleyways. Further along, the
clank of the carpenters' and coppersmiths' hammers resounds. When you
enter a street, you hardly need to ask what merchants and artisans work
there, what families live there, or where the owners of the houses originally
come from: the house fronts, smells and sounds tell you in an instant. Near
the riverside street of Binnen-Amstel in Amsterdam, a silk dyer has a 'house
and dyeworks with the Green Parrot above the door'.[1] Nearby is the home
of Egbert Ains Idtskema, where 'the Arms of Friesland hang', and a little
further along, the Portuguese widow Sara Abravanel is just selling part of
her house, identifiable by 'the Moor's head on the house front'.[2] Walking
towards the harbour, you come across the house and grounds of a furrier
'on the east side of Warmoesstraat, between Wijngaardstraetje and Armsteeg, where the Gilded Soap Barrel is on the house front and the three
Sugarloaves are on display'.[3]

Work was even more central to everyday life than it is now.
It determined not only how and where you lived – since many kinds of
work took place in the home or its immediate surroundings – but also,
unsurprisingly, what varieties of food, household objects and home furnishings you could afford. Some types of craftspeople needed ovens or
large storage areas on their property, and if your livelihood depended on
goods that had to be transported in or out of town, then you generally
preferred to live by the waterside.[4] That was certainly true of Dirck van
Dijk, the proprietor of De Drie Klaveren (The Three Clovers), which like
many other breweries in Haarlem was situated along the river Spaarne.[5]
With the help of a hoisting mechanism in front of the house, Dirck would
lift fresh dune water, brought into the city by barge, out of the canal **fig. 99**.[6]
In cities such as Enkhuizen and Purmerend, brewers had large, deep wells
on their properties that were sealed all around with a thick layer of clay to
ensure the water would be as clean as possible. Building such a well was
quite an undertaking.[7] Along with clean water, a large supply of peat was

This drawing from 1660 depicts De Drie Klaveren (The Three Clovers), a brewery in Haarlem, identifiable by the emblem on the house front and the hoisting mechanism in front of the house

99

This fireplace excavated in Amsterdam, which includes an oven door, was once part of the brewery Het Delffse Wapen (The Delft Arms), later known as De Eenhoorn (The Unicorn). Around 1608, it was used as a heat source for the soapmaking business De Clock (The Bell)

101 The Haarlem brewing complex De Windhond (The Greyhound) included a house, a brewery, a peat storehouse, a malt house, and a 'beer house' (taproom). A rough indication of the size of the complex is that later six houses were built in its place

needed to heat liquids in various stages of brewing, such as malting grains and boiling the extracted wort **fig. 100**.[8] The brewers at Haarlem's De Windhond (The Greyhound) brewery not only brewed beer at home but also served it in the adjoining beer house, where patrons slaked their thirst **fig. 101**.[9] The noise from this drinking room did not reach the house where the brewers lived, because of the intervening peat storehouse and courtyard.

The home and the workplace

Whether you had a fairly simple trade that required little specialization or a workplace with multiple rooms, working at home was the norm.[10] While many people worked from home, many others did the opposite, moving into their workplaces. Apprentices and manservants, housemaids and shop girls, all of them found accommodation at their place of employment. For the primary residents of the house, this meant less privacy, and for the employees housed there, it meant being at their workplace night and day. Not all of those employees were locals. In some parts of the Dutch Republic, especially the coastal provinces, the tight labour market attracted many migrants in search of employment.[11] One such migrant was 23-year-old Annetge Andries, who travelled from Bergen in Norway to Amsterdam to work as a domestic servant there.[12]

In addition to hiring live-in servants, you could also out-source household tasks. Laundering and starching were often farmed out to others. Maria van Nesse paid Guirt Jacopx one guilder and five stivers to tackle a mountain of laundry – five weeks' worth – in the two weeks before Christmas. Her live-in maid had injured her thumb at the fair in Alkmaar. It was a massive job for Guirt, who started work at half past four in the morning on a Wednesday and carried on until nine in the evening, continued from half past five in the morning to six in the evening on Thursday, and then spent another half day on the job that Saturday.[13]

To avoid misunderstandings, employers and live-in employees sometimes agreed on clear terms in advance. In a contract between two Amsterdam silk merchants, for example, Salomon van den Voort pledges to take Albert Fransen's son into his home for three years and teach him all the tricks of the trade, but only under certain conditions. Jan is permitted to eat at the table with the family but is required to have his linens washed and starched in his parents' home. Furthermore, Jan must 'be obedient and, under all circumstances, carry and comport himself as befits such an honest and pious young man'. The contract also makes it clear that he is not a domestic servant but an apprentice and therefore not obliged to carry peat, clean shoes, hold the family's child or perform other tasks unconnected to his training.[14] Such agreements were put in writing mainly in the case of apprentices or manservants from the upper echelons of the working middle class. The evidence that lower-class employees were much less likely to receive this treatment comes from various official documents in archives that mention disputes between households and their staff. In 1692, for example, the shop assistant Maria Jonchout, who lived in the home of her Amsterdam employers Margreta and Catarina Fabritius, complained about her sleeping arrangements. Maria threatened to leave their service unless they gave her a decent place to sleep in a box bed with a mattress, sheets, blankets and a pillow. She refused to continue sleeping on an uncomfortable wooden bench or on the stone floor, where another housemaid had slept and consequently became ill.[15]

In business together

The Delft pottery factory De Porceleyne Fles (The Porcelain Bottle) is another place where arrangements were made for the running of the household and the business.[16] The factory had been purchased in 1655 by Wouter van Eenhoorn and Quirijn Kleijnoven; Quirijn was the expert Delftware potter, and Wouter was primarily an investor. The contract between the two men specified that Quirijn's wife Engeltje would manage the shop, both organizing and selling the goods.[17] Her role in the business was honoured almost twenty years later with a plate bearing her name and the date 1673 **fig. 102**, found among the refuse in a cesspit on the factory grounds. The plate, which was in nearly pristine condition, was probably on display on a cupboard or wainscoting in Quirijn's and Engeltje's home until at some stage it fell and shattered and ended up in the cesspit.[18]

This plate was made in honour of Engeltje Kleijnoven, who worked at De Porceleyne Fles (The Porcelain Bottle), a Delft pottery factory. It was found during excavations on the former factory site

This biscuit-fired plate, found in excavations of De Porceleyne Fles, was used for bookkeeping, probably by Quirijn or Engeltje

The contract between Wouter and Quirijn also stipulated that Wouter and his wife could reside in one of the factory's outbuildings free of charge. This was compensation offered in return for Quirijn teaching Wouter the Delftware potter's trade. But it was also a practical arrangement: the Kleijnovens could keep an eye on things at night, while the kilns were being fired, an activity that posed a risk of fire.[19] An additional advantage of having a pottery factory next to their home was that they always had access to plenty of tableware. Items with minor firing errors that were too good to throw away but not attractive enough to sell could be set aside for their own use.[20]

Special provisions were also made for their daughter Ageta, as we know from the archaeological remains of a white earthenware children's tableware set.[21] She could play with that while her parents were hard at work. Painting the biscuit-fired pottery was a painstaking process, considerable energy had to be put into the shop, and there was also the bookkeeping to attend to fig. 103.

Like many other craftspeople in those days, Quirijn Kleijnoven was a member of a guild, an organization that advocated the interests of people in a particular trade. Guilds set product quality standards but also formed a crucial social safety net, which could be counted on in the event of illness, death or other adversity. As a potter, Quirijn belonged to the Guild of Saint Luke, established for people in artistic trades such as painters – including the Delft painter Johannes Vermeer – sculptors, glassworkers and book printers.[22]

In running their Delftware business as a couple, Quirijn and Engeltje were no exception. Various examples can be found elsewhere in the Northern Netherlands. In Haarlem, for instance, Abraham Casteleyn and his wife Margarieta van Bancken ran the printing house In de Blije Druck (In the Joyful Press) from 1661 onwards fig. 104. Their business was in a prime location on Grote Markt, the main square, where they printed the *Oprechte Haerlemsche Courant* newspaper and various other publications. After Abraham's death, Margaretha continued to act as the city's printer, even after remarrying in 1682. Besides continuing to print the newspaper, she also published works such as the government document *Bericht, rakende 't gebruyk der slang-brand-spuyten* (Announcement concerning the practice of fire extinguishing with hoses), the song book *Kooning en profeet Davids harpszangen, in Neederduits dicht uitgebreid. Op muzyk gebracht* ... (King and Prophet David's harp songs, expanded into Dutch poetry and set to music ...) and a print for children entitled *Speelen van Cupido* (Cupid's games).[23]

Women on their own
In contrast to the wealthy brewers, potters and printers discussed above – who needed plenty of space for their brew kettles, kilns and presses and for storage of raw materials[24] – most of the Republic's population was much poorer and lived in less spacious accommodations. Many people even lived and worked in a single room. The Harlingen home of Sibbeltje, an unmarried *matres* (teacher of young children, probably two to six years old in this case), must have been packed to the rafters during the school day.[25] After her death in 1643, a description was made of her small quarters. It states that she had a deal table and no fewer than seven school desks, as well as a large psalter, a 'home postil' (collection of Bible commentaries) and some other books. In view of the number of desks, it is possible that Sibbeltje had fifteen to twenty pupils there during the day. Her other possessions amounted to little more than some clothing, a few basic household items, a single bed and a spinning wheel.[26] In the hours of relative quiet after school, or on days without children, she could earn a little extra by spinning yarn. There were numerous *matres* schools, as businesses like Sibbeltje's were called, although some had no furniture and the women who ran them were often untrained and sometimes even illiterate.[27]

The 21-year-old shoemaker's daughter Elisabeth Strouven from Maastricht did not run a *matres* school but a boarding school for children in a wide age range **fig. 105**. Because she had many pupils in her care – eventually as many as twenty-five – she went so far as to relocate them to a larger and more suitable home, and her sister came to live with her and assist.[28] Despite Elisabeth's best efforts to teach the children 'sincere

104   This portrait by Jan de Braij depicts the married couple Abraham Casteleyn and Margarieta van Bancken, Mennonite printers in Haarlem. Visible behind them is a bust of Laurens Jansz Coster, the supposed inventor of the printing press

105 Portrait of Elisabeth Strouven, a very pious woman. After running a boarding school, she devoted herself entirely to her religion, founding the convent of Calvariënberg (Mount Calvary) in Maastricht in 1661

The poor received tokens for free loaves of bread from a bakery or the poor relief office. This token bears a scene of bread distribution: on the right, the needy recipients have queued at the counter

virtue', her work was quite an ordeal for her. She once complained to her confessor at the monastery, with tears in her eyes, 'Oh, Father, I can't go on this way. Won't you give me permission to send the children away? I can't take it anymore!'[29]

Sending children to a *matres* or boarding school was a welcome solution for families that depended on the woman's income to make ends meet. Whether women could participate in the workforce depended largely on their stage of life.[30] Before and just after marrying, women were still relatively independent. But once they had small children, the situation grew more difficult. It was a tricky time for the entire household, because one income was partly or completely lost. Poorer families often had to request financial assistance **fig. 106**. Children in the lower economic classes were expected to contribute to the household income from age six onwards, usually through unskilled or low-skilled labour such as spinning or making pins or buttons.[31] In the best cases, such work was combined with a few hours of schooling, or children had the opportunity to learn a trade elsewhere, although often not until they were older.[32]

When the Zwolle *turfmeester* (supervisor of peat diggers) Henrik Berentz fell ill, the rest of his household had to do their utmost to keep their heads above water. His wife worked as a spinner, as did one of the two adult children who lived at home. The other made buttons, and his ten-year-old child produced pins. This was piecework; they were paid a fixed amount per product, so the more pins, yarn and buttons they produced, the more they earned. The only non-earner in the family was the youngest child, a boy of five. Fortunately, the family received twelve stivers a day in poor relief.[33]

Both Sibbeltje the teacher and the wife of Henrik the supervisor illustrate the importance of spinning. This is not surprising, because yarn was always in demand, since it formed the foundation of the extensive seventeenth-century textile industry. Many girls learned to spin from their mothers from a young age, and in experienced hands the soft wool slid almost effortlessly through the fingers and into a strand of consistent thickness. Spinning had other advantages, too: it did not require

In this sparsely furnished home, a small boy prays before a meal. The spinning wheel has been placed directly under the window to make the best possible use of the daylight

Ceramic or metal whorls were slid onto a wooden stick to form a spindle, which was used for spinning fibre, such as wool or flax, into thread and yarn

a large investment and took up relatively little space in a small home.[34] This was especially true of spinning with a spindle; all that was necessary was a wooden spike with a simple whorl on top to weight it, so that it would turn properly and produce good-quality yarn fig. 108. In the course of the early modern period, the spindle was replaced by the spinning wheel fig. 107. This was more expensive to acquire, but it made the spinning process much faster because the thread was wound automatically. Sometimes an institution for poor relief would pay for the purchase of a spinning wheel. In 1637, for example, Maartge Ariens van Soetermeer took in her two grandchildren, and the Delft Kamer van Charitate (literally 'Chamber of Charity', a city organization offering poor relief) gave her extra money 'to buy a wheel for her daughter's children for spinning wool'.[35]

Since this work was done mainly by women, it makes sense that *spinster*, the Dutch word for a female spinner, came to mean an elderly unmarried woman.[36] Yet quite a few married women also turned to the spindle or a spinning wheel, for instance if their husbands spent long stretches away from home as soldiers or sailors. Other relatively straight-forward ways in which women could earn money from their homes included working as a seamstress, because textiles were expensive at the time, so they were often sent for mending and alterations.[37]

A Leiden bakery

In the middle class, which included craftspeople and small-scale traders, home life and work intersected in the front room of the house, the *voorhuis*.[38] This was where indoor life and the outside world met, and it often contained a shop or a modest workshop. Shopkeepers displayed their wares by opening the shutters at the front of the *voorhuis* or by using a *pothuis*, a low-ceilinged extension of the room. However, in most cases we should not imagine that the *voorhuis* was a shop in the modern sense of the word; instead, it was more like a parlour or reception room.

For instance, the customers who walked into the Leiden bakery run by Arent van Oostwaert and his wife Catharina van Keijserswaert must have had the feeling they were entering a cosy living room. The inventory of their belongings drawn up after Arent's death in 1695 tells us that the *voorhuis* was decorated with eight paintings and five small maps. There were five chairs with *trijpen* (wool velvet) cushions in a green floral pattern, as well as a corner bench.[39] The inventory does not mention a counter, even though it was probably present there and was not included on the list simply because it was built into the house.[40] Tellingly, the inventory of the possessions of another Amsterdam baker, Gerrit Willemsz, does not mention a counter in the *voorhuis*, but it does state that money was found 'in the counter drawer'.[41] The only items in Arent's inventory that directly related to the use of the *voorhuis* as a bakery are a cask, a trunk, a chest, a box for storing baking supplies and wooden measuring cups for measuring ingredients.[42] The shop probably also had tally sticks, notched sticks somewhat like rulers, for keeping track of the business. To keep track of who had bought how much bread on credit and when, you could scratch one line per loaf into the stick **fig. 109**.

A painting by Jan Steen offers us an impression of the warm welcome that could be expected from the baker and his wife **fig. 110**. The portrait, which hung in their kitchen, shows Arent in his work clothes, looking as if he has just taken a fresh loaf of bread out of the oven.[43] In the doorway is his wife Catharina with their wares on display next to her: loaves of various kinds, pretzels, and a decorated holiday loaf known as a *duivekater*. While this painting may not be an entirely realistic portrayal of their bakery, it demonstrates how closely the baker's trade was tied to the couple's identity.

Arent had not only the *voorhuis* at his disposal but also a special baking area, equipped solely with a stove and a variety of baking equipment. The attic was a dusty place, because the different types of flour and the wood for the stove were stored there. When Arent was on his deathbed, 'sickly of body', he was presumably no longer baking, because we find no loaves of bread or other baked goods in the inventory.[44] In contrast, Gerrit Willemsz still had all sorts of baked goods when he went bankrupt, ranging from half-loaves of wheat bread to pretzels, almost seven hundred items in total.[45]

109 Tally sticks have been in use for centuries. This one shows that a certain Mrs Volkman bought thirteen loaves of bread from a bakery between 3 and 22 May 1717; the baker made a notch in the wood for each loaf

110   Portrait by Jan Steen of the Leiden baker couple Arent van Oostwaert and his wife Catharina van Keijserswaert. The boy on the right is blowing a horn to signal that the bread is done

Home office

For bookkeeping and other administrative work, merchants could withdraw to a room known as a *comptoir* (office), after its principal piece of furniture, a writing desk that also offered storage space **fig. 112**. The *comptoir* was often off to one side near the front door, but it could also be a half-height room or area in a high-ceilinged space, or it could be in one of the upper rooms.[46] In addition to the writing desk, it often contained a money chest and a stove for heating **fig. 113**.[47]

The Amsterdam wine and timber merchant Isaac Pool had such a *comptoir* in his house, where he kept a diary for fifteen years (from 1663 to 1678).[48] For this purpose he used his almanacs, datebooks of a kind, which could have all sorts of things bound into them according to personal preference, from calendars and market schedules to moon phase tables, astrological predictions, amusing farces and extra pages for notes **fig. 111**. Isaac's entries dealt with such topics as business debts, rental income from the properties he owned, and information about his servants or building work on his house, as well as all sorts of social engagements and family matters.[49]

From the home office, you could also stay in touch with people who represented your interests abroad. The Boudaen Courten family, for example, owned not only houses in the Republic but also plantations and other properties in the colonies. The brothers Johan and Pieter were co-owners 'of a sugar plantation named De Nieuwe Hoop [The New Hope] by the Commewijne river in Suriname, including its buildings, equipment, slaves and livestock'.[50] Through correspondence, they kept as well informed as they could of developments there.[51] Johan must have been aghast when he opened a letter and learned that his shipment of sugar from Suriname would arrive a good deal later than expected **fig. 116**. The ship *'t Wilde Swijn* (The Wild Boar) had been buffeted by tempests at sea and was so heavily damaged that it could no longer sail on to Zeeland. Fortunately, it had not sunk and could return to a harbour in the northwest of Suriname, but they needed to find another ship to transport the valuable cargo.[52] Johan and Pieter kept informed not only about the ups and downs

September /   Herfst-Maendt.

1
2
3
4
5
6
7
8
9
10
11
12
13
14
15
16
17
18
19
20
21
22
23
24
25
26
27
28
29
30

C 2

This writing desk was probably a showpiece for the office, with drawers for papers and writing materials and an angled, folding writing surface

A cast-iron stove was an impressive addition to an office or other room. This one is decorated with scenes of the biblical Battle of Gibeon, exemplifying military success

of the sugar business but also about the assignment of their enslaved workers to reinforce Fort Zeelandia against a possible English or French attack in 1672, which would go down in Dutch history as the Year of Disaster.[53] This illustrates how knowledge about colonial injustice found its way into the households of the Republic on paper. Unfortunately, the readers were generally most interested in financial gain.

All this correspondence was kept in special letter bags, which could be found in many a *comptoir*. When businessman and diplomat Thomas Hees was stationed in Algiers for the States General, he ordered a pouch emblazoned with his name and position **fig. 114**. The pouch was both a functional item for protecting important documents, such as the international trade agreements he negotiated in Algiers, and a symbol of his diplomatic career. Back in the Republic, Thomas had his portrait painted with the diplomatic pouch lying casually on the table, among all sorts of other objects meant to display his learning and success **fig. 115**. To his right we see an enslaved African boy, also named Thomas, whom he bought at the Algiers slave market in 1677 and later took with him to Amsterdam.[54]

Scaling up

Overseas trade, in which many merchants took part from the safety of their *comptoirs*, led to an influx of raw materials that were turned into finished products in the Republic. Bales of rough silk and dye pigments, for example, were imported in large quantities into cities such as Haarlem and Amsterdam, and many locals there worked for businesses that shipped, dyed or wove silk.[55] These no longer exclusively served the local demand; increasingly, their products were meant for the national and international markets. In some cases, this led to serious upscaling of the home-based businesses.[56] For instance, Mathijs van der Burght of Amsterdam, who died in 1682, was no ordinary silk weaver but a 'manufacturer' of silk sheets and the proprietor of a fully-fledged velvet-weaving business. The inventory of his possessions reveals that he had three looms, three warping mills and various other kinds of weaving equipment in his home, not to mention substantial quantities of silk from Bologna and China. Mathijs also owned another 33 looms, which

114, 115 The diplomat Thomas Hees used this letter bag in his role as 'Ambassador of the States General of the United Netherlands', as the embroidered words state. In a later portrait of Thomas with his nephews Jan and Andries and an African boy, who was also named Thomas, the bag is also depicted

DE·EDELE·HEER·TOMAS
HEES·AMBASSADEUR·VAN·STAATE

116 Johan Boudaen Courten, leaning on a globe, poses in his comfortable dressing gown with a nautical chart of the Caribbean – a stark contrast to the harshness of life on sugar plantations, such as De Nieuwe Hoop, of which he was a co-owner

117 Earthenware funnels and jars were used in refining sugar. Such items are sometimes unearthed in excavations on the former sites of sugar refineries, as were these finds from Amsterdam

were not in his home but distributed among the homes of no fewer than seventeen weavers who worked for him. His other employees included silk winders, women who were paid by the pound of wound silk, and 'work girls' (including the sisters and daughter of an employee) who did various odd jobs and were paid weekly, like the weavers, for six days' work.[57]

As the century went on, women and children formed an ever larger share of the workforce, often because of deepening poverty.[58] Products from all over the world, such as tea, tobacco, cocoa and sugar, which at first had been luxury goods for the most wealthy members of society, were imported in growing quantities and became affordable to the less affluent social classes. As a result, many women opened their own small shops or groceries in their homes. Delftware potters introduced lines of cups for tea and hot cocoa, and pipe manufacturers in Gouda saw increasing demand for smoking paraphernalia. Even children under the age of twelve were recruited to help with rolling clay and polishing pipes.[59]

This type of expansion is vividly illustrated by the businesses known as sugar refineries, where crude processed sugar cane was refined into sugar. These refineries shot up like mushrooms in the course of the seventeenth century. To make enough room for the entire business, proprietors often rented or bought several adjacent dwellings and converted them into business premises, widening the front doors to make it easier to carry crates of sugar in and out. The attic floors were reinforced so that they would not collapse under the weight of the sugar. In the boiling rooms on the lower levels, raw sugar was melted into a mixture of water and eggs or oxblood in steaming vats. After various refining processes, the sugary blend was poured into conical funnels with small holes in the tip, which were placed on top of special pots into which the sugar syrup dripped fig. 117. The refined sugar remained in the funnel in a conical form known as a sugarloaf.[60] Stoves and fireplaces in the attic were used to further dry these loaves. Such refineries were a potential fire hazard, as shown by an archival document from 1670 about the sugar bakery De Zon (The Sun) on Amsterdam's Prinsengracht canal: 'Despite all efforts … the sugar bakery and the house' both regrettably went up in smoke.[61]

This quotation also illustrates that even businesses of this kind, despite their almost industrial scale, were often closely tied to people's homes. Throughout the seventeenth century, work and home life formed an almost natural symbiosis, in all social classes. In the *voorhuis* and *comptoir*, where customers were welcomed, work and private matters mingled, just as they did on the grounds outside, where the still smouldering kiln was watched over by night. Some hired a housemaid or took an apprentice to help with the work, while others scrabbled for income and a roof above their heads. It was an age when the world grew larger, new commodities and expertise were developed, and an array of commercial activities, crafts, goods and people entered the home.

parenting

Maartje Brattinga

Zeeland, November 1673. Trijntje is expecting her third child. She writes to her seafaring husband Jan Jacobsen Sloper that she misses him; she finds it hard to bear everything on her own. Her feet hurt, and she complains about her swollen ankles, which seem to sag over her shoes. By the time Jan returns home, their baby will have been born. Trijntje tells him it makes no difference to her whether it's a boy or a girl, 'as long as it's a healthy child.'[1] This was her greatest concern at a time when infant mortality was shockingly high; as a mother, Trijntje would have done all she could to bring her child into the world in good health. But her work did not end there. 'The most important contribution to giving the Republic good citizens is the raising of children,' wrote the Dordrecht physician Johan van Beverwijck in 1636.[2] A proper upbringing began with the mother, and so, for the first seven years, a child was mainly the woman's responsibility.[3] The exemplary role that she and, later, the father were expected to play only grew in importance as the child grew older.

Child development was likened to the growth of twigs, shoots or sprouts: the parents' task was to prune, tie and guide them so that they would grow in the right direction **fig. 118**. This comparison, which goes back to the Greek philosopher Plutarch, was central to many child-rearing manuals for seventeenth-century parents.[4] The Dutch parenting advice of that era was a mixture of humanist and Reformation thought. These were the two pillars of raising children to become good citizens: God-fearing, well-mannered, and respectful of the social hierarchy.

Parents' expectations for the future of their offspring varied. While some hoped for additional household income or more strong shoulders in the workplace, others were concerned with passing on their family name. For the poorest households, the birth of a child could give the final nudge into dependence on charity, both because there was an extra mouth to feed and because the demands on the mother as caregiver often made it impossible for her to earn an income.[5] Whether you had a son or a daughter made a large difference to the child's role in the household, the parents' approach to child-rearing and the family's future. No matter what challenges and expectations parents grappled with, they were not alone;

they received help from family members, neighbours and schools in nurturing cognitive and physical development, teaching manners and social skills, and providing occupational training. But first, the mother and child had to survive the delivery and the critical first few months.

Life and death

In the seventeenth century, just as today, a household with a new baby had to acquire a lot of new things. In 1628, when his wife Petronella van Vorst was pregnant with their first child, the Utrecht regent Carel Martens recorded in his account book everything he had purchased for his 'wife's layette' in preparation for the birth. This term was used for the whole set of accoutrements for the newborn child but could also refer to a literal basket (made of wicker, ceramic or silver) in which baby clothes, nappies and cloths were presented as gifts for the expectant mother **fig. 119**.[6] Carel listed absorbent cloths, nappies, '*borstrockiens*' (an additional warm layer), lace and extra linen fabric. In a fashionable household like the Martens', this baby linen could be kept in a special layette cupboard **fig. 120**.

The expectant father also bought a folding screen – to protect his wife and child from draughts – and a warm blanket for the cradle **figs. 121, 122**.[7] The infant could be nursed, changed and swaddled in a *bakermat*, a long wicker basket in which the mother or wet nurse could sit with her legs extended **figs. 123, 124**. This basket was placed close to the hearth to keep the child warm; its tall back also offered protection from cold. Despite all the care and attention that Carel devoted to his layette, things went wrong. The girl, Maria, died ten days after her birth, and her father was left with yet another expense, 'for the [burial] clothes of our dear departed child'.[8] Carel was certainly not the only parent who had to endure such a loss. Half of all children never reached adulthood, and most of those deaths occurred under the age of five.[9]

Not only cold but also poor nutrition was a threat. Clara Molenaars and her husband Herman Verbeeck in Amsterdam welcomed little Gerbrandus into the world in the spring of 1655. But the baby was unable to breastfeed. Clara most likely used all available means to stimulate

On one side of this glass a child bends a small twig; on the other, a man on horseback tugs at an old tree. Every sip of beer from this glass reminded parents to bend their young twigs in the right direction

118

The decorations on this glazed earthenware layette show the circumcision of Jesus during his first year of life

Baby linen was sometimes kept in a special layette cupboard. The carved decorations in the wood represent objects such as a cradle, a *bakermat* (see figs. 123, 124), a potty chair, a fire basket, a nursing bottle, a porringer, and a spoon

121   This cradle cover was used to protect a baby from draughts. It closed off the cradle completely, concealing the child from view, as illustrated here with a cradle from Petronella Dunois's doll's house

122 This quilted cover was laid in the cradle over a woollen blanket. Made with superbly embroidered, lustrous silk, this extra layer was not only warm but above all decorative

The *bakermat* was a type of cradle in which a child lay on the mother's or nurse's lap to be cleaned, fed, or swaddled, as the detail of a print by Willem van de Passe illustrates

123,
124

lactation, such as applying an herbal ointment with anise, fennel and dill and abstaining from sex, since it was believed a new foetus would compete for nourishment from the mother.[10] A glass breast pump was also a possibility fig. 125.[11] The mother placed the open end over her nipple so that she could suck on the long glass spout to make the milk start flowing.

But whatever she tried, her child would not drink. Clara's desperation grew. She feared the same fateful outcome as three years earlier, when she had also given birth to a son, likewise named Gerbrandus, and he too had had trouble with breastfeeding. Clara had even developed mastitis (breast inflammation), so the baby ended up drinking her blood instead of her milk, and was dead by the age of four months.[12] Determined not to let that happen again, the parents hired a wet nurse. 'And so to our dismay, our lamb must have a nurse, despite our preference and the burden on our purse,' Herman wrote in his autobiography.[13] This expense must have amounted to seven guilders a month, more than a craftsman's weekly wages.[14] For Clara and Herman, who were running a grocery at the time, it would have been a hefty sum. Furthermore, it drew criticism from the people around them: couldn't they just raise the child on porridge? If they consulted the seventeenth-century parenting literature, it cannot have made their decision any easier. Many authors, most notably Jacob Cats, insisted that mothers should nurse their children themselves: 'A woman who bears children is a mother in part, it's true; but if she nurses them she is a mother through and through.'[15] Such writers saw this as the healthiest, most natural option, claiming that it strengthened the bond between mother and child.[16] Having someone else nurse your children was seen as selfish and reprehensible.

Furthermore, hiring a wet nurse exposed the child to all sorts of risks; without a loving mother's supervision, a baby could suffocate in its sleep, for example, or be swapped for another. A more fundamental danger lay in the milk itself, which was believed to contain the woman's personal qualities, so with each sip from the breast, the baby might also imbibe any weaknesses of character she might have. That made it crucial to choose the wet nurse carefully. In practice, however, many women probably opted for

The purpose of this glass breast pump was to stimulate milk production, but it could also be used to express colostrum, a mother's first milk. Some doctors believed colostrum was unhealthy and should be disposed of

126   Frans Hals shows us how intimate the bond between a wet nurse and 'her' child could be. He may have painted this portrait when little Catharina Hooft was weaned and had to say farewell to her nurse

whoever was available and affordable.[17] The elite were much more likely to hire a wet nurse, but different households had very different attitudes.[18] While little Catharina Hooft's wet nurse even appears in her portrait fig. 126, the poet and statesman Constantijn Huygens took pride in having been nursed by his own mother. And the head of the Boudaen Courten merchant family in Middelburg noted in his family record, almost apologetically, the cases in which poor health had forced his wife to stop nursing early.[19]

The wet nurse's milk kept Gerbrandus healthy for a long while, but around his first birthday he caught a dangerous fever. After three months of continuous illness, the 'sweet sprout' passed away, to his parents' intense grief.[20] The moment he became ill coincided with the transition to solid food. Babies were breastfed for nine months to one year. Then they went on to 'drier', more solid food, as humoral theory prescribed: a porridge of milk, water and bread.[21] It is very plausible that this was when Gerbrandus ingested bacteria that caused his death.[22]

Clara Molenaars lost several children, and the emotional impact on her must have been profound.[23] Infant mortality was a danger all parents faced, and one over which they had very little control. Clara, a Catholic, prayed to St Agatha, a martyr whose breasts had been cut off, and went on a pilgrimage to Heiloo (a small town in North Holland), not once but twice, to thank and honour Mary. Parents also protected their children from everyday threats by adorning them with red coral jewellery. The coral's red colour and branching shape resemble the human circulatory system, and its properties of softness under water and hardness above water were reminiscent of clotting and therefore reinforced the association with blood.[24] Protective powers were also attributed to rock crystal. For example, it was used in rattles along with bells and a whistle, the sounds of which were thought to ward off evil. Such rattles could also have a more mundane purpose: teething babies were sometimes given the part with rock crystal to bite on fig. 127.[25] A portrait of Amsterdam's Leeuw-Hooft merchant family shows the youngest daughter Suzanna seated on her mother's lap and clutching a rattle. She cannot have been aware of its protective powers; to her, it was simply a delightful toy fig. 128.

239

Playing

The first stage of life was the most vulnerable time, and everything brought into the house, from an amulet to a folding screen, was intended to protect the infant. But even after children grew older and began toddling around on their own, their lives remained at risk. Houses were far from childproof and offered many ways for them to hurt themselves. Constantijn Huygens describes getting his head stuck between two bars of the fire screen; his brother alerted their parents to the danger by crying and pointing. Thanks to quick action by Constantijn's father, he came to no harm.[26] Parents tried to keep their children safe with special clothing. Toddlers often wore 'pudding caps', stuffed rolls of fabric, on their heads to protect their 'soft little brains'.[27] In the portrait of the Leeuw-Hooft family, Suzanna is wearing a pudding cap over her regular cap (see **fig. 128**). For children who had just learned to walk, leading strings were also convenient; incorporated into their clothing, they allowed them some freedom of movement and kept their parents in control **fig. 129**.[28]

Parents of restless young children who were not yet toilet-trained must sometimes have been tempted to leave them strapped into the *kakstoel* (potty chair). These chairs had a hole in the seat under which a chamber pot could be placed and replaced as needed, so that children could relieve themselves **fig. 130**. By leaving a toy or some food on the child's tray, preoccupied parents could keep their son or daughter contentedly busy for hours. Authorities advised against this, however. The physician Steven Blankaart warned that once children grew older, they should 'not be left in the potty chair too often, because then they'll turn into porridge sacks'.[29] Parents were expected to encourage physical exercise from a young age so that their children would not end up weak, pale and scrawny.[30]

Young children were thus given plenty of opportunity to play. Only after their minds had matured a little and their bodies had run the gauntlet of childhood illnesses were they made to sit still at their school desks.[31] Jan Kolm of Amsterdam, a merchant's assistant in Antwerp and a *rederijker* (rhetorician), depicts his children's 'daily fun' in the drawings and writings in his 'remembrance book', a unique source of

By shaking this gold rattle or blowing on the whistle, an infant could make noise. The rock crystal offered relief during teething

All the members of the Leeuw-Hooft family are making music; even the youngest daughter, Suzanna, depicted on her mother's lap, is holding a rattle. She is wearing a pudding cap

128

In Petronella de la Court's *voorhuis* (front room), the maid is strolling around with the toddler on leading strings. The manservant, holding a basket under one arm, is about to go out and run errands

130   Painted dummy boards, placed in the home to surprise guests, were both decorative and entertaining. This one showed parents what not to do; the child has fallen asleep, slumping over in the seat

words and pictures that make seventeenth-century family life almost palpable.[32] He portrayed his five-year-old son Hansje with rosy cheeks and curly hair poking out from under a tall hat, waving his whip; Hansje has just succeeded in making his top spin fig. 131a. The floor is strewn with toys: a drum and drumsticks, a spear, some marbles and a toy wagon. Hansje is holding a colf stick, a relative of the golf club, and has planted his banner with the initials H.L. in the ground behind him.[33] His father Jan says he is 'infatuated with playing' and writes that his son can generally be found in the street: '[He] would forget school and his dinner/ as long as he's out in the street with his drum and banner/ with a spear, a whip, a top, or a wagon to pull.'[34]

  Jan's younger son, three-year-old Sieuwert, was also portrayed at play by his father fig. 131d. He stands beside a child's chair with a whip in one hand and a basket in the other. Scattered on the ground are marbles, a top and a few knucklebones – pieces of animal bone used in a game. In his 'Kinderliet' (Children's Song), Jan Kolm refers to children's vivacity as they play and quarrel: 'first crying, then laughing/ first squabbling, then at peace'.[35] Kolm's reader pictures a bustling house in Amsterdam's Uilenburg district, with toys underfoot everywhere. But his home life was not always so cheerful. Little Sieuwert died a year and a half after his father drew his portrait, and Kolm's youngest daughter Lijsbet passed away four weeks after her birth.

  As Jan Kolm's portraits of his children illustrate, both boys and girls wore skirts. For very young children who were not yet toilet-trained, this had practical advantages. But despite the similarities in clothing, substantial distinctions were made between the genders. Boys had distinctively male accessories, like the hats worn by Sieuwert and Hansje.[36] But the difference becomes even clearer if we look at their toys. Kolm also depicted his daughter Anna at the age of three. She has a similar basket and almost the same chair as her late brother Sieuwert, but instead of a top, whip, drum or banner, she has a finely dressed doll on her arm fig. 131c. Kolm describes Anna doing her best to make sure her doll, Lijsgorts, won't cry. The girl also carries objects conventionally signifying a housewife: a

No. 1622 den 19 november.
Sierbert Janssoon Colm. Out 3 Jaer. en ii weecken.

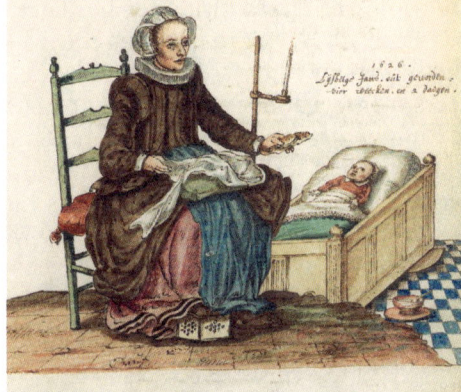

Selie Lindeman. Out 11 Jaer Ao 1624

1626.
Lesselys Jans. out geworden
vier weecken. en 2 dagen.

Anno 1625 den 19 Sant charitis In Amsterdam. Ao
Anna Jans. Dochter. out 3 Jaer. in 3 weecken.
har des smeck. 9 vier weecke. ess. en 6 sesseboe.

SK

Dit sal Hans mijn soons merck sijn haer hem geit mit Lewen

Ao. 1622 den 19 november.
Hans. Lindeman de Jonge. out 2 Jaer en 10 weecken a.
als gestelt de mom en sijn mojders vader. maer Boet
ver mij sijn vader. Hans Janssen. Kelm.

bunch of keys dangles from her right side, and on the left she has a pouch and case for sewing things or cutlery (see also **fig. 75**).[37] By playing mother to her doll, she is practising for her later role as a housewife.

When re-enacting the lives of their parents, children played with all sorts of *poppengoed* (literally 'doll goods'): miniatures of ordinary objects from weapons to cooking utensils, sometimes used with dolls and sometimes without.[38] These could be simple items like porridge bowls and cooking pots, or more complicated furnishings such as cradles and spinning wheels. They were made of materials ranging from silver, porcelain and glass to somewhat cheaper materials like wood, pewter and red earthenware. These types of toys were therefore available to children from a range of social classes **fig. 132**. Although they must normally have used these objects only in play, some small pots and pans show traces of actual soot. It cannot be said for certain whether all this sooty *poppengoed* was actually used by children, but it is possible that they learned how to prepare food and handle fire through play.[39] On the island of Vlooienburg, a multicultural area of Amsterdam not far from the Kolm family's neighbourhood, a miniature *púcaro*, a drinking cup of Portuguese origin, has been found. By playing with such objects, the children of migrants became more familiar with their parents' cultures of origin.[40]

Such toys reflected the conventional wisdom that parents should be aware that their children were imitating them. By setting a good example, they could raise good citizens. This explains why the parenting literature drew a sharp distinction between genders. But it is difficult to tell to what extent boys really did play typical male roles and how much girls limited themselves to dolls and kitchen utensils.

Jacob Cats encouraged mothers to pass on all the knowledge their daughters would need as future housewives. Taking them along to the market was the ideal way to show them how to pick out the highest-quality products.[41] One such moment was captured in the exceptional portrait of Adriana van Heusden and her daughter at the fish market **fig. 133**. Adriana is selecting the best fish and negotiating with the vendor; her daughter is watching and learning and will later do the same herself.[42] For

132a–f Children could imitate their parents, using miniatures of practically every variety of household object. Judging by the traces of soot, the little cooking pot at the top right was actually heated over a fire

boys, the future looked very different. The first step was the transition from skirt to trousers between the ages of five and eight, which children recognized as an important milestone.[43] Coenraet Droste says of the grandfather who raised him, 'He stuck me in trousers when I grew older.' He also gave his grandson his first miniature sword: Coenraet was being groomed for a military career **fig. 134**.[44]

Around the age of seven a new stage of development began, with a stronger emphasis on cognitive skills and on preparing for adult life. Not only did the paths of boys and girls steadily diverge, but so did the members of different social classes. Yet children in the Republic, unlike many of their contemporaries elsewhere in Europe, had relatively frequent opportunities to learn to read and sometimes even write.[45]

Learning

Annetje Jochems sits bowed over a sheet of paper, focusing intently. She dips her quill into the ink jar and scratches out the salutation of her letter: 'Greetings, father.'[46] Her hand, still unsteady, writes wobbly, angular words. She makes mistakes, crosses out letters and sometimes accidentally smudges the ink. The result is a spotty, barely legible note **fig. 135**. This Amsterdam girl must have learned the rudiments of writing at school; now, with her mother's encouragement, she wants to show her father her new skill.[47] She asks him to bring her a 'golden sky' – what she means by this is unclear – and wishes him a safe journey.[48]

There is also a second letter, in which Annetje writes that times are hard – it is 1672, the Year of Disaster – and expresses her wish for God to protect him.[49] At the bottom, she wrote the letters of the alphabet. But again, she couldn't reproduce exactly what she had learned. She wrote 'a b e' at first, crossed it out and started over. This letter must have been written a little later; her handwriting is quite a bit more consistent, and what she writes is more coherent.[50] The good wishes that Annetje so touchingly penned for her father never reached him. The two letters were captured by English privateers, as part of a large collection of postal items, and taken to London, where they can now be found in an archive.

In the detail of this portrait by Emanuel de Witte, Adriana van Heusden selects the best fish at the market, a skill that fits the image of the ideal housewife. She thus sets a good example for her daughter

135 Comparison of these two letters from Annetje Jochems to her father a, b at sea reveals that in the second her handwriting is much more regular

In an accompanying letter, Annetje's mother writes that she can already read the paper fairly well, but that her writing still needs a little work.[51] While today's students learn reading and writing in tandem, seventeenth-century education kept them strictly separate. Children first had to learn to read properly before taking up the quill. They usually began writing around the age of eight, when their fine motor skills were sufficiently developed for them to acquire the technique. The timing was also influenced by their parents' financial situation; learning to write made tuition more expensive, with additional costs for paper, ink and the cutting of the quill.[52]

The literacy rate in the Republic was fairly high. From around the age of three, the youngest children could attend nursery schools. Although such schools mainly provided day care rather than education,[53] they did make it possible for parents to work. Municipal authorities provided affordable city schools that offered education to many children aged five to ten.

Schools did more than teach skills; like parents at home, they were also responsible for turning children into pious, God-fearing citizens. Accordingly, they offered a curriculum centred on the Reformed faith. Learning to read, and perhaps write, was not an end in itself. Rather, it enabled you to read the Bible, a practice central to Protestantism. The primers used to teach reading and writing were therefore generally religious in character **fig. 136**. Families also put these aspects of religious life into practice at home, with encouragement from the pastor,[54] by praying, singing psalms and reading from the Bible. The father played an especially important role in such activities.[55] For example, schoolmaster David Beck regularly sang psalms with his son Adriaen, and sometimes with the children of the Roer family in Arnhem from whom he was renting a room. He also listened to Adriaen reciting from children's catechisms, books written for children to teach them the essentials of their Protestant religion through questions and answers.[56]

Parents and teachers also shared responsibility for teaching good conduct. A manual for schoolteachers tells us that great importance was attached to training in manners, such as taking off your hat, not swearing or gambling, and obeying your parents.[57] The rules of etiquette for children set down by the Rotterdam humanist Erasmus in the sixteenth century remained influential and were published in a new, rhyming translation in 1693.[58] Erasmus placed special emphasis on table manners. Much of what he wrote still seems sensible today: wash your hands before eating, lay your napkin on your lap, don't slurp, and don't lick off your fingers. Other rules included covering your mouth with your hand when yawning, neatly combing your hair before going out, and baring your head when an elderly lady or gentleman sneezes.[59] Taking off your hat was an important sign of respect in the hierarchical society of the seventeenth century and governed by strict rules.[60] If you failed to master these rules as a child, it reflected on the rest of your household. When Joan Huydecoper, the burgomaster of Amsterdam, heard from a friend that his son Balthasar had not removed his hat quickly enough in greeting, he was furious. Surely he hadn't learned such impolite, insolent behaviour at home? At the time of this reprimand, Balthasar was twenty years old.[61]

Good conduct was important, not only for the individual but above all for the reputation of the whole family.[62] Children had to be kept under control with rewards and occasional punishments. They did not receive marks at school, but better performance was encouraged through competition. The winner of a spelling or writing contest could take home a prize from the schoolteacher: a book, a print or a motto in attractive calligraphy. These prizes were all intended to contribute to their moral and religious education **fig. 137**.[63] Some parents set great store by their children's achievements. When Joan Huydecoper's eldest son Johannes was ranked only fifth in his Latin school class at the end of the school year, his father wrote to him in deep disappointment, 'I wish you had not made those two gross errors, without which you could not have failed to take first place.'[64] Such mediocre results were obviously not what he expected from his son.

Poor conduct led to punishment, occasionally corporal. For instance, David Beck disciplined his son Adriaen physically for chattering and for eating too many sweets.[65] As a schoolteacher, Beck must have owned a *plak*, a spoon-shaped paddle used for striking children, usually on the

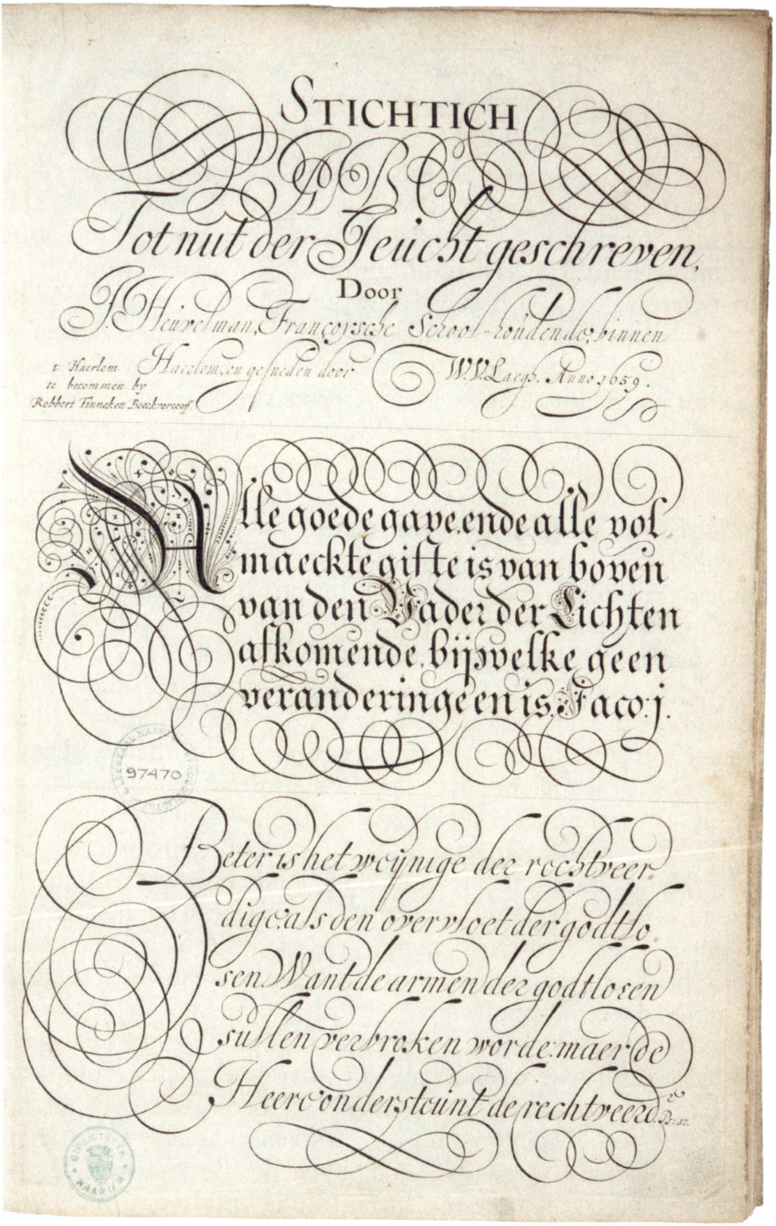

This page is from an alphabet book for learning penmanship inculcates a quotation from the Epistle of James, part of the New Testament: 'Every good gift and every perfect gift is from above, from the Father of lights'

STICHTICH

Tot nut der Jeucht geschreven,

Door

J. Heurelman, Françoysche School-houdende binnen
Haerlem, en gesneden door W. L. Laeys. Anno 1659.

t Haerlem
te bekommen by
Robbert Tinnaken Boeckvercoop

Alle goede gave ende alle vol-
maeckte gifte is van boven
van den Vader der Lichten
afkomende, bij welke geen
veranderinge en is. Jaco: j.

Beter is het weynige des rechtveer-
dige, als den overvloet der godtlosen. Want de armen der godtlosen
sullen verbroken worde: maer de
Heere ondersteunt de rechtveerd.

No. 7.   PAASCH-PRYS.

Children who did well at school could win a print. On special holidays, the entire class would sometimes receive gifts. This print of Susanna bathing, which had been in circulation since the 16th century, was given to Catholic children at Easter

outstretched hand. Some writers on education saw beating by parents and teachers as an essential method of child-rearing, as long as it was done in moderation and not on the head. But physicians such as Van Beverwijck and Blankaart were less approving of corporal punishment.[66]

Although the municipal authorities were responsible for schools and for appointing schoolteachers, the law did not make education mandatory. Many parents' top priority was for their sons and daughters to start contributing to the household income as soon as possible. Children in the poorest social strata had the least time for personal and professional development; they were often put to work at the age of eight or nine to supplement the household income. Such children were frequently subjected to exploitation and abuse.[67]

The greater the parents' income, the longer their children's formal education usually continued and the likelier it was to be tailored to their personal needs. Children from the upper classes, who could look forward to futures as merchants or officials, attended French or Latin schools. The latter type was only for boys and provided admission to university. The wealthiest families were much more likely to opt for private tutoring, so that the parents could choose both the subjects to be taught and the tutor, thus ensuring a high standard of education.

The elite, more than others, had the means to go on pruning and cultivating their tender shoots for many years. The eldest son was under particular pressure, as he was expected to become the head of the family and perpetuate the family name. A great deal was invested in eldest sons; they received a good education, were encouraged to become high achievers, and established networks that would serve them well later in life.[68] When fourteen-year-old Johannes Boudaen Courten drowned on his way from the Latin school in Dordrecht to his parental home in Middelburg, it came as a huge blow. The family was wealthy and played a key role in city administration, and Johannes, following in his father's footsteps, had been on the path to a leadership role in the Dutch East India Company. His father Pieter wrote about Johannes in exceptional detail in his family chronicle, from the number of months of breastfeeding to the recovery of his corpse from the water, still fully clothed, five months after he drowned.[69] His death suddenly made the future look very different for his younger siblings. In time, Pieter's ninth child and fourth son, named Johan, would become the new head of the family (see figs. 116, 167a).

The Amsterdam clergyman Isaac Pontanus had pinned his hopes on his only grandson, Hendrik van Beek, who had lost his father at the age of two. Pontanus took personal responsibility for part of his education and foresaw a bright future filled with virtue and assiduous study for the boy, whom he affectionately called by the pet name Heineman. Isaac himself was a gifted orator and both tolerant and visionary in his religious views. He expected Heineman to outdo him in scholarship and virtue and seized every opportunity to urge him towards that goal. For his grandson's eighth birthday, he gave him a gold medallion with Latin and Greek inscriptions calling on him 'always to be the best and to stand out above others' fig. 138. A miniature portrait had been painted for the inside of the medallion case. It depicts Pontanus putting a sheltering arm around his grandson as he presents the medallion to him with his other hand. Every time Heineman picked up the medallion, he was reminded of his mission in life, and his grandfather's eyes looked out at him from the portrait. Hendrik went on to become a Doctor of Laws and dedicated his thesis to his grandfather.[70]

Girls were not granted as much time for personal develop-ment. Besides reading and perhaps writing, they also learned needlework, a subject sometimes taught by the schoolteacher's wife. Sewing, knitting, spin-ning and embroidery were also taught at home or at separate knitting and sewing schools.[71] Needlework was associated with feminine virtues such as diligence, thrift and neatness. If you knew how to embroider, you could mark your linens to make them easily recognizable as yours – a welcome possibility in view of the high price of fabric. Embroidery could also be used to repair clothes and linens or add attractive decorations, and girls would practise the requisite skills by making samplers. They learned all sorts of stitches, patterns and colour combinations and embroidered the alphabet in a variety of fonts. Their motifs look ahead to their lives as

138   Isaac Pontanus gave this gold medallion to his grandson Hendrik van Beek
a, b   to encourage him to become a high achiever. The miniature portrait adorning
the lid of the medal case, depicts Isaac handing him the medallion

housewives and mothers: pincushions, sewing baskets, spinning wheels, linen cupboards and wedding gloves **fig. 139**.[72] Every stitch reinforced this image of the future.

After a few years of school, the sons of craftspeople often had to start learning specialized skills for their later roles in society. They continued their studies as apprentices working under masters or learned their trades at home, as did Passchier de Fijne in Leiden. At the age of five or six, he got up at four in the morning to sweep the hearths – a dirty job, since it filled the air with soot and ashes. He also helped his parents in the cloth industry after school. Like most boys, Passchier was raised to follow in his father's footsteps. At the same time, it was important to his parents to send him to school.[73] His autobiography tells us that he developed a ravenous appetite for reading there, and especially for religious writings. After submitting a piece that confirmed his mastery as a cloth worker at the age of sixteen, he remained interested in theology and had the opportunity to retrain as a clergyman. Passchier was eager to do it, but it was not his decision to make.[74] Even though he was already a fully qualified craftsman, it was still his father who made his career decisions for him. In this case, he acceded to his son's wishes. While mothers were in charge of child-rearing at home for the first seven years, and after that focused mainly on their daughters, fathers were more involved in the education and career choices of their older children, especially their sons.

Leaving home

The age at which children left their parents' house was highly variable. Boys learning crafts and trades began their apprenticeships at the age of twelve to fourteen, often taking up residence in their master's home.[75] Girls from the elite moved in with relatives for a while to learn to run a household, while upper-class boys attended Latin school. Since not all cities had a Latin school of their own, this often required them to live elsewhere for a time. Religion could be another reason not to attend a local school. Andriese Lucia Bronkhorst, a fabulously wealthy Frisian aristocrat, sent her eight-year-old daughter Lucia Helena all the way to Gouda in 1643 for a five-year

139 This sampler is embroidered with three alphabets and various objects associated with housewives: a linen cupboard on the left, a sewing basket and wedding gloves at the upper right, and underneath them a pincushion, fireplace tongs, a spoon, and a key. The clasped hands in the centre symbolise eternal fidelity

programme of Catholic education. Andriese saw few other opportunities for her daughter in the immediate vicinity. This was in large part because Catholicism had been outlawed since the Reformation, and this ban was ever more strictly enforced as the seventeenth century went on.[76] Primary sources suggest that her mother visited only once, to mend her clothes.[77]

The death of a parent could be another reason for leaving home. After a father or mother died, a surviving child might be taken in by a relative, whether temporarily or permanently. In the lower classes, the loss of one or both parents often drove a child to the orphanage; the children of burghers were admitted to special orphanages for their social class, while others had to make do with orphanages for the poor, established by the Church or private individuals. They would remain there until they came of age.[78] In the upper classes, orphans were often cared for by relatives. After Maria van Nesse's brother died, his three- or four-year-old daughter Geertruijt stayed with her for a while. She lived only a couple of doors down the street, and they already had a close relationship. It must have been a difficult time for Geertruijt, and Maria did her best to brighten the girl's days. She sent for toys from Amsterdam and went to especially great lengths on Sinterklaas (Feast of St Nicholas), a traditional Dutch holiday, when Geertruijt was showered with gifts, such as a miniature spinning wheel, a doll's cradle and table, and an alphabet book. She also enjoyed marzipan, white and red biscuits in the shape of letters, and sugared almonds.[79] Her mother Dieuwertje Hooghelandts remarried twelve years after her husband's death and had children with her new husband, in addition to her two surviving daughters from the previous marriage. Complex family structures like these, with half-brothers and half-sisters, were quite common because many children lost one or both parents.

Around the age of eighteen to twenty, young people ceased to be seen as children. In the years that followed, they became more independent with every step – earning an income, marrying and moving into homes of their own – and the pressure from their parents began to ease. After men turned twenty-five and women twenty, they no longer needed parental consent to marry. Once they were leading lives of their own, it eventually became clear whether all the pruning and cultivating had been effective, whether they had become good citizens as their parents had hoped. At this stage, their father and mother's influence over their development probably varied a great deal from family to family and between social classes. Young men from elite families, in particular, continued to feel parental pressure long after officially coming of age.[80]

Moralists believed that parents should continue advising their children throughout their lives, and even from beyond the grave. The pastor Petrus Wittewrongel, for instance, saw it as a father's last duty to give advice from his deathbed. He acknowledged, however, that not everyone would possess the mental clarity to do this in the final moments of their life. Other authors recommended putting down one's wise words on paper in advance, since these last pieces of parental advice would never be forgotten.[81]

140 Yfke Tjesma's wedding casket is decorated on four sides with biblical scenes: the cardinal virtues and Jacob and Rachel on the front and back, and Susanna and the elders and Tobias and Sarah on the sides

engagement

David Beck, a schoolteacher, is so lovesick that he can't stop talking about Geertruijt, the neighbour of his good friend Theodore Calaminus, a pastor in Arnhem. In his diary, David marks the day of his first encounter with her, 17 November 1627, with an asterisk.[1] Ever since then, he has visited the home of Theodore and his wife regularly, hoping for a glimpse of Geertruijt. He tries to win her heart by writing poems and giving her little presents. At first, she rejects David's advances, leaving him inconsolable. The strongest opposition to their liaison comes from Geertruijt's father and brother, perhaps because David, aged 34, is a widower and has three children from a previous marriage. Furthermore, he has become infatuated with one woman after another since his wife's death.

Although young people were reasonably free to find their own partners, parental consent was essential. But Geertruijt later shows renewed interest, and in the late summer of 1628 they meet in secret and regularly exchange gifts – often pears and hazelnuts, which are in abundant supply in that season. One beautiful day in mid-September, she kisses him for the first time, in the vineyard behind the houses. That night, David is too elated to sleep, and this date is also marked with an asterisk.[2] When she offers him bunches of flowers and pieces of fruit, he takes it as encouragement to go on visiting her in the garden. These tangible tokens of affection were an important way of making one's intentions clear, especially when they could not be spoken aloud.

Sadly, David Beck's diary ends in November 1628, and we don't know exactly how he won his suit, but David and Geertruijt did eventually win over her family. They must have become engaged some time in early 1630 and married that same year. The engagement – or promise to marry – was a serious step, because as a rule it could only be broken by mutual consent.

This strict rule was meant to prevent those who had premarital intercourse from making overhasty promises and later reneging on them.[3] To add force to his pledge, a man would give his bride-to-be as valuable a gift as he could afford. If a silver or gold medal was beyond his means, a small ring or an engraved copper or silver thimble was an acceptable alternative.[4]

Women kept and cherished such engagement gifts for the rest of their lives. Take Yfke Tjesma, who died in 1668. In the large sealed cupboard in the front inner room of her house in Voorstraat in the Frisian city of Harlingen, she kept two silver caskets. She had received one of them from her husband Frans Reiniers Tempelar 35 years earlier, when they became engaged.[5] Such caskets stood in a long Frisian tradition of putting great effort into lavish engagement presents – both the packaging and the contents. In earlier times, gifts of a few coins or medals had been wrapped in a *knottedoek* (Frisian for 'knotted cloth'), often richly embroidered by one of the young man's female relatives. He would offer the cloth to his beloved with a loose knot in it. If she tightened the knot, it signalled that she accepted his marriage proposal. In Yfke and Frans's day, and in their social circles, the cloth had been replaced by a more valuable silver casket **fig. 140**.[6]

The casket delivered numerous messages about Yfke's future role as wife. The front was decorated with the seven virtues, accompanied by the inscription 'Blijft hoop, geloof en liefd' ons bij:/ Soo houdt ons Godt van tweedracht vrij' (Hope, faith, and love, remain with us/ God keeps us free of discord thus). A virtuous life was the key to a harmonious marriage, because only when a husband and wife had a good relationship with each other could they serve the household and thereby God.[7] One side of the casket bears a scene of Susanna and the Elders.[8] This story of a woman raped and then nearly condemned to death because of her attackers' lies is linked not primarily to their crime but to her conjugal fidelity: 'Waer trou falieert: ist heel verkeert/ Bemint: daer gy trou in vindt' ('Where fidelity fails, nothing avails/ Where fidelity is found, let love abound'). Despite the relatively free choice of partners, all these engagement customs still hint at very traditional views. Men were expected to take the lead in courtship, while young women were supposed to hold back and remain chaste. An engagement gift not only confirmed a couple's marriage plans but also symbolized the deeply felt importance of honour and fidelity.

141 This *ketubah* was designed by Salom Italia, a Jewish engraver from Mantua who lived in Amsterdam from 1641 onwards. Six vignettes, surrounded by scrolling foliage, show the steps taken by the future spouses in the community in preparation for their marriage

Femke Diercks

marriage

'My Dear Aunt!', writes Cornelia Johanna van Beveren in Batavia (present-day Jakarta, and the location of the Dutch East India Company headquarters in Asia) on 14 December 1689, with all the enthusiasm of a young bride. Her letter to Maria Sweers de Weed in the Netherlands reports on her wedding earlier that year to the merchant Jurriaan Beek. She says there were around 80 guests, 'both the second and the first day, most of them young people'.[1] A seventeenth-century wedding had two important parts: the oath of conjugal fidelity on the first day and the consummation of the marriage that night, which was the occasion for continued celebration the following day.[2]

Weddings took place in church or at city hall, depending on your religion. The Reformed could simply marry in church, while others had to go to city hall, separately from their own religious ceremony, to make the marriage legally binding. For Christian spouses-to-be, *ondertrouw* (registering to marry) and signing the prenuptial agreement were important steps in the weeks preceding the wedding. Such agreements, customary across social classes, listed the property to be contributed by each spouse and stated how it would be distributed if one spouse died. *Ondertrouw* was the official declaration of the couple's intention to marry; this was similar to the reading of the banns, but under the authority of the city government. The document was signed at city hall, and the marriage plans were then announced three Sundays in a row in church, in the case of a Reformed couple, and on the steps of city hall for members of other denominations. A Jewish man would also sign a *ketubah* in synagogue, establishing his duties to his bride-to-be **fig. 141**.

The wedding ceremony was almost always followed by a collective meal, usually in the home of the bride's parents. Wedding gifts as we know them

269

142 The handles of this cutlery set, which Anna Roelofsdr de Vrij received from her husband Jacob Bicker, are decorated with foliage and birds in translucent enamel. Birds symbolised marriage and procreation

today, brought by the wedding guests for the couple, were uncommon in the seventeenth century.[3] The groom did, however, generally give presents to the bride.[4] They frequently combined symbolic significance with practical utility, as in the case of the cutlery Anna Roelofsdr de Vrij received from her husband, the merchant Jacob Bicker, in 1608. Since cutlery was not kept on the table but carried in a small cylindrical case attached to a belt, it was the perfect gift – it could be worn on her person and serve as a daily reminder of her conjugal duties fig. 142.[5]

Among both Protestants and Catholics, a seventeenth-century wedding was not complete until the marriage had been consummated. Cornelia received a bridal crown from her husband-to-be, 'made entirely of strings of pearls and diamonds'.[6] Such crowns symbolized the bride's virginity. As

143 Brigitta Stuyling's bridal crown is decorated with glass and enamel ornaments suggestive of marriage and family life, such as the couple's initials, flowers, birds, layettes, and porringers

they were usually made of flowers, it is rare to find less perishable examples, such as the pearls described by Cornelia or the silver crown that belonged to Brigitta Stuyling from Alkmaar, who married the Amsterdam pastor Petrus Schaak in 1667 fig. 143. According to Jacob Cats, the bride offers up her virginity by marrying and 'after this crown, becomes the husband's crown'.[7] When the crown was still on display on the second day of Eva van Ceulen and sailmaker Willem Karmichel's wedding celebration in Amsterdam, their guests asked in surprise, 'Why, Bridegroom, how can it be that the Bridal Crown is still hanging? It's said in Holland that, when that happens, the Bride is still a virgin.' The bridegroom confirmed that sexual intercourse had not yet taken place.[8]

144 Aaltje Anslo's wedding ring has two parts that join to form a circle. Only when separated do they reveal the spouses' names and the wedding date

The importance of the consummation of marriage as a transition to married life also explains why bedrooms were often richly decorated. In Cornelia's case, even the decor in church matched that of her bedroom: 'The cushions placed on an oriental carpet in church, as custom demands, were made of green velvet with gold, in perfect harmony with the use of green fabric to adorn everything in the bridal chamber.'[9]

The wedding ring was worn only by the wife in the seventeenth century and reminded her of her bond with her husband and her duties to him.[10] Cats wrote that in giving his bride a ring, the groom 'attested that he had roundly, sincerely, and without the least deception entered into that holy Covenant with his beloved'.[11] The ring's design could reinforce this

145   This bowl is covered with symbols of matrimony, from clasped hands
       and a burning heart to rings and birds. There are also symbols of mortality,
       such as a death's head and an hourglass

message; examples include fede rings with two clasped hands, or rings
with a house, worn in the Jewish community as a symbol of the future
household and the Temple in Jerusalem.[12] Very occasionally, the ring had a
more personal meaning, as in the case of the ring decorated with enamelled
landscapes worn by Aaltje Anslo when she married the merchant Michiel
Block in 1658 **fig. 144**.[13] Not only marriage itself but also its appurtenances
were imbued with symbolism, which consistently returned to the themes
of faith, duty and the marriage bond **fig. 145**.

146 In the centre of this silver tazza is a dome with a hinged lid. When the vessel is filled, the gilt figure of a child emerges from it: 'Hansje in the cellar'

Maartje Brattinga

birth

During the beautiful, cold winter days in Leiden in February 1663, the expectant father Pieter de la Court is looking forward to what he hopes will be the happiest year of his life – second only to the year of his wedding – and, as he can see from his wife Catharina van der Voort's 'sweet, swelling belly', his seed fell on very fertile soil.[1] Two months earlier, Catharina excitedly wrote to all her brothers to let them know she was about three months pregnant with the couple's second child; their daughter Magdalena had by then turned one year old.[2] The pregnancy is progressing well, and Pieter writes 'that not one meal goes by without a toast to the health of our Hansken in the cellar' – in other words, the unborn foetus.[3]

For these toasts, Pieter may have used a silver tazza with a special surprise inside. When wine was poured into the cup, the ball in the middle opened, slowly revealing a small figure **fig. 146**.[4] Hansken came out of the cellar – a direct reference to the expected birth. Even though this was a festive toast, the participants must not have felt entirely carefree as they drank, considering the risks attendant on pregnancy and childbirth. Proposing the toast, taking a sip and passing round the vessel were, in fact, ritual acts intended to ensure a favourable outcome.

To remain healthy and safe throughout their pregnancy, women would seek advice from friends, relatives and neighbours, and might also turn to medical handbooks for the general public. Some recommendations are still familiar to the modern reader: eat well, get plenty of rest, wear loose clothing and avoid extremes of heat and cold.[5] Other tips now strike us as less sensible. For example, pregnant women were instructed to be careful of what they saw and even what they thought, because it was firmly believed that such things could directly influence the unborn child. By keeping a painting or figurine of a charming young boy in the house during her pregnancy, a mother

147 Jacob Cats tells the story of an ugly woman who gave birth to an attractive child and was therefore suspected of dishonourable conduct. When a beautiful figurine with a striking resemblance to her child was found in her home, her honour was restored

could supposedly bear a similar-looking baby **fig. 147**.[6] Repeated toasts to a successful outcome, performed while watching a 'birth' take place in a silver vessel, also formed an expression of this idea. The negative implications of these beliefs were also accepted. When Catharina's pregnancy ended in a miscarriage, this was attributed to the fact that she had witnessed a fight two days earlier.[7]

After the miscarriage, Catharina's haemorrhaging continued for an entire month. She ultimately made a full recovery, but many women contracted life-threatening infections after a miscarriage or childbirth – infections that lingered for weeks or even months.[8] With that in mind, many women had their wills drawn up during pregnancy or the postpartum lying-in period.[9]

148   In Petronella Oortman's lying-in chamber, the mother could sit in a comfortable lying-in seat while receiving guests. Coffee and tea were served from a costly silver urn and tea kettle while they admired the newborn

The midwife's presence was a crucial factor in delivering a child successfully, but the pregnant woman's loved ones also played an important role. On 24 October 1660, Sophia Coymans, whose pregnancy had reached full term, seemed to have begun to 'krack' (have contractions, literally 'crack'), her husband Joan Huydecoper wrote in his diary. The contractions cannot yet have been very serious, because Joan went on receiving visitors and his mother came for dinner with them. Two days later, the time had come, and events moved very fast. The midwife had not yet arrived, but fortunately, Sophia's mother was there to help. The child, a girl, had almost been delivered by the time the midwife arrived.[10] She helped with the post-delivery stage, but what most impressed Joan was his mother-in-law's decisive action. He wrote to his cousin that everything had moved so fast that his mother-in-law, to the astonishment of everyone present, 'had to receive the child, thus playing the midwife'.[11]

When the mother and child both survived, the relief must have been immense. The upper echelons of society had numerous post-childbirth rituals, in which children were shown off to the world by their parents and welcomed by family and friends. For example, considerable thought was put into furnishing the special, temporary lying-in chamber where visitors were received **fig. 148**. When Magdalena de la Court was born in 1661, her family served cinnamon biscuits and handed out sugar wreaths to the children.[12] At festive gatherings of this kind, alcoholic drinks such as caudle (which was similar to eggnog) and brandy with raisins were also often served. Toasts were drunk again, as they had been during the pregnancy, this time to the baby's successful arrival and the health of the new mother **fig. 149**.[13]

149 This glass, filled with white wine and sugar, was used to toast 'The Health of the New Mother'. The people present would drink together, relieved that the child was born and that the mother was doing well

150 The baby was wrapped in a warm, padded cover (*doopluur*, literally, 'baptismal nappy') for the baptismal ceremony. The excellent state in which this one has been preserved suggests that it was always cherished as a family heirloom

Maartje Brattinga

baptism

A milk dish, six spoons and a salt cellar, all silver, for Isaac. A gold medallion on a chain and a sum of money for Joost. Twelve napkins, a tablecloth and a towel for Maria. These are just a few of the varied baptismal gifts presented to the children of Maria van Swanenburg and Willem van Heemskerk. The Leiden cloth merchant kept a meticulous record of them all in his family chronicle, along with the dates of baptism and the names of the godparents who had bestowed the gifts.[1] All of Willem and Maria's fifteen children were baptized a few days after their birth, some at home and others in church. They must have been beautifully dressed for this special occasion **fig. 150**.[2]

Children in Catholic and most Protestant families began their religious lives with this baptismal rite, their first introduction to their social and church communities.[3] The ceremony also formed the ritual beginning of their relationship with their godparents, who acted as witnesses and had the important responsibility of supporting their godchildren throughout their lives. This moment was marked by a special present, the *pillegift*, which reinforced the ties between households or families.[4] A *pillegift* could be a rattle or an attractive necklace, but in many cases it was not a conventional present for a baby or child. Instead, it was an object that would remain significant for life (or longer) and serve as a memento of the baptism. In addition to this symbolic meaning, a *pillegift* also had monetary value. Often made of silver, it served as a kind of insurance that could be cashed in if necessary. This was consistent with the role of the godparents as providers of assistance to their godchild. Not everyone was lucky enough to receive an expensive baptismal gift, however, a fact illustrated by the discovery of a brandy bottle in Konijnenstraat in Amsterdam. The inscription engraved into this square glass bottle, which was found in an excavation, suggests that it was very likely presented as a *pillegift* **fig. 151**.[5]

Roeltje, the daughter of the schoolteacher David Beck, received a silver rummer from her godmother Geertruyt. The gift was not presented during her baptism, however, but only nine months later, because of the very real risk of her dying in those intervening months. She bore the same name as her mother, Roeltje van Belle, who had died in childbirth.[6] During the baptismal ceremony, the child's name was officially recorded. Naming children after family members, including deceased siblings, was a common practice. Siblings' names sometimes speak volumes about the terrible impact of the high mortality rate within a family.[7] In the Frisian Van Juckema family, three girls in a row bore the name of Aelke, because of the deaths in the family; all were named after their grandmother.[8] In a surviving portrait of the first Aelke, born in 1605, the one-year-old girl appears to be sleeping peacefully in her cradle fig. 152. But a closer look reveals her pale complexion, the straw she lies on and the wreath of rosemary twigs around her head. This evergreen herb symbolized immortality, and straw was said to ward off evil. This is a mourning portrait commissioned by her father Ruurd after he lost his wife and then his daughter.[9]

151 This small bottle of brandy was possibly a gift in honour of Salomon Verbeeck's birth or baptism in Amsterdam in 1601. The shards are inscribed with his father's name, Cesar Verbeeck, the date 1601, and the letters 'SA' (for 'Salomon')

The high infant mortality rate made it very important for parents to have their children baptized as soon after birth as possible. When children died very young, as Aelke did, then at least the ceremony had brought them into the church community and ensured their spiritual welfare, in the hope of eternal life after death.

152 Aelke van Juckema did not live beyond the age of two. Her father, who had also lost his wife – Aelke's mother – used this small portrait of Aelke in death to keep her memory alive

153 In this drawing by Gesina ter Borch, which accompanies the lyrics of the song 'Minnaers klacht Over sijn storven Maistresse' ('A lover's lament over his dead mistress'), we see a man in mourning with pallbearers and a funeral procession in the background

death

In 1637 Maria van Nesse in Alkmaar, overcome with grief, wrote in her *memorieboek* (notebook): 'My dear departed brother's child, Gijsbertus van Nesse, died … on the 17th of October … 5 and a half weeks after his late father … at 2 years of age minus 8 and a half weeks. And had my late brother lived 6 weeks longer, he would have turned 38 years old.'[1] Her family was in deep mourning after losing her brother and nephew in such quick succession.

After a death, the closest neighbours made the practical arrangements. A window or door was opened to let out the departing soul. The family was asked to leave, because otherwise their strong emotional bond with the deceased might make the soul unwilling to leave the house. After that, darkness prevailed: curtains, shutters and doors were closed to prevent the soul from returning. Mirrors were turned to face the wall or covered with cloths, so that the spirit of the deceased could not settle there.[2] From the time of death until the coffin was carried to the final resting place, the entire household was shrouded in mourning.

Extended family members, neighbours and possibly others in the same occupation were visited by an *aanspreker* – a type of undertaker whose responsibilities included going around in person to announce the death – and sometimes asked to close up their houses too. Isaac Pool describes this in his diary: 'On the 12th of January [1674], an *aanspreker* came to ask if we would be so kind as to close our house, because our cousin Van Raeij had departed this world around two o'clock.'[3]

Written remarks of this kind that have been preserved, as well as lists of 'death debts' (expenses resulting from a death), tell us more about the rituals surrounding mourning and funerals in the seventeenth century.

154 This bier was made for a bakers' guild in 1666, to carry members to their final resting place. It bears the inscription 'the bakers' bier,' along with a poem and painted images of various types of bread

These varied by region and religion, but there were certain constants. For one, it was not family members who undressed, washed and then dressed the body of the deceased, but neighbours or close friends or associates, or someone hired for the task. The dead were conventionally dressed in a linen shroud tied shut with black ribbons and a cap.[4] The body was laid out on a bed of straw. A carpenter was hired to make a coffin, and those who could afford it had it lined with cloth. The decorations, flowers, herbs and other parting gifts offered by mourners depended on their financial means, but also on the religious affiliation of the deceased and the rules of the church and city.[5] The baker Arent van Oostwaert's death debts tell us that mourning garments could be rented: his friends, who had served as pallbearers, had incurred rental costs for their mourning cloaks.[6] Despite attempts by Reformed city leaders to suppress certain customs linked to death, many ancient rituals stubbornly persisted. For example, putting a bundle of straw in front of a house as a sign that a person had died there – an especially common practice in Zeeland and the Southern Netherlands – was sometimes prohibited, or permitted only on a small scale and without ostentation.[7]

On the day of the funeral, the mourners walked in a long, silent procession, two by two, to the final resting place, which was usually in the church or on its grounds, or often in a cemetery outside the city if the deceased was not Reformed **fig. 153**.[8] The coffin was covered with a pall, and if the funeral had been arranged by the guild, the pall was decorated with the guild's coat of arms and related images.[9] Some guilds also owned a bier for use at their members' funerals, as is clear from the inscription on a surviving example from the

155 When a guild member passed away, funeral medals were distributed, such as this one from the carpenters' guild. After the ceremony, they were returned as proof of attendance

Hindeloopen bakers' guild: 'The baker kneads the bread and bakes it for the people's good, this bier was made exclusively for bakers young and old' **fig. 154**. Guilds required their members to be present at the funerals of their fellows in the same trade and collected their funeral medals as proof of attendance **fig. 155**.[10] Those directly involved were sometimes given money or a gift, such as a medal or silver spoon, in return for their help.[11]

A funeral was almost always followed by a shared meal.[12] For Geertje Claes's farewell meal in Amsterdam, for example, 'two hams, half a cask of beer, biscuits, wheat bread and white bread, butter and cheese' were purchased, and the items rented included 'napkins, tablecloths, jugs and glasses'.[13] This form of collective closure, like all the other rituals of mourning, helped surviving family members to say goodbye and commemorate the deceased.

156 During the eight-day Hanukkah festival, an additional light was lit each day. The form and exuberant floral decoration of this *hanukkiah* are characteristic of the Netherlands

Sara van Dijk

winter festivals

One by one, from left to right, Anna Osorio lit the eight wicks in her brass Hanukkah menorah while reciting the blessings **fig. 156**.[1] It is sundown and the last day of Hanukkah, the eight-day Jewish 'festival of lights'. In Lisbon, where she and her husband were born, they had been unable to celebrate it because they had been forced to convert to Christianity. They had both come to the Netherlands as children with the first generation of *conversos* (converts) who fled to Amsterdam, where, thanks to the relative religious freedom in the Dutch Republic, they had been able to rediscover their Jewish faith.[2] Learning all the prescribed religious laws had been a difficult study, particularly since they had not been brought up with a command of Hebrew. For people like them, in 1645 the Amsterdam Rabbi Menasseh Ben Israel – a *converso* himself – published an instruction manual in Portuguese on the application of Jewish law.[3] In this you could read that Hanukkah was celebrated to commemorate the miracle during the rededication of the Second Temple in Jerusalem. After the destruction of the city by the Greeks, there was only one day's supply of oil left for the seven-branched temple menorah, but it continued to burn for eight days. Menasseh described how the *hanukkiah*, the Hanukkah lamp with eight oil containers, should ideally be hung outside by the front door or in front of the window, but in a non-Jewish environment it sufficed for it to stand inside on the table.

Hanukkah was not the only festival that was celebrated indoors (and hence out of view of the authorities) during the dark days of winter. Both Sinter-klaas (Feast of St Nicholas) and Epiphany had Catholic origins, which was a thorn in the side of the Reformed Church. The government also tended to take an ambivalent attitude towards festivals; people needed some form of release, but there was always the risk of squandering money, excessive drinking and fights breaking out. As a result, city councils tried to ban the

157 The 'amusing three kings game' began with the assignment of roles. Each lot represents a member of the royal household, from the jester all the way up to the king

markets with their stalls full of sweets and gingerbread on the eve of the Feast of St Nicholas, and pastors complained about Protestant children putting their shoe by the hearth at bedtime in the hope of finding a gift in it in the morning. But to no avail. The Feast of St Nicholas, on 5 December, continued to be a popular children's festival; as Jan Steen's painting shows, the eve of the feast, when gifts were exchanged within the family, was a joyful event with songs, treats and presents for the youngest family members **fig. 159**.[4]

The Church had even stronger objections to Epiphany. This festival on 6 January was the final day and the climax of the Christmas period. Before the Reformation it was elaborately celebrated in public, with masked

158 During the Epiphany celebration, the king received a paper crown. This one is probably based on a 16th-century design that was reprinted for hundreds of years. You could cut it out and colour it in yourself

singers who went around knocking on people's doors on the eve of the festival and performed religious plays in the street on the day itself. All these Catholic – and some much older – 'frills' were placed under a ban. The result was that the festivities took place behind closed doors, where three (referring to the Three Magi) or thirteen (alluding to the number of days of Christmas) candles burned. Family and friends came together to play the *koningsspel* (Epiphany game). By drawing lots, one of the gathering was elected king for a day, along with a complete royal household from cook to physician **fig. 157**. The king was adorned with a paper crown **fig. 158**, but the doctor was equally important for the revelry, advocating wine as the best medicine, which then flowed liberally.[5]

159 The painting *The Feast of St Nicholas* (1665–1668) by Jan Steen shows a wide range of December treats in the left foreground: a basket of gingerbread, waffles, and spiced biscuits, an apple with a coin in it, and a large loaf of the sweet white bread known as *duivekater*

A delicacy we encounter at all these Christian festivals, from the Feast of St Nicholas to Epiphany, is *duivekater* (also known as *vollaard* in the Southern Netherlands).[6] This sweet white bread is prominently featured in the foreground of Jan Steen's *Feast of St Nicholas* as well as in his portrait of the baker Arent van Oostwaert **figs. 159, 110**. The bread might be decorated with small pipe-clay discs **fig. 160**. Sometimes the decoration, such as a swaddled Christ Child, would refer to a specific festival, but examples of scenes from the Old Testament, such as Adam and Eve by the Tree of the Knowledge of Good and Evil, are also known. More unusual are pipe-clay discs depicting Stadtholder Willem III on horseback, who as a right-minded Calvinist viceroy had many followers in Protestant circles. Thus, religion and politics were also brought to the table in this festive treat.[7]

160 Pipe-clay discs for decorating holiday bread, with Adam and Eve under
a, b the tree of knowledge of good and evil on the left and Stadtholder Willem III
on horseback on the right

During the shortest days of the year, festivals were celebrated by every denomination, with sweetmeats and by candlelight. Even though these festivals were of a religious nature, they punctuated the winter and formed part of a larger cycle of seasonal festivities. The advent of spring was celebrated with Carnival, followed by Easter or Passover halfway through spring; Whitsun marked the beginning of summer, and St Martin's Day (11 November) heralded the winter festivals. In this way the seasons, which we come across so often as decorations in home interiors, lent colour and rhythm to the year.

at home

Sara van Dijk

Emblem books such as Roemer Visscher's *Sinnepoppen* (1614), which includes a motto and a moralistic explanation on each page, were immensely popular. The motto on this page beautifully expresses the emotional value of the home: 'East or West, home is best'

161

XXXVII

T'huys best.

DOe alle beesten van Iupiter te
gaft ghenoodt waren, foo heeft
hem de Schildt-padt alleene achter
ghehouden, ende is niet ter Feefte
ghekomen : Iupiter verwondert,
foude gheerne de oorfaeck daer af
weten, liet hem vraghen, waerom
hy niet ghekomen was in foo goe-
den grooten gefelfchap, die van den
opperften God gheroepen waren.
Antwoorde : **Oost/ West/ t'huys
best**. Waer over hy verwefen worde in den hooghen Raedt der Go-
den, altijdt zijn huys voor hem te
draghen, ende by zijn leven daer
niet uyt te gaen.

T'huys best.

Abnormally changeable weather with rain and hail kept the schoolmaster David Beck indoors on the morning of 14 June 1627. Sitting in his rented room in Arnhem, he wrote in his diary, 'I was doing absolutely nothing, being lazy and occupied solely by my thoughts.'[1] In the seventeenth century, lounging around was regarded with suspicion; the biblical idea that 'idleness is the devil's pillow' held sway. Man had to make himself useful, for there were serious risks to free time. Hence, in your own house, concealed from the eyes and moral judgment of others, doing nothing was (and still is) possibly the ultimate feeling of home.

'*T'huys best*' (Home best) is also the motto of the emblem that the poet Roemer Visscher adopted in 1614 **fig. 161**. His explanatory text accompanying the picture is based on an amusing fable by the Greek poet Aesop and tells how the tortoise came by its shell. The reptile was invited to a great feast by Jupiter, king of the gods, along with all the other animals, but he failed to turn up. Asked why, he answered, in Visscher's clever translation: 'East/ West/ Home best'.[2] As a punishment, Jupiter fittingly gave the tortoise his shell, so that he would always be at home but would also have to lug his house around with him forever. The maxim shows that '*t'huys*' denoted more than just a location; here you were safe and able to withdraw and relax. '*T'huys*', then, already meant home.

The feeling of home is created by all the ordinary things you do there, day in, day out: sleeping and dressing, cooking and eating, housekeeping, working and raising children – all the activities that have been discussed in the previous chapters. Once all these tasks were completed, home was also the obvious place in which to do something entirely different – even if that meant doing nothing at all for a while. It was also where you practised your personal religion, relaxed, received visitors and amused yourself. Pleasing furnishings completed the sense of home.

Decoration

As today, people furnished their houses with all manner of personal objects to make it feel their own. Those who had money to spend were influenced by the latest fashions, and in the course of the seventeenth century it became increasingly fashionable to coordinate the colours and patterns of fabrics – for instance, by matching the tablecloth to the fireplace cover – which brought greater visual unity to the interior. The blue valance and matching tablecloth of Anthony Oetgens van Waveren and Anna Spiegel are an early example (see **fig. 88**).

Displaying Asian porcelain on top of cabinets, wainscoting and mantelpieces likewise became a rage that gradually spread throughout the population. Porcelain was a material hitherto unknown in Europe, and people were fascinated by its sheen and hardness. It was not long before the scenes on vases, bowls and saucers were adapted to European tastes. The world depicted on these objects was inspired by a Western fantasy of Asia, and it rapidly secured a place in the Dutch interior, though this rarely attested to a genuine interest in China or Japan. As a result of its growing supply to the Dutch Republic, porcelain became progressively cheaper and hence a typical example of affordable luxury. Blue-and-white Delft pottery was produced as an imitation of these Asian porcelains. While it was painted in the same colours and patterns to resemble real porcelain, being a local product, it did not enjoy the same prestigious status. People were generally aware of the difference between the two. The bulk of earthenware was utilitarian and was usually kept in a kitchen cupboard rather than displayed on the mantlepiece.[3] However, the two holes in the foot rings of many bowls and saucers show that they were also intended to be hung up **fig. 162**.

The walls in most homes were of white plaster, but they were far from bare. Paintings were extremely popular. Maria van Nesse from Alkmaar had no fewer than 74 paintings towards the end of her life – in addition to an assortment of prints and alabaster figurines – distributed throughout her rooms. Some of these were heirlooms; others she had commissioned from local painters or purchased from an art dealer, a second-hand merchant or simply at the market along with other household goods.[4] It was common in the Dutch Republic, where the Catholic Church was no longer the principal patron, for artists to work largely for burghers, who decorated their interiors with still lifes, biblical and mythological scenes,

162 The decoration on this Delftware dish, 33 inches in diameter, is inspired by Chinese porcelain. A wire could be run through the two small holes in the back to hang it up

genre pieces and landscapes. Paintings were found in every room, from the *voorhuis* to the kitchen, and not just in the houses of the rich but also in middle-class homes.[5]

The subjects were seldom chosen specifically for the spaces where they hung, although personal preferences can certainly be detected. In 1627, Maria commissioned the artist Zacharias Paulusz to paint a panel showing 'Our Lady seated with her sweet child on her lap placing the wedding ring on [the finger of] St Catherine'.[6] The mystical marriage of the saintly Catherine, who refused to wed and devoted her life to God, must have appealed enormously to Maria. As a convinced Catholic, she did the same, and she too would like to have entered a convent as the bride of Christ. Since it had been impossible to become a nun since the Reformation, Maria lived in chastity as a spiritual virgin: unmarried and serving the Catholic Church.[7] At thirty guilders, it was one of her more expensive paintings, but it was entirely in keeping with her religious convictions.

The Jewish merchant David de Abraham Cardozo from Amsterdam likewise owned a painting close to his heart. In the will he drew up in 1687 (a year before his death), he determined that the painting 'depicting the Portuguese Jewish Church of this city, painted by Emanuel Wit [Emanuel de Witte]' should go to a good friend **fig. 163**. It is remarkable that of all his effects – furniture, jewels and works of art – this is the only object that was specifically mentioned by name.[8] It shows how fond he must have been of the painting, which is not surprising when we consider that the Sephardic Jews had fled their native Spain and Portugal, where they were persecuted because of their religion. In Amsterdam, Cardozo was able to practise his faith, and the Portuguese synagogue was the ultimate symbol of this.

Although to our eyes, Maria owned a considerable number of paintings, she was not a collector.[9] For most people art was primarily a decoration to brighten up the house, while it naturally reflected their personal religious or political views. Those who were unable to afford paintings could resort to a variety of cheaper printed works, from illustrated news pamphlets to engravings of the ten commandments, to pin on their walls.[10]

163 Emanuel de Witte made a number of paintings of the interior of the Portuguese Synagogue in Amsterdam. This version, signed and dated 1680, may have been in the possession of David de Abraham Cardozo

The highest echelons in society opted for tapestries, but even the wealthiest of burghers could not afford more than one tapestry chamber. In 1660, for her house in Rapenburg in Leiden, Sara L'Empereur bought a 'set of tapestries' with a total length of 191 ell (over 13 metres), priced at four guilders per ell. She was given a small discount and 'only' had to pay 749 guilders.[11] A set like this covered all the walls in the room, occasionally from floor to ceiling, though more often they hung above the wainscoting. Although Sara says nothing about the subject, it is likely that it was a landscape. Tapestries with boscages and idealized gardens were so popular that they could be supplied from stock. Sometimes different designs were thematically linked and formed a series, such as the four seasons, but the exact subject was less important than their decorative quality, and depending on the available space, you could purchase a complete set or only part of one **fig. 166**.

Because the tapestries were not made to size, they were regularly – certainly in the early seventeenth century – hung over doors **fig. 165**, instantly stopping the draught. Later it became more customary to make special pieces to place above windows and doors. Despite their high cost, tapestries were not always handled with care: they were pushed aside, moved elsewhere, or became sooty or stained with wine, beer and grease.[12]

And yet a tapestry was the ultimate luxury, not merely because of its price but also on account of the greenery it depicted, which offered an escape from the daily grind of the bleak low country, as we can read in the poetry of the period. Jan Vos, the Huydecoper family's poet, devoted a poem to the tapestries in the *zaal* (main reception room) of their house in Singel: 'Who transports me from the IJ to the Greek Tempe?/ Here it flaunts its gay flowers, there the lush land laughs./ Winter has no power to temper this arbour./ Lent, which adorns spring, is eternal here.' He continues with a lyrical description of trees and birds, only to conclude that the 'lush life' is in the shade of a leafy canopy.[13]

A similar effect could be achieved with a cheaper alternative, a painted linen wallcovering, as can still be seen in the main reception room of Petronella Oortman's doll's house **fig. 164**. The painted pieces in the *zaal*

In the *zaal* (reception room) in Petronella Oortman's doll's house, you stand amidst a panoramic landscape painted by Nicolaes Piemont. A cloud-filled sky with birds on the ceiling reinforces the sense of being outdoors

165 Adriaen van de Venne drew this opulent interior around 1620. The walls and doors are covered with tapestries. It was customary to place all furniture, including chairs, against the walls

166
a, b
Tapestries such as these, from François Coppens's series *Park Landscapes*, brought the outdoors indoors. Many details allude to the seasons, such as the billing and cooing doves in the spring and the animals with their young in the summer

of the house of the Amsterdam regent Cornelis Backer in Herengracht were, according to a praise poem, 'surpassing tapestries' because their colours did not fade. They created 'a summer for the eye' on which the master of the house could 'feast' and 'relax' after state business.[14]

Family and friends

The *zaal* was not just a place to rest the mind. Being the most representative room in the house, it was intended for formal receptions, the tapestries and other decorations ensuring a fitting grandeur.[15] The immensely rich merchant Johan Boudaen Courten and his wife Anna Maria Hoeufft had furnished the *zaal* in Het Grote Huis in Noordstraat, Middelburg, with two mirrors set in gilt wooden frames, delicately carved with garlands of flowers and their family arms **figs. 167, 168**. The two matching gueridons – tall stands on which candlesticks were placed – take the form of a sculpted angel bearing the tray on its head while loosely holding the family coat of arms with one hand.[16] Such an impressive set of mirrors and gueridons was highly fashionable at the close of the seventeenth century. It must have been a wonderful spectacle when the candles were lit in the evening, the warm flickering light reflected in the mirrors, heightening the lustre of the elegantly carved gilt frames.

The room was further decorated with a mythological painting and a print of the town of Middelburg, as befitting a person with a position on the city council and in the local chamber of the Dutch East India Company. The family portraits hung here too **fig. 169**. Johan attached great importance to these. He attached handwritten notes to the back of the paintings, identifying the sitters, such as 'Hortensia del Prado, Mother of my Mother Sr. Joh. Boudaen 1678'.[17] Later, probably after his death in 1716, when the estate was divided among his four surviving children, someone made a list on which all these notes were carefully copied, including the exact position of the portraits on the wall.[18] Johan's parents, Pieter and Catharina, were prominently placed 'above the mirror with the Van Hoeufft coat of arms' **figs. 169f, g**.[19] A large, full-length portrait of Sir Peter Courten – a second cousin from the English branch of the family –

hung above the chimneybreast fig. 170. That he, too, was accorded such a prominent place and a genealogical explanation on the back shows the enormous importance of enduring family ties.

Johan's inscriptions give a brief account of the whole family history. His forefathers originally came from Meenen in the Southern Netherlands, where his great-grandfather Guillaume Courten was arrested under the regime of the Duke of Alva on account of his Protestant sympathies. He managed to escape in 1568 with the help of his wife Margarita Cassier, an event that the couple – or one of their children – commemorated by having a silver tazza (drinking cup) made, picturing Guillaume behind bars fig. 171. It was a centrepiece in the family mythology, and over the years a further three tazzas were made for the various descendants. Johan came into possession of one of these, and through inheritance it has always remained with the portraits.[20]

After his escape, Guillaume fled with Margarita and their like-named young daughter Margarita to London, where he continued his textile business, and his sons William and Pieter were born. William took over the business in London, and when the political situation in the Northern Netherlands had become more settled, the other two children moved there: Margarita to Rotterdam after her marriage to Matthias Boudaen, and Pieter to Middelburg. Together with William, Pieter built the family business into a flourishing international trading house. He was also the one who, as Johan wrote on the back of the portrait, built the 'Great House' in Middelburg along with his Italian wife Hortensia del Prado. It did its name justice. It was virtually an Italian palazzo, extending over two plots, with a large Renaissance style garden fringed by arcades – a new home for these successful immigrants.[21]

Hortensia and Pieter remained childless. Their nephew – the son of Margarita and Matthias, who was also called Pieter – joined his uncle from a young age to learn the trade and later inherited the trading company and the house in Middelburg. By then he was married to Catharina Fourmenois and had taken his parents' combined surnames, Boudaen Courten. The family book that he kept tells of the vicissitudes of his family,

167   Johan Boudaen Courten and Anna Maria Hoeufft had their portraits painted by Caspar Netscher in 1676.
a, b   These are copies by Philip van Dijk. Copies of portraits were typically painted for all family members

This luxurious set of two mirrors and gueridons is decorated with the family arms, Boudaen Courten's on the left and Hoeufft's on the right. The combination with the dazzling gilt exudes prestige

168

Guillaume Courten ⚭ **Margarita Cassier**
(1540–after 1580)   (died in or after 1616)

Matthias Boudaen ⚭ **Margarita Courten**
(died before 1606)   (1564–1640)

Pieter Courten   ⚭   **Hortensia del Prado**
(1581–1630)   (died 1627)

Pieter Boudaen Courten ⚭ **Catharina Fourmenois**
(1594–1668)   (1598–1665)

Jacob Pergens ⚭ **Anna Boudaen Courten**
(died 1681)   (1599–1622)

169a–i, Johan Boudaen Courten's family portraits formed a gallery of ancestors, which graced
170   his home's foremost reception area, the *zaal*. The full-length portrait of Sir Peter Courten,
        a type reserved for the high nobility, held a place of honour there

door sijn huijsurouve Marghueriete Victorie ghegheuen * ... *
... in meenen 1567 dach ...

171 This silver tazza is decorated with an image of Guillaume Courten behind bars. The inscription states that Alva meant to 'rob him of his life', but God 'gave [him] victory', through the agency of his wife, who helped him to escape

including the removal of his wife's bladder stone and the birth of their twin sons Pieter and Johan (who would later live in the 'Great House' with his wife Anna Maria).[22] Above all, the personal entries give an insight into how closely interlaced work and personal matters were, which was typical for the elite. Family members, including those by marriage, were referred to by the term 'friends' and were both business partners and confidential advisers, and were therefore strongly dependent on one another.[23]

In the *zaal*, Johan and Anna Maria were thus surrounded by their 'friends': physically when they received them in this room for business or pleasure, but equally in the form of their portraits. The presence of many Courten generations and the flamboyant gilt furniture with the family coats of arms lent prestige, and at the same time would have been a constant reminder of the task that rested heavily on their shoulders. Whenever Anna Maria Hoeufft looked at herself in the mirror bearing her own family coat of arms, she in effect joined the ancestral gallery along with the portraits of her parents-in-law above her. Her task was clear: to continue the family line. For Johan the pressure was no less great. His forefathers had steadily built up a global trading emporium from scratch. They looked down on him from the wall. It was his duty to uphold the honour of the house of Boudaen Courten.

Religion
The family line was of great importance, certainly for the upper echelons of society, among whom there was a growing interest in noble titles. The Boudaen Courtens were not the only ones who were preoccupied with their ancestry. There are other family books and series of family portraits (whether or not fictitious), but genealogical notes were more often recorded in the family Bible.[24]

The earliest notes that the Frisian Lucia Hester van Aylva made in her Dutch authorized version of the Bible, which would remain at Hania State, the landed estate in Holwerd, for several generations, were about the death of her father on 2 December 1665, followed by that of her mother on 8 January 1669 fig. 172. Within a month she married

Mourits Lodewijk, baron of IJsselstein. Lucia subsequently recorded the births of their five children: three sons who died shortly afterwards, all named Mourits, a girl stillborn at seven months, and a daughter Hester Jasperina. The third Mourits, born on the evening of 21 October 1674, died on 2 January of the following year, 'having reached the age of 10 weeks and 2 days'. Lucia's grief is almost palpable when she continues, 'buried on 5 January 1675, that evening being the eve of Epiphany, in the church of Holwaedt in the crypt with his ancestors and brothers and sister'.[25] Despite the young age at which he died, the child remained an integral part of the family line, together with the other Mouritses and his tiny stillborn sister, who was never baptized and therefore never given a name. The precious family Bible was an appropriate place for these entries. The Book of Genesis relates how God made a covenant with Abraham that would also apply to all his offspring.[26] He is one of the patriarchs of the chosen people. Extensive genealogical registers, showing how all the protagonists relate to their forefathers, are found in both the Old and the New Testaments. When people recorded the births and deaths of grandparents, parents and children on the endpapers time and again, these relatives, too, become a part of this long line.

The Bible was omnipresent in the daily life of the seventeenth century. Most people who owned books at home had a Bible and other religious literature.[27] Richly decorated with a silver or brass mount (like Lucia's copy) and kept on a lectern, the Bible represented the word of God at home. The Church strongly advocated reading the Bible every day. Both the best-selling writer Jacob Cats and the pastors Petrus Wittewrongel and Simon Oomius, two exponents of the Further Reformation (a Puritan movement within the Reformed Church), advised doing this every morning the moment you got up and every evening before going to bed. For Wittewrongel and Oomius, the whole of life was steeped in religion, but these were the moments of the day when you could devote yourself exclusively to reading because there were no other chores waiting. All three stress the importance of self-study and contemplation as well as of reading together. According to Cats, a good family man created 'a small church in

Den 2 Decemb: 1665 op een saturdagh de klok half 4 uair na
noen is binnen Liewaerden inden heere ontslapen mijn heer d'
Ernst van Aijlua oudt 48 jaren en is den 5 dito, van Ste
burghe huijs uit gedragen na de jacobiner kerk van waer
lijk des draghs daer na, na holwerdt is gevoert, en aldaer
kelder binnen de kerk ondergesit

Ano 1669 den 8 januarij is op een vrijdagh seer christelick
klok 3a 4 uair na noen inden heer gerust mijn vrou
moeder Jacomina Hester van Loo oudt in haer 52 ja
en is den 25 den dito van het huijs hania vijf gedragen
ook inde kerk tot holwerdt begraven

Den 31 january 1669 ben ik Lucia Hester van Aijlua 13
onsen Predicant Jacobs Reuius tot Holwerdt getrount me
mijn man de heer Meurs Lodewijk baron van Isselstein

Ano 1669 den 31 desembris op een vrijdagh morgen de klok ontr
7 uren, ben ik door godts zegen verlost van een jonge ze
de welcke na dat hij des eerste januarij 1670 bij den christely
ontvangenen doop, Is genoemt geworden Mouritius Vincent D
3 den van january verschreven is inden Heere ontslapen, en
daer op Den sesten dito sijnde een Donderdagh begraven

Den 28 Novembris 1670, sijnde een Maandagh, b
ik de klok ontrent twee uir de nacht verlost van
dochterken van ontrent sesen maanden dragens [ge]
en is getroch tot holwart bij haer voor vader inde ker

Anno 1672 den 8 februarij zijnde een donderdagh de
ontrent ses uijren, is geboren onsen zoon Mouris Erns
die daar op den elfsten dito in de kerck alhier tot
door onsen Predicant Reuius verschreven den christen
doop heeft ontfangen wiens geboorts Godt zegene

Ano 1673 Den 25 Julius sijnde op een sent Jacobs dagh op een Verijdagh
de klok half seven ben ik door Gods genade verlost van
dochter en is den 27 door onse Predicant Reuius den chri
doop ontfangen en is genaem Hester Juneriza wiens geboorts g

Den 22 April 1674 is in den Heere ontslapen onse zoon M
Ernst Vincent, nae dat hij door snure accidenten van sijne t
en teeringh teere mael was uijt geteert, oudt zijnde 2 j
thijn weecken en drie dagen waer op hij den 26 dito op
sondagh avens tot holwaerdt in de kerke in de kelder
bij sijn voor ouderen en brouter en sijn sester

Ano 1674 den 23 October synde op een Woensdagh savons tusschen
acht en negen ben ick door Gods genade verlost van mijn derste soon
de welcke aan dat hij op den 25 october bij der christelijcken ontfangene
doop is genoemt geworden Mourits Ernst Vincent en die doop is aen het
sijn Predicant door onse Predicant Jacobs Reuius wiens geboorte Gods godt
wil zeegenen

Welcke onse Zoon Mourits Ernst Vincens den 2 Januaris snachts
ontrent 2 uijren deser werelt door den doot overleeden is out sijnde
geworden 50 weecken en 2 dagen ende den 5 Januaris 1675 des
avonds sijnde drie koonige avondt inde kerck tot Holwaerdt
inde kelder bij sijn voor-oders en broeders en suster gestelt

. . . .

De 9 junij 1692 is gebooren mijn broer syn oudste dochter of een donderdagh tus
schen elf en twalif uijren smiddaegs en heeft des sondags daer aen den heiligen
doop ontfangen en is Frouck Elisabeth genaemt

Den 2 October 1713 op een Saterdag smorgens tusschen negen en tien uiren is onse outste Dochter gebooren, des
sondags daer an, den heijligen Doop ontfangen, en is genaemt
Helena Amerentiana Catharina
× door de predicant Nordbeck tot Holwert,

Den 27 December 1714 op een donderdagh is onse outste Soon gebooren, smorgens tusschen seven en agt uiren, en is des vridaegs daer an tot Leuwarden in de groter kerck door de predicant Tinius gedoopt en is genaemt
Ernst Samuel,

Den 5 den Februarius 1716 op een woensdag savons tusschen 5 en 6
uiren, is ons tweede Soon gebooren en vriedags daer aen volgende
tot Leuwarden in de water kerck door predicant Siccama
gedoopt, en is genaemt Ulbe Aylva en is den ...
April des selvigen jaers overleeden en tot Holwert bij geset

Den 19 Julius 1717 savons omtrent tien uiren is onse derde Soon
gebooren en is des sondags daer aen volgende door predicant Holom
tot Holwert gedoopt en is genaemt Ulbe Aylva en is den ...
September des selvigen jaers overleeden, en tot Holwert bij geset,

Den 17 xber 1718 is onse vinde Soon gebooren, smiddags om twalif uiren en is gedoopt
in de groote Kerck tot Leuwarden door Predicant Siccama en is genaemt Lodewijck Carel
en 30 Januarius 1719 tot Leuwarden overleeden en tot Holwert ingeset,

Den 26 Augustus 1721 des nade-middags omtrent 5 uiren is onse
sijlde Soon gebooren en den 30 Augustus van deselve maent
overleeden, en is bij sijn Broeders geset ... en is voor den Heijligen
doop over leden,

his house', and the authors were unanimous that it was his task to actively involve the whole family in reading and contemplation.[28] Those who were unable to do so should ask their neighbours to read to them, advised the straight-thinking theologian Gisbertus Voetius.[29]

Reading the Bible was compulsory, and the advice of preachers was indeed followed. There were all kinds of schedules in circulation for studying the complete book (from Genesis to Revelation) in one year. The schoolmaster David Beck was one such conscientious reader. From his diary entries in 1624, when he was living in The Hague, we learn that he started his new French Bible on 21 January and finished the 'reading' in mid-December. He probably followed the *Kalendier der Bybelen* (Bible Calendar), a daily reading schedule that prescribed passages from the Old and New Testaments, the Psalms and the seven books of the Apocrypha **fig. 173**.[30] David did indeed regularly read his Bible at the beginning and end of the day, but he also studied in the afternoon and even during school time when his pupils were quietly at work. Although his classroom at home was not heated, he would withdraw there to read when he was not teaching. His study, which was more comfortable, was another favourite reading spot.[31]

This reading schedule was not confined to a group of strict Calvinists. The more free-thinking Delft regent Pieter Teding van Berkhout, who read progressive philosophers such as Blaise Pascal and was familiar with the ideas of Benedictus de Spinoza, used such a calendar. Unlike David, though, he was not always very particular about attending church. If it was raining, he considered reading the Bible to the whole family an excellent alternative.[32]

The spiritual virgin Maria van Nesse was likewise in possession of a Bible as well as of typical Catholic religious aids, such as books of hours (with prayers and psalms), devotional prints and a rosary.[33] Moreover, in 1642, she made a home altar in the *voorkeuken*, the room in front of the kitchen, in a corner by the hearth. It was a huge undertaking, which she carefully planned in her *memorieboek* (notebook). She considered resting a bed board on a wooden chest and the pull-out leaf of her writing

Junius heeft xxx. daghen, by de Hebreen de vierde, *Sivan* genaemt.

De dagh.	De Psalmen.	't Oude Testam.	d'Apocryp. Boecken.	't Nieuwe Testam.
1		13.14	14	21
2		15.16	15	
3		17.18	16	
4	67	19.20.21		22
5	68	22.23		23
6	69	24.25		24
7		Paral.j.1.2		25
8		3.4	mac.j.1	26
9		5.6	2	
10		7.8	3	
11	70	9.10.11		27
12	71	12.13		28
13	72	14.15		Rom. 1
14		16.17		2
15		18.19	4	3
16		20.21	5	
17		22.23	6	
18	73	24.25.26		4
19	74	27.28		5
20	75	29.Par.ij.1		6
21		2.3		7
22		4.5	7	8
23		6.7	8	
24		8.9	9	
25	76	10.11.12		9
26	77	13.14		10
27	78	15.16		11
28		17.18		12
29		19.20	10	13
30		21.22	11	

(∴) 5

desk, but in the end she had a bench and two stools made to support it, adding the two large foot stoves that had been her mother's. Above it she hung three alabaster reliefs depicting the Nativity of Christ, the Last Supper and the Adoration of the Magi, and she dressed the altar with a cover, four gilt wooden candlesticks, a crucifix from the box bed in the *voorkeuken*, two small jugs that she painted gold and purple (each to hold an artificial flower), two larger gilded jugs that she fetched from the mantelpiece of the best room (each with two artificial flowers), and a small bell.[34] Maria's *voorkeuken*, with a hearth, a long table covered with a tapestry tablecloth, her writing desk, a portrait of her father and probably a box bed, was a pleasant and much used room in the house, to which she could also withdraw for private worship.[35]

At the same time, Maria described how her altar could easily be dismantled if visitors called, possibly because it would then be in the way, or because she could not always openly bear witness to her faith in a Reformed world. However, she was not the only Catholic with a special place for prayer or meditation at home. Her altar is an ambitious home-made structure, but ready-made groups of figurines and altar vases were also on sale, a pair from the Klaeuwshofje – a group of almshouses for poor unmarried Catholic women – in Delft dated 1667 being an example **fig. 174**.[36]

As in Catholic homes, ritual objects, such as Torah scrolls and *tallits* (scarves worn over the head at home as a reminder of God's commandments), played an important role in Jewish households. Inventories of Sephardic Jewish estates in Amsterdam and The Hague list Shabbat lamps, which could be found in the kitchen, the dining room or the *binnenkamer*, the 'inner room' between the front and back rooms. Here the mistress of the house lit the Shabbat candles and recited the blessing over them in the presence of the whole family.[37] Religion was more integrated into daily Jewish life than in Christianity, and living according to the laws was an indissoluble part of this. For this reason, a kosher household needed two sets of plates, one each for milk and meat dishes, for instance, in addition to purely ritual objects.[38]

The need for a place for spirituality in the home, for both communal and private use, was no different for Protestants than for Catholics or Jews, but for Protestants the emphasis lay on reading and memorizing passages from the Bible and reflecting on these throughout the day.[39] Other than books, no specific objects were needed for this, and hence there are no typical Reformed counterparts to Shabbat lamps or altar vases. However, since Protestants in these settings were so well-versed in the Scriptures, objects with biblical decorations resonated deeply and reinforced the exhortations of pastors, such as Oomius and Wittewrongel, to reflect on the word of God as they went about their daily duties.

Through ordinary, everyday objects, such as a fire curfew picturing the explorers searching for the Promised Land, or a linen cupboard showing the ordeals of Susanna and the Elders, the presence of the Bible was virtually taken for granted (see **figs. 80, 96**). The tale of Susanna and the Elders would have acted as an example for a housewife or maid going to the cupboard, while the story of the expulsion of the Jewish people from Egypt and the subsequent discovery of the Promised Land by two explorers who returned with bunches of grapes as proof of the abundance they had encountered, could easily be related to their own times. Just as the people of God were driven out and led by Him to a new and prosperous homeland, so the Protestants from the Southern Netherlands found a new home in the Dutch Republic.[40] Besides encouraging good conduct, the sight of familiar stories on opening a cupboard door or banking a fire would have been comforting and reassuring.[41]

Relaxation

While religion played a major role in the private domain in the seventeenth century, this did not mean that daily life was all religious devotion. There was a very different and much more light-hearted side to free time. Many households had a copy of the Bible and Cats's books on their shelves, but there was plenty of choice for those looking for real diversion. During long winter evenings, Pieter Teding van Berkhout liked to read in a chair by the fire or – nice and warm – in bed.[42]

174 With a pair of altar vases, you could set up your own home altar. The letters 'IHS' and
a, b 'MAR' stand for Jesus and Mary. On the other side is 1667, the year they were made

There was something for everyone: from books of pure entertainment, such as farce and joke books and novellas, to more informative texts, such as history books, newspapers and travelogues.[43] For intellectual stimulation, there were poetry anthologies and emblem books, theatre plays and philosophical works.[44] All these could transport the reader to other times and other worlds. This was, of course, less the case with the perpetual stream of lampoons and pamphlets, with their sharp commentaries on topical issues, serving readers who were politically or religiously engaged.[45] Bookworm David read it all, from a pastoral romance when he was in love and had his head in the clouds, to a news pamphlet that a friend pressed into his hand during a walk through the Hague Forest.[46]

A similarly wide range of games was available, which, unlike reading, were more of a shared activity. In addition to card games, board games were popular for indoors. One of the best-known was trictrac. Several fine, luxury trictrac boards have been preserved, but the only one that is more or less complete – with some of the checkers and one of the two dice – is the miniature version in the *zaal* of Petronella Oortman's doll's house **fig. 176**. It still even has the tiny tokens that served as gambling money.[47] The *zaal* was an ideal space for this type of game. Johan Boudaen Courten also had a trictrac board, by the family portraits and mirror and gueridon set.[48] Trictrac was a game of chance and of fluctuating fortunes, but it also demanded patience, focus, and strategic insight, as did Johan's working life as a merchant.

Another popular game was the Game of the Goose, which is still well known in the Netherlands, although it was not played by children then. It was an adult game of chance, symbolizing man's journey through life with its ups and downs and emphasizing the role that chance plays in real life. It could also be played for money, or – as a cheaper alternative – for simple tokens, such as those made from shards of household earthenware pots, since retrieved by archaeologists **fig. 175**. The Game of the Goose was well known throughout Europe, but the finest Dutch edition by the printer Claes Jansz differs from most of the foreign variants on one point: a player landing on square 61 found a cup and had to make a toast **fig. 177**.[49]

175 Betting games were popular. Those who could not afford to bet money or buy attractive tokens used homemade substitutes such as these, made from shards of pottery

176 This miniature game board comes from the *zaal* (reception room) of Petronella Oortman's doll's house. Chess and nine men's morris can be played on the two outer sides, and trictrac (a game similar to backgammon) on the inner board

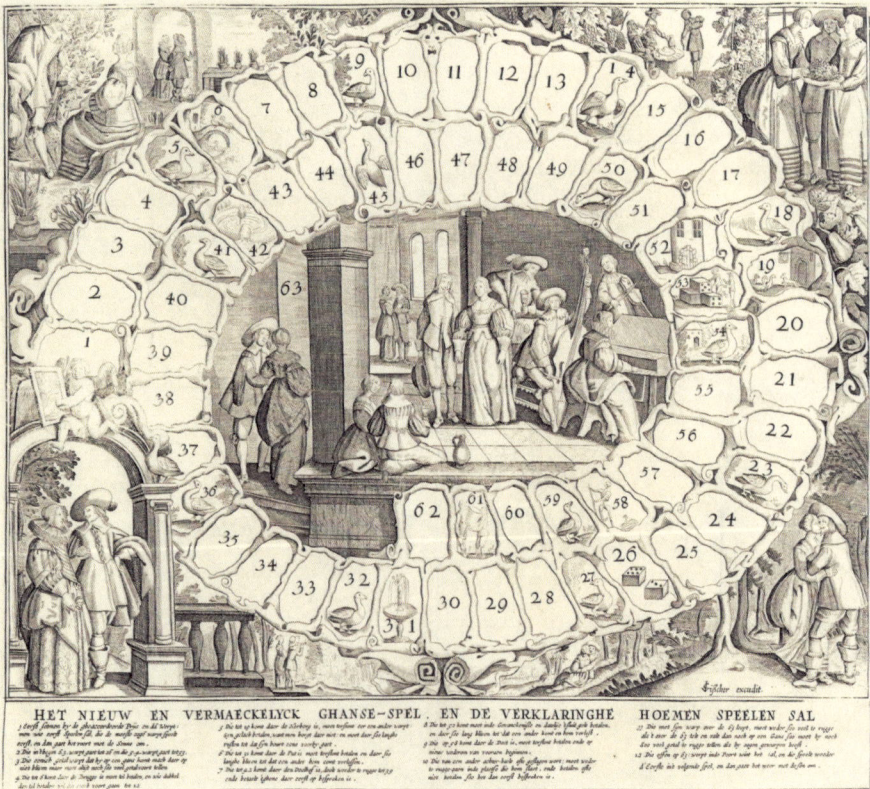

HET NIEUW EN VERMAECKELYCK GHANSE-SPEL . EN DE VERKLARINGHE HOEMEN SPEELEN SAL

This wine glass, engraved by Willem Mooleyser, shows a man with his hat in his hand raising his glass in a toast, with the inscription, 'The Welcome of the Friend'

The combination of drinking and gambling games was not just harmless amusement; in the eyes of the Church, it was one of the greatest hazards of free time. There are countless examples of losing money and alcohol abuse leading to fights, unwanted pregnancies and broken marriages.[50]

In most cases, however, drinking and toasting was a significant part of social interaction. Unsurprisingly, alcohol played a major role in the diary of the Amsterdam wine merchant Isaac Pool. He regularly treated his visitors to one or more rummers of Rhine wine, and on a Monday morning, straight after breakfast at a friend's house in Gouda, he drank a 'farewell glass of gratitude'.[51] It was very customary to toast one's company, as a late seventeenth-century wine glass shows **fig. 178**. The bowl is engraved, 'De Wellekomst van de Vriende' (The Friend's Welcome) with, in between the words, the figure of a man raising his hat and his glass as a greeting.[52] This is a very common type of wine glass, and even without this sort of telling decoration, toasts would have been made to friendship and other happy times.

Friends came in all shapes and sizes. In the seventeenth century they could be close relatives with a business and a family dependency relationship, as we have seen with Johan Boudaen Courten and Anna Maria Hoeufft. There was also a concept of friendship that went back to antiquity. Johan (who wrote poetry and was a member of the local *rederijkerskamer*, the rhetoric chamber)[53] and David both had such friends, in the humanistic sense of the word: men with whom they shared cultural and literary interests and whom they met because they enjoyed each other's company. The Roman orator Cicero had described such male friendships in his *De amicitia* (44 BCE), and the concept had become widely disseminated in the Netherlands through the Rotterdam writer and thinker Erasmus, even among people like David who had no command of Latin. He would usually sit by the fire in the kitchen chatting to family members and acquaintances who had come to visit him in The Hague. He received only a select group of friends in his *comptoir* (study) to discuss art and literature. It was his personal refuge, where few people came and where he liked to read, write poetry or make music.[54]

Music thrived in Dutch homes, and David was one of the many amateur musicians.[55] A spinet, virginal or even a harpsichord could be found in well-to-do houses, and occasionally even in middle-class homes. David himself had managed to get hold of a second-hand harpsichord for fifteen guilders in Arnhem, which he cleaned and freshened up by painting it green and grey.[56] Besides this, he played the flute, the violin and the zither. In middle-class as well as upper-class circles, making music together was a common and intimate way of whiling away the time and enjoying one another's company. Sara L'Empereur, for example, had learned to play the theorbo (a string instrument from the lute family). She also owned a lute (at 150 guilders, by far the most expensive instrument she had at home), two violas, one viola da gamba and two small zithers, which probably belonged to her husband and her children.[57]

The Netherlands also had a flourishing song culture; people rich and poor, young and old whistled and sang in the seventeenth century, including at home.[58] Little was needed for this: just your voice and only a small repertoire of songs, for most of these were contrafacta, new lyrics written to tunes that everyone knew. You did not have to be able to read music to sing these songs as you did to play the expensive instruments of the elite. Printed songbooks – a typical Dutch phenomenon – were in circulation for those seeking variety and wanting to learn new melodies, in addition to sheet music as in the rest of Europe.

Two splendid examples of contrafacta can be found in an album compiled by the amateur painter and calligrapher Gesina ter Borch from Zwolle between the ages of 21 and 30. It is an exceedingly rare and above all personal collection of lyrics of over 90 songs, which she copied from a variety of sources and illustrated with her own drawings. The genres vary from drinking songs to lamentations, but the majority are pastoral songs. One of these was written to the melody of the famous Italian madrigal 'Amarilli mia bella' by the composer Giulio Caccini, which is still a classic for those who take singing lessons. The Dutch text that Gesina recorded is not a literal translation but a reinterpretation: a lament of a man upon losing his beloved Amaryllis (see **fig. 153**). Caccini's melody crops up with

Alongside the lyrics 'Rosamonde mijn beminde' ('Rosamonde my beloved'), sung to the tune of 'Amarilli mia bella', Gesina ter Borch drew a man tying (*strikken*) his beloved's shoelaces, a punning reference to snaring (*strikken*) a partner

180   Virginal dating from 1640, made by renowned instrument maker Joannes Ruckers.
A virginal was suitable for smaller rooms, since it took up less space than a harpsichord.

other lyrics elsewhere, such as a love poem featuring not Amaryllis but another beauty named Rosamonde fig. 179. She is still very much alive and sets the poet's heart on fire.[59] Gesina would not have collected the songs and made her fine illustrations merely for her own pleasure but for her friends and relatives to enjoy and to pass around at lively get-togethers when singing together.

Making music was enjoyable as well as being good for your health. A virginal made by the renowned Antwerp instrument maker Joannes Ruckers reminds the audience of this during recitals with the words *MUSICA LABORUM DULCE LEVAMEN* (Music is a sweet relief from work) inscribed on the lid fig. 180.[60] This belief in the beneficial property of music has a medical background and relates directly to the fundamental humoral principle of maintaining good health: the balance between the four humours. Working too hard led to melancholy and consequently to an excess of black bile, an imbalance that could be corrected with a little relaxation.[61] This explains why even the stiffest of Calvinists encouraged music-making and singing in a domestic setting.

Music played an important role in all denominations. Wittewrongel believed that singing revitalized the mind, for the angels and the departed sang songs of praise to God in heaven. Naturally, it was psalms that should be sung in such instances, as David frequently did with his younger brother and sister, who were living in with him in The Hague, and any other guests, sometimes accompanying the singers on his violin. The psalms, 'comforting fortifications of the heart' as Wittewrongel was later to dub them, brought David, who had been widowed the year before, welcome consolation.[62]

Cats, on the other hand, warned against overly frivolous lyrics, which were even more dangerous if they were beautifully sung, because they stuck in your mind all the more. The enormous popularity of songbooks with tantalizing titles, such as *Cupido's lusthof* (Cupido's Pleasure Garden, 1613) or *Venus minne-gifjens* (Venus' Love Gifts, 1622), shows that his words fell on deaf ears.[63] A bit of fun and eroticism were all part of free time.

Comfort

Gradually, a new pastime made its appearance and led to new forms of social interaction as well as the need for all the accompanying trappings. From the beginning of the seventeenth century onwards, the Dutch East India Company had imported small quantities of tea, particularly for medicinal use, but in the 1670s imports swiftly increased, and within no time social life was unimaginable without tea-drinking calls. Porcelain, which had initially served mainly as decoration, came to be used as teaware, and the need arose for a new item of furniture at which you could sit with all the tea bowls and saucers, tea canisters, teapots and tea kettles: the tea table, larger than a side table but much smaller and more intimate than an extendable dining table.

One of the earliest images of such a table appears in a 1689 portrait by the amateur painter Cornelia van Marle, which probably depicts her half-sister Aleida Greve (right foreground) with her other half-sister and a maid **fig. 181**. The women are set in an opulent room decorated in gilt leather, possibly in their parental home, the Gouden Kroon (Golden Crown) in Zwolle. They are drinking tea out of tiny porcelain bowls, sweetened with white rock candy from the small basin on the table. Both the portrait and the actual tea table have been preserved in the *hofje* (almshouses) founded by Aleida posthumously for destitute elderly women in her native town. Although the table has been radically restored, it still has its typical oval top with its shallow upstand, which can be folded away when not in use.[64] In one corner of the *zaal* in Petronella Oortman's doll's house is a tea table that can actually be folded open; it features a beautifully decorated top with a parrot and garlands that looks like a precious painting **fig. 182**.[65]

Tea-drinking soon became commonplace across the classes. In Het Grote Huis in Middelburg, Johan and Anna Maria even had a *posteleijn comptoirtie*, a small space that was cosier and more comfortable than the *zaal* and which was fully equipped for a tea party, with a painted tea table, four chairs with cushions, tea cannisters and above all a vast collection of porcelain. There was so much china that after their deaths, the children did not take the trouble to have the individual pieces inventoried

181 In 1689, Cornelia van Marle portrayed her half-sisters at the tea table. The maid is serving tea from a porcelain pot. On the floor beside her is the copper kettle of hot water

182 The miniature tea table in the *zaal* (reception room) of Petronella Oortman's doll's house can actually be folded into a vertical position. The tripod and the oval tabletop with the raised edge are typical of tea tables

but had the assessor divide everything into four lots of equal value to be drawn blind by them.[66] Even the Amsterdam tailor Steven Stams and his wife Abigael Tefferi had a tea stand, teaware (including two kettles) and a tiny tea table in their small basement apartment in Sint Antoniesbreestraat at the time of their deaths, within nine days of each other, in 1709.[67]

The shift in the use of porcelain from decoration to table-ware and the rapid spread – partly through colonial exploitation – of luxury consumer goods, such as tea and sugar, throughout the population were not the only changes at the close of the seventeenth century. New medical scientific ideas were gaining ground. The prevailing fundamental theories about how the world worked and how the human body functioned within it gradually began to topple. Earlier in the century the physician Johan van Beverwijck had integrated new products, such as sugar, into the ancient humoral theory, in which all foodstuffs were classified according to their alleged warming or cooling and dry or wet properties. The new generation of physicians embraced the new medical insights, and their eyes were all firmly fixed on tea as a stimulant. It was the 'healthiest drink', according to Steven Blankaart, and that applied 'not only to old people but to children as well'.[68] This was a remarkable statement, for according to the humoral theory the constitution gradually changed from warm and moist to cold and dry in the course of a person's lifetime, and children were advised to eat and drink very different things from elderly people. In a treatise entirely devoted to tea, the physician Cornelis Bontekoe was more explicit still and stated 'that one should not judge any herbs by that old and false measure of the 4 qualities'.[69]

Bontekoe was, moreover, the first to stress the importance of comfort. After initially bemoaning the excessive popularity of Asian luxury goods, from textiles to porcelain, and consequently the impending decline of Christian morals – complaints often heard – he changed his tune. He propagated the invention of a tea urn from which both hot water and strong tea could be dispensed: ideal for serving large gatherings. With such an urn and porcelain bowls, you had 'all the equipage for drinking tea with ease and pleasure', he concluded.[70]

Ease and pleasure are intrinsic to the feeling of homeliness. A house had first to fulfil the primary need for shelter from the weather. Once this need was met, seventeenth-century houses were equipped with all manner of paraphernalia to make daily life easier and more agreeable, from a silver beard brush to a self-rotating spit in the hearth, from educational children's toys to tapestries to keep out the draughts. In the course of the century, more and more people secured access to these luxuries. The number of objects in the house grew, rooms were given more specific functions and comfort was further enhanced. Reading books in bed, reflecting on the Bible by the fire, lighting Shabbat candles in the kitchen, drinking tea out of beautiful bowls in the *zaal*, cherishing a wedding casket or a baptismal gift in a locked cabinet: together, all these things and activities made a house a home.

notes

People and Possessions

1 'Veel bedden nadt, kleeren van mijn vrou inde kas bdurfen [bedorven] ende foort alles soo diselaat [desolaat] gestelt dat het nauwelyck sonder schryen aan te sien was', Duquesnoy and Salman 2018, p. 121. See ibid., p. 103, on extreme weather in the period 1673–1675.
2 Ibid., pp. 80–82.
3 De Vries and Van der Woude 1997, pp. 57–63; Frijhoff and Spies 1999, pp. 154–162.
4 Unlike surrounding countries, the Dutch Republic (including the Generality Lands) did not, for instance, experience famine or food riots. See De Vries 2019.
5 For the ewer and basin set, see The Hague 2005, pp. 198–199, and Amsterdam 2018, pp. 190, 260, no. 26; for the candlesticks Amsterdam 1999, pp. 59–60; for the spice box The Hague 2005, p. 205, and R.J. Baarsen in Amsterdam 1993, pp. 443–444, no. 103.
6 This approach is indebted to the concept of 'assemblages' currently popular in archaeology and material culture studies. See Antczak and Beaudry 2019 for the reconstruction of assemblages of people and objects.
7 See pp. 89, 238, 256 and 307 of this publication.
8 Quantitative inventory studies have been carried out in various cities in the Netherlands, whereby descriptions of goods from large numbers of inventories from different social layers have been systematically categorized and counted. This gives an idea of changes in consumption patterns and the rise of new consumer goods, although individual users and articles are lost sight of. See for instance Dibbits 2001.
9 De Vries 2007.
10 Josina Schade van Westrum lived in the house De Munt in Postelstraat 42 in Den Bosch and died in 1704. Otto Copes had already passed away in 1674. EsH, 0072, Notarissen met standplaats 's-Hertogenbosch, inv. no. 2963, Minuutakten, fols. 43r–65v. The article by De Mooij 1999 on

this inventory is an example of qualitative research that establishes the relationship between the house, the floor plans, the function of the rooms, the furnishings and the occupants, as advocated by Fock 2000, p. 131.
11 NEHA, Collectie Familie du Tour, inv. no. 1, Huishoudboek van Sara L'Empereur van Oppyck (1632–1685). See also Lunsingh Scheurleer et al. 1986–1992, vol. 6b (1992), pp. 530–534; Mourits 2016, pp. 93–94.
12 NEHA, Collectie Familie du Tour, inv. no. 1, fol. 31r.
13 Maria van Nesse lived in Langestraat 89–91 in Alkmaar. RAB, Henegouwen, Archief van de familie De Clerque Wissocq de Sousberghe, inv. nos. 652, 653, Memorieboek van Maria van Nesse (hereafter referred to as Van Nesse 1623–1646). Scans, transcriptions and a glossary can be consulted via www.regionaal archiefalkmaar.nl/mariavannesse (consulted 20 May 2024). See also Noorman and Van der Maal 2022.
14 Duquesnoy and Salman 2018, p. 102.
15 Haks 1985, p. 147.
16 Beck 1624 (1993), pp. 8–11; Blaak 2009, p. 43.
17 Schmidt and Van der Heijden 2016, pp. 22–32.
18 Noorman and Van der Maal 2022, pp. 168–203.
19 Schmidt and Van der Heijden 2016, pp. 32–33.
20 'ghij weerwolff, ghij onrust, ghij leugenachtige claddige vrouw', Duijn et al. 2018, pp. 72–73, 142–143.
21 This metaphor is used by numerous clergymen. See Haarlem 1986, p. 62, in. 16, for an overview.
22 Cats 1862, vol. 1, p. 391.
23 Bedaux 1990, pp. 109–112; De Mooij 1999, p. 90; P. Huys Janssen in Den Bosch 2000, pp. 100–101.
24 Roberts 2012, pp. 15, 215–216.
25 Cf. Descola 2013, pp. 201–231, on the analogical world view.
26 Pijzel-Dommisse 1987, p. 17.
27 See Fock 1998 for the portrayal of interiors in genre painting and R. Baer in Boston 2015, pp. 237–238 for the stereotypical depiction of the lower class.

Praz 1982, pp. 124–127 and Rybczynski 1986, pp. 51–75 considered 17th-century Dutch genre painting to be a literal representation of interiors and domestic life, and regarded this period as the start of bourgeois domesticity, a stereotypical view which persists to this day. Provided they are cautiously used, however, paintings and doll's houses continue to be important visual sources in certain respects. See in this connection Pijzel-Dommisse 2000, pp. 49–51; Fock 2001; Denver/ Newark 2001.
28 'eenen inventaris ... van al onse meublen, middelen, goet, gewaet, Boecken ende Juwelen, zoo veel dies waren ten tijde van R[oeltjes] overlyden', Beck 1624 (1993), p. 132; Blaak 2009, p. 65.
29 Beck 1627–1628 (2014), pp. 50, 56, 59 (resp. 14 March, 5 and 17 April 1627).

House

1 Most of the insights in this chapter are drawn from Van den Heuvel (in preparation); Fock 2001; Loughman and Montias 2000; and Lesger 2024.
2 De Vries and Van der Woude 1997, pp. 57–63.
3 Dibbits 2001, pp. 54ff.
4 Pierik 2022, pp. 60–61.
5 Kuijpers and Prak 2002.
6 Lesger 2024, p. 13. It is exceptionally difficult to quantify poverty and socio-economic security in the early modern period. Rough estimates indicate that 40 to 60 per cent of the population lived at approximately subsistence level. Another 20 to 30 per cent were just above this level, but still quite vulnerable (Van Nederveen Meerkerk 2007, p. 206). One quarter of the Leiden population qualified for poor relief in 1614 (Orlers 1614). The figure in Delft was around 15 per cent (Van der Vlis 2007, pp. 57, 64).
7 Lesger 2024, p. 13; Schrevelius 1750, pp. 346–347.
8 'aansienelijcke en rijcke coopluijden', Dekker 1979, p. 45. The quotation is from an eyewitness account of the Undertakers' Riot of 1696 by Amsterdam trader Joris Craffurd.

9 'eerlijke armen', Van der Vlis 2001, pp. 274–276. See also Van Deursen 1991, pp. 58, 73*ff*.
10 It was mandatory for such hovels to be made of wood, so that they could be demolished if the city was attacked; Lesger 2024, p. 132.
11 Ibid., p. 83.
12 Walle 2005, p. 68. The neighbourhood was not simply a geographic reality but above all a social unit.
13 Stone-Ferrier 2022, p. 6.
14 Walle 2005, p. 61.
15 Ponte 2018, pp. 47–48. For other examples of Black women running boarding houses, see Ponte 2022, p. 139.
16 Van der Heijden 1998, pp. 56*ff*.
17 Lenarduzzi 2019, pp. 46–49.
18 Kooijmans 2016.
19 Ekkart 1978–1979.
20 'van malcander een vruntlic [vriendelijk] seggen te hooren', Walle 2005, p. 78.
21 Ibid., pp. 78, 113.
22 Eibach 2011, pp. 621–664. See also Pierik 2022, p. 87.
23 Dekker 1979, pp. 44–45. According to Lesger 2024, pp. 124–125, the crowd was not out to disrupt the established order but rather to restore moral solidarity within it.
24 'De behangsels kerfden zij van boven tot beneden met messen en verscheurden deselven sooverre als zij konden. Kostelijcke schilderijen wierden aan stukken geslaagen en met voeten getreeden. ... Thin en kooper sloegen zij tot malkanderen en wierpen het in de burgwal. Het porcelijn wierd altemaal in stukken gesmeeten en vertreeden, hoe mooij en kostelijck het ook was. ... Wijn en bier liet men door de kelder loopen, de botervaten in stukken geslagen en op straat geworpen.' ('They slashed the wall hangings with knives from top to bottom and tore them apart, as far as they were able. Valuable paintings were smashed to pieces and trampled underfoot ... They bashed in tin and copper objects and hurled them into the city moat. All the porcelain was smashed to pieces and trampled, no matter how fine and valuable

it was ... Wine and beer was spilled onto the cellar floor, and the butter churns were broken to pieces and thrown out into the street.') Quotation from an eyewitness account by Joris Craffurd (see note 8); Dekker 1979, p. 56.
25 Smashing windows was a typical part of popular riots throughout Europe. Lesger 2024, p. 108.
26 See note 6.
27 Van Oosten et al. 2017, p. 39.
28 Van Wijngaarden 2000, pp. 97–102; see esp. p. 100, on dwelling outside the city gates.
29 Ibid., pp. 32–33.
30 Hell 2024, p. 30. The Leprozenhuis was originally intended solely for lepers, but in the course of the 17th century the institution came to rent rooms to a larger range of people in need.
31 'Ja wel vier huys gezinnen zomtijdts in een huys, als in de voorhuyzen, achterhuyzen, kelders, voor en achterkamers, dat het ongelooffelijk is', Van Domselaer 1665, p. 212. Lesger 2024, pp. 123, 128.
32 'een blindt peert seude daer geen schade in huis gedaen hebben'. Van Wijngaarden 2000, p. 103. CO, IA 025 3120741, Stadsarmenkamer te Zwolle, inv. no. 312, Register van bedeelden, 5 February 1696, fol. 280v.
33 Van Wijngaarden 2000, pp. 102–104.
34 Van Elburg 2022, pp. 128–136, with references to Meischke et al. 1993–2000.
35 Lesger 2024, p. 65.
36 The specifications were officialized by a notary and served as a contract between the owners, Gosen Nicasius van Florij and Lucas Cuylaert, and the carpenter Jan Jochemsz Pol. SAA, 5075, Archief van de Notarissen ter Standplaats Amsterdam (hereafter ANSA), inv. no. 863, notary Jacob van Zwieten, 1 April 1634, fols. 146–161. See also Fock 2001, pp. 22*ff*.
37 Loughman and Montias 2000, pp. 23, 30.
38 Van Elburg 2022, p. 20.
39 'en straf of streel uw vrouwe niet,/ daer 't iemandt hoort, of iemant siet./ de bed-gordijn/ dient dicht te zijn', Cats 1862, vol. 1, p. 833.

40 Goeree 1681, p. 154, is vehemently opposed to kitchens in cellars, 'because what need is there for a living body to dwell under the earth? There will be plenty of time for that when one is dead.' ('want wat is het noodig met den levende lijve onder d'aarde te wonen? Dat doet men lang genoeg, als men doot is.')
41 See p. 71 of this publication.
42 According to the specifications, 'opde deur salder een reus geschilderd werden' ('a giant shall be painted on the door'). No conclusive evidence has yet been found of whether a more general association was drawn between giants and privies.
43 Lesger 2024, pp. 73–75.
44 'van binnen met overkostelijke vercierselen gemaakt/ dat eer koninks-palleijzen dan kooplieden Huysen gelijkken', Fokkens 1662, p. 69.
45 Steenmeijer 2005, pp. 228–229; Ottenheym and Terwen 1993, p. 130.
46 For Rapenburg 48, see Steenmeijer 2005, pp. 228–232.
47 Ibid., pp. 230–232.
48 De Jonge and Ottenheym 2007, p. 242.
49 Steenmeijer 2005, pp. 250–252; Ottenheym and Terwen 1993, pp. 130–139.
50 Ottenheym and Terwen 1993, p. 136.
51 For example, Constantijn Huygens wrote that his wife Suzanna van Baerle's contribution to their house was equal to his own; Fock 2001, p. 18. Margaretha Turnor, the wife of Godard Adriaan van Reede, supervised the rebuilding of Amerongen Castle after it had been set on fire by French troops in 1673; Van Burkom 2001, p. 70.
52 'De Zalen zijn in alle Huisgebouwen die iets willen zijn, gemeen en oorbaar [algemeen en nuttig]. ... [Ze] dienen om iemant te onthalen, groot bezoek en Statie te houden' and 'verdrietzame donkere Kamertjes, onderscheiden', Goeree 1681, p. 149.
53 He was picturing coloured marble with white capitals and bases. The ultimate execution was somewhat simpler; a local

Dordrecht stonecutter used petit granit and white marble. Ottenheym and Terwen 1993, pp. 137–138.
54 Den Haag 2015, p. 13.
55 Ottenheym 1989, pp. 40–41.
56 'De Knechts Slaapkamer en die van de Meiden dienden zo wijd van den anderen gehouden te werden, als 't vier [vuur] van de verbrandelijke dingen', Lesger 2024, p. 82; Carlson 1993.
57 Van der Veen 2000, p. 149, tempers this claim, noting that many collections of curiosities ended up spread throughout the house, and studies were often sparsely furnished.

Body
1 'silver baertborsteltjen', Mourits 2016; Mourits 2017.
2 'ceukenhuijsraet en t'geen men dagelijxs gebruijckt', 'borstel van ebbenhout met silver, een scheerteijl' and 'kniptangetjen'. ATH, inv. no. ATH 434, Kasboek, c. 1635–1653, pp. 154, 176. In 1638, Johannes had bought a case containing a 'knife', 'fork' and 'shaving [knife]'. ATH, inv. no. ATH 438–439, Kwitanties 1638.
3 '½ jaer scheren', ATH, inv. no. ATH 434, Kasboek, c. 1635–1653, pp. 256–257.
4 Van Beverwijck 1636, vol. 2, p. 159. In the early modern period, the terms *kamer* (room), *secreet* (secret), *privaat* (private), *gemak* (comfort), *heymelicheit* (concealment) and *stille* (quiet place) were used for the toilet. See, for example, Bitter 2022, p. 527.
5 'vuyligheyt', 'sobere luyden' and 'en voor de gene, die wat veel eten, tweemael', Van Beverwijck 1636, vol. 1, p. 501. In most cities in the Dutch Republic, some of the earliest privies were in public space – under bridges, for example. In the course of the 15th and 16th centuries, relieving oneself came to be seen as more of a private matter, and when a household built a privy, the city began to require an accompanying cesspit. This change took place in Leiden as early as 1463, and Amsterdam followed suit in 1528. See Bitter 2022, p. 527; Van Tussenbroek 2023, pp. 267, 444.

6 'Soo drae dan yemandt opftaet, sal hy sijn hooft kemmen, den mont spoelen, de tanden ende tonge reynigen, oiren ende neus schoon maken, de oogen ende t gheheele aensicht met kout water afwassen, het lichaem, ende insonderheyt armen en beenen wrijven.' Van Beverwijck 1636, vol. 2, p. 160. Ten years earlier, an almost identical routine had been described in Jacobs 1626, p. 15.
7 Vigarello 1988, pp. 58–61; Sarti 2002, p. 196; Du Mortier 2010, p. 144; B.M. du Mortier in Van Suchtelen 2021, p. 59. In the scholarly literature, the standard reference for this subject is Vigarello 1988 (originally published in French in 1985). His conclusions about personal hygiene and the importance of clothing and underclothing were widely endorsed in major works on social and dress history. Recent research has shown, however, that the theoretical objections to washing were not dominant throughout Europe. See, for example, North 2020 on England.
8 Du Mortier 2010, pp. 143–144.
9 Van Beverwijck 1636, vol. 1, p. 501: 'drooge ende dampige vuyligheyt, die de huyt uyt-werpt, ende waer van de hemden vuyl werden' ('dry and damp dirt excreted by the skin, which soils the smocks'); Vigarello 1988, pp. 58–61.
10 'Mijn moeder was een seer sindelijcke vrouw … [wij droegen] onse hemden by de winter [nooit] langer als een week, en by de zomer [nooit] langer als een halve week', Vrouwaart 1699, pp. 15–16, quoted in Du Mortier 2010, p. 144; Du Mortier 2012, p. 32.
11 See p. 210 of this publication.
12 She uses the Dutch term *rijchlijf* for stays. Van Nesse 1623–1646, fols. 85r, 86r (for Sijfert), 42r, 83r, 85r (for herself). On bodices and stays, see Der Kinderen-Besier 1950, pp. 184–185.
13 Daleman 2021, p. 179.
14 Some bodkins had small spoons at one end that could be used to collect earwax, since earwax or candle wax made it easier to draw lace or ribbon into the small holes. See for instance the bodkin with spoon that belonged

to Fedt van Goslinga in Friesland (Leeuwarden, Fries Museum, inv. no. Z2014-001). Akkerman 1987, p. 214; Akkerman 2017, p. 46; Minderhoud 2017, p. 21. The ribbons on the sleeves of the salmon-pink corset each have an aglet (or eyelet), which made it easier to lace them up (fig. 33).
15 Maria van Nesse's sister Adriana is also wearing a bejewelled needle in her hair in her portrait (Valenciennes, Musée des Beaux-Arts, inv. no. P.46.1.1 52).
16 'nieuwe silferen naelt', Van Nesse 1623–1646, fol. 71r.
17 For large collars, see the following portraits in this publication: the family portrait by an anonymous artist (fig. 65), Eva Wtewael (fig. 76), the Sonck family (fig. 55) and the Boudaen Courtens' gallery of ancestors (fig. 169).
18 Du Mortier 1986, pp. 45–49; Du Mortier 2023, pp. 205–206.
19 The Dutch term, *portefraas*, is from the French *porte-fraize*: *porter* means to carry or support, and *fraize* means a pleated collar or ruff. Du Mortier 2023, pp. 204–208. Few supportasses have been handed down; most are archaeological finds.
20 Du Mortier 2023, p. 208; Van Nesse 1623–1646, fol. 88v.
21 The Hague 2005, pp. 151–153. For example, Johanna tho Borcken from Doetinchem had a silver toiletry box and brush with her family coat of arms made in 1663 by a silversmith in Zutphen (Stedelijk Museum Zutphen, inv. no. V1849); Van Dijk 1999, p. 31.
22 For a recipe intended to prevent wrinkles, see for example Piemontese 1602, vol. 2, p. 10.
23 Jacobs 1626, pp. 45, 123; Nylandt 1670; Witgeest 1684.
24 Witgeest 1684, p. 480.
25 Ibid., p. 485; Antwerp 1998, p. 106.
26 Witgeest 1684, p. 489.
27 Apothecaries referred to alabaster salve as *unguentum alabastrinum*; see www.regionaalarchief alkmaar.nl/images/Documenten/ Artikelen/Verklarende_woorden lijst_bij_het_memorieboek.pdf (consulted 20 September 2024).
28 Jacobs 1626, p. 136; Witgeest 1684, pp. 492–494.

29 Jacobs 1626, p. 135.
30 Christen and Christen 2003, p. 62.
31 Witgeest 1684, p. 489; Vincent 2018, p. 36.
32 Van Nesse 1623–1646, fol. 29r.
33 Du Mortier 2010, pp. 128–129.
34 'Waterlandsche Boerinnen', 'onaensienlijk hayr' and 'sterck water', Witgeest 1684, pp. 268, 488.
35 See, for example, the nearly identical Roman lice combs in Lange 2017, pp. 151, 269–270.
36 Vincent 2018, p. 44.
37 For example, probate inventories in Amsterdam City Archives mention 'schilpadde kammetjes' (tortoiseshell combs). See, for example, SAA, ANSA, inv. no. 5142, notary Joannes Boots, 2 June 1690; SAA, ANSA, inv no. 5065, notary Michiel Servaes, December 1695, fol. 4v. Elephant ivory combs have been found during excavations – for Amsterdam's North–South metro line, for instance; see find numbers NZD1.00044FAU012, NZD1.00028FAU011 and NZR2. 00657FAU001. Boxwood combs were the most common variety, however, and many have been found in a variety of urban archaeological contexts. Examples from the North–South line excavations include find numbers NZD1.00040 HT001, NZD1.00088HT004 and NZD1.00393HT002.
38 Platteschorre-Weurman 2008; Du Mortier 2010, pp. 129–130.
39 Personal communication Bianca du Mortier.
40 'met hair regt neder hangende als een pond Kaersen', Witgeest 1684, pp. 486–488.
41 'als een die uyt Brasyl gekomen is', ibid.
42 'Konste om ghesont te leven', Van Beverwijck 1636, vol. 1, p. 48.
43 'niet-natuerlijcke', Knoeff 2017, pp. 13–17; R. Verwaal in Knoeff 2017, pp. 16, 98–111; Verwaal 2021. See Van Beverwijck 1636, vol. 1, p. 69, describes this as follows: 'Affecten ofte Bewegingen des Gemoets, Lucht, Spijs ende Dranck, Oeffeninge en Ruste, Slapen ende Waken, Af-setten ende Op-houden' ('Affects or Emotions, Air, Food and Drink, Exercise and Rest, Sleeping and

Waking, Excretion and Retention'). See also p. 21 of this publication.
44 'lucht', Knoeff 2017, p. 13.
45 Raimond-Waarts 2014, p. 57.
46 'hersenne, hert en lijff' and 'Christelijck sterven', Beck 1624 (1993), p. 168.
47 'Gave Gods' and 'haestige siecte', ibid. In 1624 almost one-fifth of Delft's inhabitants died of the plague. Noordegraaf and Valk 2020, p. 233.
48 Caspers 2003, pp. 255–256.
49 Welch 2011, pp. 16, 19–21.
50 'perfumeerde hanschoenen', ATH, inv. no. ATH 434, Kasboek, c. 1635–1653, p. 212.
51 A portrait from 1611 of Maria's sister Adriana van Nesse (note 16) shows her wearing an openwork pomander.
52 Van Nesse 1623–1646, fol. 50r. Two years earlier, in 1638, she had had the plague amulet fixed because it was broken. Ibid., fol. 43v.
53 Van Nesse 1623–1646, fols. 3v, 36r, 37v. Noordegraaf and Valk 2020, appendix 2, p. 231. *Sint-Nicolaasbroodjes*, or *Tolentijnbroodjes*, were rolls baked annually on 10 September, the day of St Nicholas of Tolentino's death. These consecrated rolls were thought to have special power to cure disease. See Nannings 1932, p. 14.
54 'reyn en suyver' and 'fenijnige wester- en zuyder-lucht', Anonymous 1655, p. 6; Noordegraaf and Valk 2020, pp. 190–191.
55 L. Marx in Van Suchtelen 2021, p. 65.
56 Jacobs 1626, p. 116.
57 'twatermaken', 'verzachten', 'soet amandelen' and 'in Godes naam de steen te laten afneemen', Boudaen Courten *s.a.* (2005), pp. 55–56. See Van Beverwijck 1637, p. 8, for a verse description of treatment with almond oil.
58 Houtzager and Verschuyl 2001, p. 1371; Kooijmans 2004, pp. 186–188. See Van Beverwijck 1637 for a few astonishing recipes for removing bladder stones through urination.
59 Kooijmans 2004, p. 189.
60 Willem Boenaert's library consisted primarily of books written in Dutch or translated from Latin. The inclusion of a dictionary of

Latyn en Duyts (Latin and Dutch) suggests that he was unable to read Latin. Houtzager and Verschuyl 2001, p. 1373.
61 Boenaert was in possession of an edition of *De chirurgie …* (Surgery …) by the French surgeon Ambroise Paré, which discussed and depicted various instruments for removing bladder stones. See Paré 1655, pp. 497–500. Present at the operation, besides Boenaert and Pieter Boudaen Courten, were two Middelburg city doctors, a pastor, a midwife and two family members. Several people were needed to hold down Catharina during the operation, which was conducted without anaesthesia.
62 Boudaen Courten *s.a.* (2005), p. 55.
63 HUA, 26, Familie Des Tombe, inv. no. 1080, Familiekroniek, fol. 22.
64 Kooijmans 2016, p. 166. The exact note is 'CIV' (coitus, 1 time, V – regrettably, the meaning of 'V' is unknown).
65 HUA, 67, Familie Huydecoper, inv. no. 55, diary notes, 1659, pp. 95, 108.
66 Kooijmans 2016, p. 167.
67 Van Beverwijck 1636, vol. 2, pp. 33–34; Venette 1687, pp. 132–133; De Mare 2003, p. 276; Cats 1862, p. 385.
68 'af-schieten van het natuerlijck zaet' and 'fris', Van Beverwijck 1636, vol. 1, p. 505, vol. 2, p. 160.
69 Van Beverwijck 1636, vol. 2, pp. 22–23.
70 'in omhelsing'. The term 'omhelsing' (embrace) is used frequently in Venette 1687 for sexual intercourse.
71 Buisman 1996, p. 560.
72 'Ick ben kout', De Moederloose 1695, vol. 2, pp. 169, 170–171, vol. 3, pp. 70–71, 78; Roodenburg 1993, pp. 329–330.
73 'niet alleen schadelijck, maer dickwils doodelijck' and 'koude en drooghe luyden', Van Beverwijck 1636, vol. 2, p. 162. In that event, Isabella could have given her husband a few 'suyckerwortels' (skirrets) to eat: 'Sy hebben oock eeenige windachtigheyt in haer, waerom dat sy den lust tot by-slapen verwecken, en werden daerom van de goede Vrouwen

de Mans dickwils te eeten geghe-ven, segghende dat se seer ghe-sondt zijn' ('They have a certain airiness to them that makes them rouse the urge to lie together, and good Wives therefore often give them to Husbands to eat, saying they are very healthy'). Van Beverwijck 1636, vol. 1, p. 324.
74 'saet gegeven' and 'eerst de natuer opwecken en dan het saet wegsmijten', De Moederloose 1695, vol. 3, p. 185.
75 Roodenburg 1983, p. 333.
76 'lijfmoeder te suyveren', 'afgaen van het mannelijck saet', 'Teel-zaet verdooven', 'van onderen geset' and 'Geyligheyt ende 't Saet', Van Beverwijck 1642, pp. 230, 236. Nylandt 1670, p. 238, also mentions rue (in powdered form) for 'removal of Semen' ('ontvloeinge des Zaets'). This effect could also be achieved with the help of nut-meg (p. 320), lettuce mixed with other herbs (p. 303), artichoke (p. 170), water lily (p. 124), tansy (p. 115), hemp seeds (p. 65) or pine (p. 28).
77 'van boven ende onderen' and 'ingespeut', Treffers 2009, p. 203. A number of Dutch museum col-lections include 19th- and 20th-century *vrouwenspuiten* (literally, 'women's syringes'), often made of Bakelite and rubber instead of wood; see Grooss 2001.
78 Jan Steen, *The Doctor's Visit*, c. 1665, Rotterdam, Museum Boijmans Van Beuningen, inv. no. VdV 76. In the painting, a slip of paper lies on the ground, bearing the rhyme, 'Hier baet geen mede-syn,/ want het is minnepyn' ('No medicine can help here,/ For this is the pain of love').
79 According to city archaeo-logist Hemmy Clevis in Zwolle, boxwood was very well suited to this purpose, because it 'is very smooth and does not splinter', Clevis 2001, pp. 118–120.
80 Hirsch 2023, pp. 95–97. Ac-cording to Annabelle Hirsch, a vaginal syringe could also be used to simulate ejaculation.
81 'stanck', 'als een nieuwe bruidt of versche roos' and 'met schoon goetjen aen en wel gereynight', De Moederloose 1695, vol. 3, p. 357.

82 'zy souden seggen dat wij Joods waeren' and 'ick sal 't wel gewent werden', Roodenburg 1983, pp. 330–331.
83 Longman 2002, p. 149; Gawronski and Jayasena 2007, p. 12.
84 Underpants made of various materials are mentioned in pro-bate inventories, but whether they were intended for a man or for a woman is often unclear. Women did wear underpants; the inven-tory of Jacob Rotgans's possessions drawn up after his death (1624–1672) lists a 'vrouwe onderbroeck' (pair of women's underpants) among his 'lijwaet' (underwear). It may have belonged to his de-ceased wife Magdalena Timmer-man. The estate of the Amsterdam needle maker Pieter Brouwer and his wife Trijntje Hendrix also evi-dently included a pair of women's underwear. SAA, ANSA, 2262B, notary Adriaen Lock, 21 March 1675, p. 888; SAA, ANSA, inv. no. 1201, notary Jan de Vos, 1652, p. 369.
85 'pessaria' and 'steeckpillen', Paré 1655, p. 754; Sennert 1656, p. 472; Crawford 1981, p. 55.
86 Crawford 1981, pp. 50–53.
87 Verwaal 2023, p. 122.
88 'losinghe'. The ages are re-ferred to as the *tweede seven jaer* ('second seven-year') and the *sevende seven jaer* ('seventh seven-year'), respectively; Van Bever-wijck 1642, pp. 620–621.
89 Stoter 2014, p. 359.
90 'maent-stonden', Crawford 1981, p. 53.
91 The juice and pulp of aloe vera were (and still are) used for such purposes as oral and dental hygiene, eye conditions and staunching blood flow from wounds. See Dodonaeus 1644, p. 583; Van Beverwijck 1651, p. 16; Nylandt 1670, p. 338.
92 'maeg te suyveren en te ont-lasten' and 'in soethout', Van Nesse 1623–1646, fols. 75v, 83r.
93 The Dutch term used by Maria, *galiga*, refers to *Aloe gallica*, an-other name for the great yellow gentian. See Dodonaeus 1644, p. 584.
94 'zachte kamergangh', Van Beverwijck 1636, vol. 1, p. 498.

95 Ibid., vol. 2, p. 157.
96 'natuerlijcke wermte' and 'Minder als ses uren te slapen, is naeulijckx genoegh: al wat boven de negen uren gaet, dat is te veel' ('Less than six hours of sleep is barely enough; anything beyond nine hours is too much'), Van Bever-wijck 1636, vol. 2, pp. 154–156.
97 Humorism recognized four stages of life, each with its own properties: childhood (moist and warm), youth (warm and dry), adulthood (dry and cold) and old age (moist and cold). Raimond-Waarts 2014, p. 38.
98 Strouven 1638–1649 (2020), p. 51.
99 Beck 1627–1628 (2014).

Mealtime
1 Van Nesse 1623–1646, fol. 52v.
2 'Reijst', 'Gepalde Gerst', 'Gort', 'Groen Erreten' and 'Tarwen Meel'. Pijzel-Dommisse 1987, p. 50.
3 See also p. 342, note 10.
4 NEHA, Collectie Familie du Tour, inv. no. 1, fols. 69v–70r.
5 Van Nesse 1623–1646, fols. 55v, 69r. See also Noorman and Van der Maal 2022, p. 119. Foreign visitors frequently mentioned Dutch people eating bread rolls with meat or cheese, see Bartels 2021, p. 34. See Willebrands et al. 2022, pp. 246–258, for the butchering season and the popularity of beef.
6 'butter die starck is weder soet te maken', Van Nesse 1623–1646, fols. 9v, 25v; Noorman and Van der Maal 2022, p. 123.
7 'een houten bier oft wijnstel-lingh in de wijnkelder', De Mooij 1999, p. 93; EsH, 0072 Notarissen met standplaats 's-Hertogenbosch, inv. no. 2963, Minuutakten, fol. 61v.
8 Pijzel-Dommisse 2000, p. 158.
9 Such partitions were prob-ably quite common but are seldom mentioned in inventories. Maria is therefore a unique source in explicitly recording that she had a carpenter repair the metal fittings of the cellar door and the wooden slats. Van Nesse 1623–1646, fol. 67v. See Noorman and Van der Maal 2022, pp. 119–120, on tallying, with illustration.
10 Pierik 2023. See Soetens 2001, pp. 170–172, for mineral water bottles and pitchers.

11 Inventory of Cars Janssen, 14 October 1691. Published in Van Wijngaarden 2000, p. 263.
12 Cats 1862, vol. 1, pp. 484–485. See also De Mare 2003, p. 272.
13 'de konst van te kooken verstonden', Anonymous 1660, p. 13. Specialized kitchen staff seldom seem to have worked in Dutch burgher households, although little research has been done on the subject. Cooking was one such a skill, resulting in a higher wage. In the 18th century, kitchen maids (who were well in the minority) earned considerably more than servants (Carlson 1993, pp. 116–117). See also Hell and Meijer 2019, pp. 55–57, and Barlösius 1991, on professional cooks and women home cooks.
14 See p. 21 of this publication.
15 Gentilcore 2016, pp. 11–22; Van Winter 2016; Willebrands 2023.
16 Personal communication Anna Laméris, Friedes Laméris Kunst en Antiek. See also Blijleven 2022, pp. 127–131.
17 Muusers and Willebrands 2020, pp. 31–32. See Landwehr 1995, pp. 14–23, for an overview of cookery books that were published in the Northern and Southern Netherlands in the 17th century.
18 Stoter 2016, pp. 53–54. Andriese Lucia Bronkhorst started her housekeeping book shortly after her marriage to Schelte van Aebinga in the autumn of 1632 and wrote daily entries until her death in 1666.
19 Sara's note about salmon, for instance, is in accordance with a fish calendar in a cookery book from 1560 and an older German treatise, J.M. van Winter in Utrecht 2004, p. 149. See also p. 176 of this publication.
20 'Sij moet wel een uur geroert worden', 'anderhalf fierendel rijs in een mengelen melck' and '3 fierendelen rijs', Van Nesse 1623–1646, fols. 27r, 38v.
21 Jobse-van Putten 1996, pp. 150–152; Willebrands et al. 2022, p. 47.
22 Willebrands et al. 2022, pp. 117–118.
23 De Mooij 1999, pp. 91–92; EsH, 0072 Notarissen met standplaats 's-Hertogenbosch, inv. no.

2963, Minuutakten, fols. 58r–61v. Descriptions of cooking utensils and their use are derived from Witteveen 1992, pp. 14–29.
24 'een blicken panneke om appelen in te braden', 'klein keukentie' and 'eenen grooten koperen ketel, in den bodem gelapt'. Cf. Corbeau 1993, p. 372.
25 NEHA, Collectie Familie du Tour, inv. no. 1, fols. 5r, 27v.
26 R. Ekkart in Hoorn 2016, pp. 236–237; Enschede 2018, pp. 156–157.
27 Van Oosten 2015, pp. 101–152; Bitter 2011.
28 Schrickx 2025 (forthcoming).
29 In 2024, macrobotanical research was carried out on the cesspit finds by Merit Hondelink and Oda Nuij. All the animal remains (bones, fishbones and fish scales) were analyzed respectively by Tijmen Moesker (Moesker Archeologie) and Amy van Saane (Nehalennia Archeology).
30 RAA, 0685, Familiearchief Van Foreest, inv. no. 61, letter from Jacob van Foreest to his children, 15 September 1629. See www.regionaalarchiefalkmaar.nl/images/Documenten/Artikelen/transcripties/overige/Brieven-aan-Jan-van-Foreest.pdf for the transcription (consulted 8 August 2024).
31 Gentilcore 2016, pp. 50–51, 55–56. See De Rijk 2015, pp. 24–35, for hunting rights and the kinds of birds that were hunted.
32 See J.M. van Winter in Utrecht 2004 and Willebrands et al. 2022, pp. 173–196, for fish and preparation methods.
33 Gentilcore 2016, pp. 70–73.
34 Van Beverwijck 1636, vol. 1, p. 291.
35 Ibid.
36 Blankaart 1683, pp. 9–10. See also Rotterdam 1983, p. 61; Voskuil 1983, pp. 470–472.
37 NEHA, Collectie Familie du Tour, inv. no. 1, fol. 12v.
38 See De Vries 2019, pp. 287–298, 306–371, for the consumption of wheat and rye bread in relation to price and income in different parts of the Dutch Republic.
39 'Steden die belegert zijn', Van Beverwijck 1636, vol. 1, p. 297.
40 Noordegraaf 1995; Prak 1998, pp. 61–67, 73–74. Zwolle was an

exception; only money was handed out here (Van Wijngaarden 2000, p. 109), whereas poor relief in Groningen consisted of money and bread as well as butter (Buursma 2009, p. 99).
41 Van der Vlis 2001, pp. 110–113.
42 '17 dosijn pannekoecken' made from '3 mettgis meel' and '2 mengelen melck' ('17 dozen pancakes' using '3 measuring cups of flour' and '6 pints of milk'), Van Nesse 1623–1646, fol. 81r.
43 De Vries 2019, pp. 287–288, who, for want of other evidence, based this on the menus of orphanages.
44 Beck 1624 (1993), pp. 131, 185.
45 Ibid., pp. 120, 205; Van Beverwijck 1636, vol. 1, p. 294; Voskuil 1983, pp. 474–476.
46 Amsterdam 2004, pp. 287–288.
47 Bruijnen 2002, p. 67.
48 Fock 2001, pp. 24, 88, 163.
49 Koldeweij 2001, pp. 188–189. The gold leather fragments from the house at Ramen 1 in Hoorn are small and do not show the complete pattern.
50 Cited in King James Version 1611. Franits 1986, pp. 36–40; Schama 1987, p. 158; De Jongh 2014, pp. 20–22.
51 Muusers 2015, p. 51, see also pp. 52–55 for the influence of the fasting rules on the recipes in cookery books.
52 Stolk 2022, pp. 50–51, 112–116, 133–137; Bakker 2020; IJzereef 2005.
53 Stolk 2022, pp. 67–78.
54 'che cava dalla terra abbruciata e polverizzata dai soli della state na spruzzaglia d'acqua in sul tardi', Magalotti 1945, p. 70. See Stolk 2022, pp. 76–82; Casimiro and Newstead 2019, p. 45.
55 See Van Eeghen 1960, pp. 97–103, for Agneta's family history, her complicated relationship with her son Jan and her many successive wills.
56 'silvere kruytdoos … als meede de gedreeven lampet en gieter ende vier gedreeve silvere kandelaers', Van Eeghen 1960, pp. 106–109.
57 Amsterdam 2018, pp. 190, 260, no. 26.

58 The marine theme was adopted more often for ewer and basin sets. Hague inventories include the specimens 'Neptune and water gods' and 'Lobsters', but also cosmological subjects such as 'Time' and 'The four seasons of the year'. The Hague 2005, p. 198. See V.J. Avery in Cambridge 2019, pp. 149–150, for French and Italian examples.
59 Van Eeghen 1960, p. 109.
60 SAA, 234, Archief van de Familie Deutz, inv. no. 275, Journaal van Elisabeth Coymans, 1649–1653, p. 598. With thanks to Dirk Jan Biemond, who drew this archival document to our attention.
61 Amsterdam 1999, pp. 59–60.
62 See, for instance, the following recipes in *Het excellente kookboek* by Carolus Battus from 1593: Muusers and Willebrands 2020, nos. 18, 28, 31, 38, 39, 46, 48, 79, 103, 105, 154, 178, 189, 210, 252, 265, 267–270, and *De verstandige kock*: Willebrands et al. 2022, nos. 12, 15, 20, 27, 42, 143.
63 The Hague 2005, p. 205; R.J. Baarsen in Amsterdam 1993, pp. 443–444, no. 103.
64 Van Nesse 1623–1646, fols. 12r, 83v, 86v.
65 De Mooij 1999, p. 91.
66 Beck 1624 (1993), pp. 39, 86, 117, 197.
67 'Of schoon u onverhoets eens gasten over quamen,/ Al is uw keucken slecht, j'en hebt u niet te schamen;/ Doet brengen dat'er is, al waer het zout en broot.' Cats 1862, vol. 1, p. 484.
68 See Muusers and Willebrands 2020, p. 62, for the use of baking pans.
69 Van Nesse 1623–1646, fols. 15r, 26r.
70 Hell and Meijer 2019, pp. 55–57. See Willebrands et al. 2022, pp. 233–243, for the preparation of pies.
71 NEHA, Collectie Familie du Tour, inv. no. 1, fol. 16v.
72 ATH, inv. no. ATH 433, Kasboek, 1641. The following is written on the back of a pile of loose bills from 1639: 'Reeck. verscheijden tot der maeltijt uut school scheijdende, kost met de wijn tsamen

*f*40: 8' ('Bills for the school-leaving meal, cost together with the wine, 40 florins: 8'). See Fock 1982 for Pieter de la Court's wedding banquet, with very similar dishes.
73 H.H. Pijzel-Dommisse in The Hague 2015, pp. 23–24, 73–74; M. Willebrands in ibid., pp. 50–51.
74 Muusers 2013, pp. 123–127; Willebrands et al. 2022, p. 259.
75 See, for instance, Cats's 'Tafel-manieren en tafel-wetten' (Table Manners and Table Etiquette) in Cats 1862, vol. 2, pp. 827–829; Blankaart 1683, pp. 137–154.
76 Cats 1862, vol. 2, pp. 828–829.
77 'De vrou moet op de spijs en op de keucken passen,/ Op schotels wel gescheurt en lijnwaet net gewassen,/ Moet toonen metter daet, en even metten schijn,/ Dat haer de gasten lief en waerde vrienden zijn', ibid., vol. 1, p. 484; vol. 2, p. 828.

Housekeeping
1 'dit heb ick vergeeten', NEHA, Collectie Familie Du Tour, inv. no. 1, fols. 5, 6.
2 Petrus Wittewrongel's influential work *Oeconomia christiana ofte christelicke huys-houdinge* (Oeconomia Christiana, or Christian Housekeeping) was published in 1655. Menasseh ben Israel described 'perfecta Oeconomica' (perfect Oeconomica) in his book on housekeeping for the Jewish community, *Thesovro dos dinim* (Thesaurus of Laws, 1645).
3 On honour, see p. 37 of this publication.
4 Groenendijk 1984, pp. 105–106.
5 'een sleutel van het huys en al het huys-bedrijf', Cats 1862, vol. 1, p. 484.
6 Proverbs 31:10, 31:27, cited in King James Version 1611.
7 Haarlem 1986, pp. 73–75.
8 Duijn et al. 2018, p. 75.
9 'moei-al' and 'vrouwe-kweller', Cats 1625 (1993), p. 72.
10 The contemporary meaning of 'curfew' in English derives from the medieval laws that regulated the covering and extinguishing of household fires in the

evening at a set time. See *Oxford English Dictionary*, s.v. 'curfew (n.)', December 2024, https://doi.org/10.1093/OED/5148513221.
11 Christian housemaids in Jewish households sometimes worked on Shabbat, even though this was not officially permitted. Levie Bernfeld 2020, p. 14.
12 Pierik 2022, pp. 60–62.
13 The invention of the pendulum clock by Christiaan Huygens in 1656 had made this form of timekeeping more accurate.
14 NEHA, Collectie Familie du Tour, inv. no. 1, fol. 65; see also Lunsingh Scheurleer et al. 1986–1992, vol. 6b (1992), pp. 531–532.
15 Noorman and Van der Maal 2022, p. 163.
16 For Maria van Nesse see ibid., p. 164. For the Huydecoper family see Kooijmans 2016, p. 398, n. 6.
17 NEHA, Collectie Familie du Tour, inv. no. 1, fols. 9r, 14v, 26r.
18 Fock 2001, p. 37.
19 Van Wijngaarden 2000, p. 109; Van der Vlis 2001, p. 107.
20 NEHA, Collectie Familie du Tour, inv. no. 1, fol. 17v.
21 'Als het bezit niet past bij de man, geldt net als bij schoenen: te ruim doet zwikken, te klein knelt.' Blom et al. 1999, p. 25.
22 Muinck 1965, p. 312.
23 Nijboer 2007, pp. 97–101. For an example of a tally stick (a tool for keeping track of unpaid debts), see fig. 109.
24 Compare Van Wijngaarden 2000, p. 201.
25 Beck 1627–1628 (2014), pp. 20–21.
26 Blom et al. 1999, p. 68.
27 'Teen en tander tot de maeltyt', NEHA, Collectie Familie du Tour, inv. no. 1, fol. 9v.
28 Cats 1862, vol. 1, p. 484; see also Franits 1993, p. 92.
29 NEHA, Collectie Familie du Tour, inv. no. 1, fols. 11v, 16r.
30 These German Jews may have played a role in the re-education of the families for whom they worked, because of their knowledge of dietary laws and the general rules of Jewish life. After the expulsion of the Jews from Spain and Portugal in 1492, the Sephardim who remained in those countries had been compelled to

renounce their religion, and they could not return to the faith of their forebears until after their arrival in the Republic. Levie Bernfeld 2020, p. 16.

31 On Margaretha van Berensteyn, see Duijn et al. 2018, p. 123; on Josina Schade van Westrum, see De Mooij 1999, p. 98.

32 For example, Sara paid a tailor fourteen guilders for 'making the manservant's clothes and something for my husband' ('het maken van de kneghs kleeren en iets voor mijn man') in the week of 8 May, and in the week of 23 May she paid two guilders, eight stivers and sixteen cents for a ribbon for her husbands 'garment' ('cleet'), and two guilders and two stivers to Gert Andriessen to mend the piece of clothing. NEHA, Collectie Familie du Tour, inv. no. 1, fols. 8v–9r.

33 Instead of peat, firewood was more often used in the countryside, and coal was imported for brewing. Saelens 2020, pp. 46, 48.

34 Van Wijngaarden 2000, p. 109.

35 Van Nesse 1623–1646, fol. 3v; Wagenaar 1765, p. 353.

36 Muinck 1965, p. 238.

37 NEHA, Collectie Familie du Tour, inv. no. 1, fols. 9r, 16r. The volume of a barrel of peat was 227 litres, according to the Amsterdam measurement standard, which was probably also adopted in other cities. See Muinck 1965, p. 238.

38 Dibbits 2001, p. 82.

39 Lunsingh Scheurleer et al. 1986–1992, vol. 6b (1992), pp. 529–530.

40 Fock 1997b, p. 462.

41 Van Wijngaarden 2000, p. 98.

42 Fock 2001, p. 32.

43 Duijn et al. 2018, p. 97.

44 Amsterdam 1971, nos. 1, 29.

45 Lunsingh Scheurleer et al. 1986–1992, vol. 6b (1992), pp. 529–530.

46 Fock 1997b, pp. 464–465, 474; Lunsingh Scheurleer et al. 1986–1992, vol. 6b (1992), p. 530.

47 This is consistent with probate inventories. See Pijzel-Dommisse 2000, p. 150.

48 ATH, inv. no. ATH 433, account book, 1653, p. 31.

49 Van Wijngaarden 2000, p. 109.

50 Fock 2001, p. 109.

51 ATH, inv. no. ATH 434, account book, 1649, p. 136.

52 Duijn et al. 2018, p. 104.

53 Sarti 2002, p. 105; Muinck 1965, p. 235.

54 Van Nesse 1623–1646, fol. 2r.

55 Muinck 1965, p. 236.

56 Oil lamps are often found in archaeological excavations. Pijzel-Dommisse 2000, p. 151.

57 Muinck 1965, p. 236.

58 NEHA, Collectie Familie du Tour, inv. no. 1, fol. 6r.

59 Pijzel-Dommisse 2000, p. 151.

60 Bitter 2016, p. 151.

61 NEHA, Collectie Familie du Tour, inv. no. 1, fol. 6v.

62 Ibid.

63 Muinck 1965, pp. 287, 288.

64 NEHA, Collectie Familie du Tour, inv. no. 1, fols. 14v, 15r; Noorman and Van der Maal 2022, p. 125, n. 100.

65 'swartsel', Van Nesse 1623–1646, fols. 12r, 83v.

66 Anonymous 1753, pp. 29–30.

67 'besloten lucht' and 'ongezonde dampen', Van Beverwijck 1636, vol. 1, pp. 227, 254.

68 A 17th-century bed stick has been preserved in Petronella de la Court's doll's house; see Pijzel-Dommisse 2000, p. 168.

69 'geen spinne-koppen, vliegen of ander venyningh ongediert', Anonymous 1660, p. 13.

70 Kloek 2009, p. 95.

71 From 75 to 90 per cent of servants were women, a much higher proportion than in other countries. Only in more rural areas was the percentage of male servants higher. Carlson 1993, pp. 18, 73.

72 Ibid., p. 18; Kloek 2009, p. 95.

73 Levie Bernfeld 2012, pp. 13–15, 19.

74 Sorber 1988, p. 111.

75 Van Nesse 1623–1646, fols. 70–72.

76 Van Ysselsteyn 1946, p. 95.

77 Anonymous 1658 (1670), n.p.

78 De Vries 2007, p. 232.

79 Coarse linen has sixteen threads per square centimetre on average, while fine linen has as many as forty threads. S. de Zoete in Boston 2015, pp. 75, 84.

80 Burgers 1960, pp. 126, 128–129.

81 S. de Zoete in Boston 2015, p. 83. Van Ysselstein 1946, p. 146, works with an estimate of 750 to

1,000 home textiles in the average large house. This figure probably includes clothing, because even the probate inventories of the wealthiest families rarely list such large quantities of home textiles.

82 De Mooij 1999, p. 98.

83 Compare North 2020, pp. 237–238.

84 Sorber 1988, p. 116.

85 Pijzel-Dommisse 2000, p. 170.

86 De Mooij 1999, p. 94.

87 Moerman 2021, p. 54.

88 Van Beverwijck 1636, vol. 1, pp. 464–465; Loughman and Montias 2000, pp. 146–147.

89 Moerman 2021, pp. 73–74; De Mare 2001, p. 37, n. 19.

90 Van Ysselsteyn 1946, p. 146.

91 Regtdoorzee Greup-Roldanus 1936, pp. 98–100.

92 Van Nesse 1623–1646, fol. 30r.

93 Green soap was made of whale oil, which was produced by boiling baleen whale blubber. This soap was very suitable for cleaning but had a disagreeable smell. Chomel and De Chalmot 1778–1793, pp. 4066–4067, 4316.

94 Van Eeghen 1960, p. 114.

95 NEHA, Collectie Familie du Tour, inv. no. 1, fols. 7v, 9v, 14r, 16r, 18r.

96 Peelen 1908, pp. 51, 58.

97 Glass slickstones first came into use in the 7th century and have been found by archaeologists in many areas of Europe. These simple, inexpensive tools were used to smooth fabric and making it more lustrous. Their shape and the inertness of glass also makes them suitable for other purposes, such as grinding herbs in the kitchen and making paper. See Bartels 2009; De Kreyger 2011.

98 Sorber 1988, p. 118.

99 Den Besten and Den Bestenden Burger 1983, p. 72.

100 S. de Zoete in Boston 2015, p. 87.

101 B.M. du Mortier in Van Suchtelen 2021, p. 62.

102 GA, 0439, Huizen Waardenburg en Neerijnen, inv. no. 513, Testament van Sara L'Empereur van Opwyck, p. 59.

Work

1 'huis en ververij waar de Groene Papegaeij boven de deur

staat', Hell 2024, pp. 134–135; SAA, ANSA, inv. no. 951C, notary Benedict Baddel, 10 November 1637, fols. 1014–1015.
2 'het Wapen van Friesland uithangt' and 'Het Moriaanshoofd in de gevel', SAA, 5062, Archief van de Schepenen: kwijtscheldingsregisters, inv. nos. 44, no. Z, 28 February 1651; 55, no. O2, 7 March 1668.
3 'in de Warmoesstraet aen d'Oostzijde, tusschen het Wijngaardstraetje en de Armsteeg, daer d' Vergulde Zeepton in de gevel staet en de drij Suijckerbroden uijthangen', SAA, 5061, Archieven van de Schout en Schepenen, van de Schepenen en van de Subalterne Rechtbanken, inv. no. 2173, 24 September 1689. On sugarloaves, see p. 222 in this chapter.
4 See, for example, Veerkamp 2021 on the use of the grounds and on the equipment required for a beer brewery and soap works.
5 NHA, 3615, Parochie Onze Lieve Vrouw Rozenkrans en Heilige Dominicus (Spaarnekerk) te Haarlem, inv. no. 269, Verkoopakte, 1666.
6 Van Dekken 2009, p. 88; Unger 2001, pp. 166–167.
7 This was true of De Hoek brewery in Enkhuizen (Schrickx and Stellingwerf 2020, p. 33) and De Dubbele Arent brewery in Purmerend (Moesker (forthcoming)).
8 Malting involves germinating grains and then drying them prior to fermentation. Wort is a watery, sugary intermediate product in beer brewing, derived by filtering water that has been mixed with malted grains.
9 Breweries, like other businesses, were not infrequently run by women rather than men. The women in question were often widows who took over the business after their husband's death. Van Dekken 2009.
10 This did not change until the end of the century, when a greater separation developed between work and home life. See, for example, De Vries and Van der Woude 1997; Van den Heuvel 2018; Poelwijk 2003.
11 See, for example, Kuijpers 2005; Songer and Van Lottum 2007; Janssen 2017.

12 SAA, ANSA, inv. no. 942, notary Daniel Bredan, 9 February 1633, fol. 123.
13 Van Nesse 1623–1646, fol. 70r.
14 'gehoorsaem sijn ende sich in alle gevalle houden ende dragen als sulcx een eerlijck ende vroom Jongman betaemt', SAA, ANSA, inv. no. 513, notary Jacob Jansz Westfrisius, 16 March 1616, fol. 184.
15 SAA, ANSA, inv. no. 5844, notary Joan Hoekeback, 13 December 1692, fols. 523r–525v.
16 Van Aken-Fehmers 1999–2001, vol. 2, p. 185.
17 Ibid., vol. 1, p. 65; SD, 161, Oud Notarieel Archief (hereafter ONA), inv. no. 2041, notary Melchior van der Borcht, 19 March 1655.
18 Ostkamp 2003.
19 A report drawn up by the city's fire inspection office in 1668 shows that Kleijnoven's business had two kilns; see also https://delftsaardewerk.nl/ontdekken/plateelbakkerij/de-porceleyne-fles-1653-1876 (consulted 10 October 2025).
20 The objects found in the cesspit at De Porcelyne Fles included tableware with slight manufacturing errors that showed some traces of use. Ostkamp 2003, p. 188.
21 On 4 January 1660, Quirijn and Engeltje Kleijnoven had their daughter Ageta baptized in the Nieuwe Kerk of the Dutch Reformed congregation in Delft. Ostkamp 2003, pp. 189–190; SD, 14, Doop-, trouw- en begraafboeken Delft, inv. no. 14.57, 4 January 1660, fol. 160v.
22 Buijsen 2010, pp. 18–23; https://delftsaardewerk.nl/en/ontdekken/plateelbakkerij/de-porceleyne-fles-1653-1876 (consulted 10 October 2025).
23 Hell 2014; Molhuysen and Blok 1912, p. 85.
24 Van Dekken 2009, p. 222.
25 The death certificate for Sibbeltje (Sibbeli) does not give a surname, but it does state that she was a *matres* (schoolmistress). Tresoar, 13–16; Nedergerecht Harlingen, inv. no. 196, Inventarisatieboeken, 1642–1645.
26 'huijs postille', Otten 2019, Tresoar, finding aids 13–16;

Nedergerecht Harlingen, Inventarisatieboeken, inv. no. 196.
27 Otten 2019; Bakker et al. 2006, pp. 439–441, 483–487.
28 Koorn 2013; Koorn 2021; Strouven 1638–1649 (2020).
29 'tot oprechte deugd' and 'Och, pater, ik kan niet meer. Geef mij toch toestemming de kinderen weg te zenden. Ik kan niet meer!', Strouven 1638–1649 (2020), p. 24.
30 Van Nederveen Meerkerk 2007, p. 188; Van der Vlis 2001.
31 It was permissible for orphans from the Heilige Geest Weeshuis (Holy Spirit Orphanage) to go to work from as early as the age of six, and the children of poor relief recipients in Zwolle had often already begun working by that age; see Van Nederveen Meerkerk and Schmidt 2006, pp. 30, 46–47.
32 See also p. 259 of this publication.
33 Van Nederveen Meerkerk 2007, p. 213; CO, 0741, Stadsarmenkamer, inv. no. 311, register van bedeelden, 1683–1692, fol. 71v.
34 Van Nederveen Meerkerk 2007; Van den Heuvel 2018.
35 'om een wiel voor haer dochters kint te coopen om wol te spinnen', Van der Vlis 2001, p. 89.
36 Van Nederveen Meerkerk 2007, p. 192.
37 Lugtigheid 2021, p. 127; Teunissen and Stolk 2024, pp. 11–12.
38 See also p. 46 of this publication.
39 De Vries 2007, pp. 218–241.
40 See also Lesger 2013, p. 124.
41 'de lade vande toonbanck', SAA, ANSA, inv. no. 2410, notary Jacob de Winter, 24 June 1673, fols. 149–152.
42 De Vries 2007, pp. 218–241.
43 Ibid.
44 'sieckelijc van lichaeme', ibid.
45 SAA, ANSA, inv. no. 2410, notary Jacob de Winter, 24 June 1673, fols. 149–152.
46 Fock 2001, p. 154.
47 Fock 1997b, pp. 465–466.
48 Isaac Pool owned a number of ships, which he used for trade with countries including France, England, Norway, Latvia and Russia. Ibid.

49   Ibid.
50   'van een suykerplantagie gelegen in Suriname aan de rivier Commewijne genaemt De Nieuwe Hoop met sijn huijsinge, gereetschappen, slaaven en bestialen', HUA, 26, Familie Des Tombe, inv. no. 1100, Johan Boudaen Courten and Anna Maria Hoeufft's will, p. 6; Weterings 2011, p. 341. At first, the entire plantation probably belonged to Johan and Pieter Boudaen Courten, who later sold part of it to their contact person, Pieter Heerense. On the origin of the Boudaen Courten trading house, see p. 307 of this publication.
51   Some ten letters from the brothers have been preserved as part of a large group of postal items captured by English privateers in 1672, commonly referred to as the Year of Disaster. These items never reached their destinations, but today they offer insight into the subject matter and frequency of the brothers' correspondence. See HCA, inv. no. HCA30-223, for a digital copy. See also Brouwer 2014.
52   NA, 1.05.01.02, Tweede West-Indische Compagnie, inv. no. 733, Net-resoluties, 12 May 1692, fol. 397.
53   Pieter Heerense, their contact person and the co-owner of the plantation, kept them informed about this. Brouwer 2014, pp. 185–186.
54   Teske 2011, p. 64. Although slavery was outlawed in the Republic, it is unclear whether this boy was actually paid for his work as Thomas Hees's servant.
55   See, for example, Van Nierop 1930; Colenbrander 2013; Teunissen and Stolk 2024, pp. 33–62.
56   De Vries and Van der Woude 1997; Van den Heuvel 2018; Poelwijk 2003, p. 12.
57   'zijdelakenfabrikeur' and 'werck meijsies', Colenbrander 2013, pp. 43–44.
58   Van den Heuvel 2018; Schmidt and Van Nederveen Meerkerk 2012.
59   Van Nederveen Meerkerk and Schmidt 2006.
60   Poelwijk 2003, pp. 67–73.
61   'Alle pogingen vergeefs … de zuiker-bakkerij en 't woonhuis', ibid., pp. 107–110.

Parenting
1   'als het maer een gesont kint is', Brouwer 2014, p. 253; HCA, inv. no. HCA 30/645, letter from Trijntje to Jan Jacobsen Sloper, 30 November 1673.
2   'Om de Republiek goede borgers te geven, is meest gelegen aen de op-voedingh der kinderen', Van Beverwijck 1636, vol. 2, p. 101.
3   'Het kint is uw beslagh tot aen de seven jaren', Cats 1862, vol. 1, p. 537.
4   By way of Plutarch's treatise *De liberis educandis* (The Education of Children) – which was translated, adapted and reprinted in countless editions from the 15th century onward – Dutch authors such as Desiderius Erasmus and Jacob Cats were profoundly influenced by Aristotle's views. These were, in brief, that natural inclinations (*natura*) had to be corrected by rules (*ars*) and practice (*exercitatio*). Aristotle's ideas found their way into advice literature and life writings. The leading manuals of parenting were written by physicians (Van Beverwijck and Blankaart), clergymen (Wittewrongel and Koelman), schoolteachers (De Swaef), and the poet, lawyer and moralist Jacob Cats.
5   Prak 1998, pp. 76–77.
6   'huysvrouws luijermant', Knoester and Graafhuis 1970, p. 205; Lunsingh Scheurleer 1971, pp. 315–316. Later in the paragraph: 'pislappen', 'luyeeren', 'borstrockiens' and 'linnewat'.
7   On the use of lying-in chambers for receiving guests in the 17th century, see Pijzel-Dommisse 2000, pp. 60–67.
8   'voor de klederen van ons kintie saliger', Knoester and Graafhuis 1970, p. 205. The girl was interred in the presence of dozens of invited guests; see Heurneman 2002, p. 133.
9   A full 80 to 85 per cent of these deaths were of children under the age of five. See J. Dekker, L.F. Groenendijk en J. Verberckmoes in Haarlem 2000, p. 57.
10   See, for example, Rösslin 1650, p. 39; Nylandt 1669, p. 17. Sexual abstinence was motivated by the assumption that a mother's milk

was actually menstrual blood transformed on its way from the womb to the breasts. It was believed that women had just enough for one child at a time; see Matthews Grieco 1991, p. 18.
11   Breast pumps (initially made of ceramic and later of glass) had been in use since ancient times to encourage lactation, stimulate inverted nipples and reduce breast inflammation, but also to express colostrum, a mother's first milk, which was believed to be unhealthy for the newborn. On the glass breast pump, see Matthews Grieco 1991; Obladen 2012; Verwaal 2023. There were also silver nipple cups that could aid in breastfeeding. These items were probably part of the toolkit of the 17th-century surgeon; see Scultetus 1657, p. 51; Paré 1655, p. 738.
12   Verbeeck *s.a.* (1999), pp. 91–92, 105–106.
13   'zodat met groot verdriet dit schaapje moet te min, tot groote kostenlast, al waer et tegen zin'. Ibid., p. 106. On Herman Verbeeck and Clara Molenaars, see also Dekker 1994; Dekker 1995, pp. 47–57.
14   Dekker 1995, p. 154. The Huydecopers, a family of Amsterdam regents, paid 50 guilders for half a year; see HUA, 67, Familie Huydecoper, inv. no. 30, Kasboek van Joan Huydecoper, 10 December 1627, fol. 21r. This account book also shows that the wet nurse earned considerably more than the housemaid.
15   'Een die haer kinders baert is moeder voor een deel; Maer die haer kinders sooght, is moeder in 't geheel.' Cats 1862, vol. 2, p. 533.
16   De Swaef, Cats, Van Beverwijck, Wittewrongel (see note 1) and the physician Steven Blankaart all stress the importance of breastfeeding by the mother. It is difficult to determine how widely this advice was followed.
17   Van Beverwijck 1636, vol. 2, pp. 75–85; Blankaart 1684, pp. 2–4; Cats 1862, vol. 2, p. 537. In Leiden, there was even a family business that provided care for nursing babies. Children delivered

by the midwife Hillegont's Cornelis could be breastfed by her daughter Trijntgen, who worked as a wet nurse. Hillegone's eldest daughter Aeffgen provided childcare in her mother's home. See Schmidt 2001, pp. 139–140.
18 Dekker 1995, pp. 142–155. Hiring a wet nurse became less unusual towards the end of the century.
19 Constantijn Huygens believed he had a special bond with his mother thanks to breastfeeding; see Huygens *s.a.* (2003), vol. 1, pp. 141, 143. Pieter Boudaen Courten describes how his eldest son was breastfed by a wet nurse from the age of two months onwards, because his wife Catharina Fourmenois had fallen ill; their sixth child was weaned by the early age of five and a half months; see Boudaen Courten *s.a.* (2005), pp. 53–54.
20 'soete spruijt', Verbeeck *s.a.* (1999), pp. 109–110. Clara Molenaars gave birth to eight children in total and had several difficult pregnancies, dangerous deliveries and breastfeeding problems. Five children died in the first, vulnerable eighteen months of life.
21 It was important for food to be suited to the child's makeup, in accordance with the dictates of humoral theory. Food therefore had to be moist for the first three years, and then increasingly dry; see Van Beverwijck 1636, vol. 2, pp. 86–99, 101; Blankaart 1684, pp. 13–15, 28–29.
22 Dekker 1995, p. 52.
23 On psychological trauma after a child's death in the 17th century see Kooijmans 2023, pp. 158–162.
24 Van Beverwijck regularly mentions coral in combination with blood; see Van Beverwijck 1642, pp. 193–194, 241. The outward resemblances between blood vessels and coral are not mentioned there but are part of a tradition of associative thinking that Van Beverwijck carries forward.
25 Willemsen 2003, p. 65; Naaktgeboren 1987, p. 80; Keijser et al. 2021, p. 73.
26 Huygens *s.a.* (2003), vol. 1, p. 67.

27 'weeke hersentjes', Blankaart 1684, p. 15. Blankaart points out that the infant brain is still weak and could also be damaged by rocking the cradle.
28 S. Kuus in Haarlem 2000, p. 70.
29 'moet men het niet te veel in de kak-stoel laten sitten, want dan werden zy pap-sakken van kinderen', Blankaart 1684, p. 26.
30 Van Beverwijck 1636, vol. 2, pp. 90–91.
31 'Maer men moet de kintsche jaren/ boven reden niet beswaren want/ jonge kinders moeten spelen/ Of van pijn en sieckte quelen' ('But the early childhood years/ are no time for toil and tears/ little children need to play/ lest they sicken and pine away'). Cats 1862, vol. 1, p. 759.
32 'daegelijcke pret' and 'gedenck boeck', SAA, 15030, Inventaris van de Collectie Stadsarchief Amsterdam, inv. no. 77884, 'Ghedenk boek' van Jan Sijwertsz Kolm, 1618–1630. For the manuscript, see Smits-Veldt 1991 and Goedings 1998.
33 The initials stand for 'Hansje Lindemans'; 'Lindemans' was his mother's surname.
34 'speelziek', 'sou [hij] wel vergeeten school en dis/ als hij maer op de straet met trom en vaendel is/ met spiets, met sweep, en tol, off wagen om te sleepen'.
35 'dan huyllen, dan lagh/ dan kijven, dan vree'.
36 See S. Kuus in Haarlem 2000, pp. 78–80, and Kuus 1994 for more differences between boys' and girls' clothing.
37 In a portrait by Jan Kolm of his family (1624) that recently resurfaced, he depicted his children in much the same way as in the drawing in his *gedenkboek*. In the painting, Anna is holding a basket filled with cherries but does not have a doll on her arm. Around her neck she wears a red coral necklace with a heart-shaped pendant. Although both her brothers are depicted in this painting, Sieuwert had already died by the time his father made it, as the hourglass at his feet indicates. Courtesy of Lawrence Steigrad Fine Arts, New York.
38 When miniatures are found in archaeological excavations, it is

often difficult to tell whether they were used as children's toys, were collected by adults, and/or formed part of a doll's house. A distinction is made between two sizes, and it is assumed that the smaller category of miniatures were not suitable for use as toys but intended for doll's houses. Both categories are referred to as *poppengoed*. See Willemsen 2003; Bitter 2009; Bitter 2012.
39 Further investigation is needed in order to determine whether the pots really were used for cooking.
40 Stolk 2022, pp. 141–160; Stolk 2020. On how *púcaros* were used, see also p. 137 of this publication.
41 Cats 1862, vol. 1, pp. 484–485, 760.
42 In the scholarly literature, this portrait has been linked to Cats, but greater emphasis has been placed on the role of the good housewife than on that of the mother educating her daughter. De Vries 1990, pp. 55–56; E. de Jongh in Utrecht 2004, pp. 345–346.
43 In exceptional cases, however, the boys are known to have been even younger; see S. Kuus in Haarlem 2000, pp. 80–82.
44 'Toen ik groter werd stak hij mij in de broek', Dekker 1995, p. 159.
45 The Republic had higher literacy rates than other European countries and showed improvement over the course of the century. Education was, however, a consumer market, in which more money meant a higher level of educational attainment. On this topic, see for example Dekker 1995, pp. 167–199; Roberts 1998, pp. 99–100; Van Deursen 1994, pp. 131–132.
46 'West gegroet min vader', HCA, inv. no. 30/652.2, letter from Annetje Jochems to Jochem Jansen, May 1672; see Brouwer 2014, pp. 55–56, 118–119.
47 Geertruijt, Maria van Nesse's niece, likewise wrote a brief letter to her aunt at the age of nine to show how well she could already write. Her aunt gave her a schelling coin; see Van Nesse 1623–1646, fol. 71r.
48 'gouden hemel'. Many children requested and received

attractive gifts from their seafaring fathers. This term may have been meant figuratively. Personal communication Judith Brouwer.
49 HCA, inv. no. 30/652.2, letter from Annetje Jochems to Jochem Jansen, May 1672.
50 The two letters must have been enclosed with the letter sent by her mother Jannetje Jans in May 1672. HCA, inv. no. 30/652.2, letter from Jannetje Jans to Jochem Jansen, 2 May 1672. Personal communication Judith Brouwer.
51 HCA, inv. no. 30/652.2, letter from Jannetje Jans to Jochem Jansen, 2 May 1672.
52 Boekholt and De Booy 1987, pp. 39, 40; De Booy 1977, p. 219.
53 Such nursery schools were known as *kleinkinderschooltjes* (small-child schools) and *matressenschooltjes* (schoolmistress schools). On the latter, see p. 203 of this publication.
54 For example, the Amsterdam pastor Petrus van der Hagen urged parents to teach them to pray: 'Soo ras uwe kinderen verstant toonen, leert se haer gebeden selve stamelen, haren Godt kennen. Die halve gebroockte woorden zijn haren schepper soo aengenaem, die kintsche tale klinckt in sijn ooren als een aengename melody' ('As soon as your children show any sense, teach them to stammer their prayers for themselves and become acquainted with their God. Those half-mangled words are so pleasing to their Creator; that childish language sounds like a sweet melody to his ears'); see Groenendijk 2004, p. 97; Van der Hagen 1699, pp. 8–9.
55 On Christian education, see Boekholt and De Booy 1987, pp. 33–37; Van Toorn and Spies 1990; Utrecht 1991, p. 12.
56 On the Sundays 30 September, and 4, 11 and 25 November 1627, David Beck sang psalms with his son Adriaen; see Beck 1627–1628 (2014), pp. 108, 118, 120, 125. On Protestant *kindercatechismussen* (children's catechisms), see Van Toorn and Spies 1990, pp. 143–148; Exalto 2023.
57 Valcooch 1591 (1875), p. 21.
58 Erasmus' *De civilitate morum puerilium* (On Civility in Children; 1530) was published in 1693

under the title of *Van de borgerlyke wellevendheid der kinderlyke zeden* (On the Civil Courtesy of Children's Morals), in a translation by the Noordwijk schoolteacher Michiel Komans.
59 Erasmus 1530 (1693).
60 Oddens 2020.
61 Roberts 1998, pp. 181–182.
62 On the importance of honour in the 17th century, see p. 37 of this publication.
63 Boekholt and De Booy 1987, pp. 32, 36.
64 'Ick hadde wel gewenscht dat gij die 2 grove fouten niet had begaen, sonder dewelcke U de eerste plaets niet had kunnen ontgaen.' Kooijmans 2016, p. 190.
65 On 12 September 1627 and 20 October 1628, see Beck 1627–1628 (2014), pp. 103, 199.
66 Blankaart 1684, p. 31; Van Beverwijck 1636, vol. 2, p. 102; Dekker 1995, p. 174.
67 Van Doorninck and Kuijpers 1993, pp. 41–43; Van Nederveen Meerkerk and Schmidt 2006, p. 30.
68 Johannes, Joan Huydecoper's eldest son, left home at the age of ten. His father introduced him to influential contacts and put pressure on him to succeed. See Kooijmans 2016, pp. 61–62, 190.
69 Boudaen Courten *s.a.* (2005), p. 53.
70 'Altijd de beste te zijn en boven anderen uit te steken', Van der Ham 2010.
71 Van Doorninck and Kuijpers 1993, p. 33; Boekholt and De Booy 1987, pp. 50, 59, 79.
72 Arnolli en Sloof 2004.
73 De Fijne 1694, p. 2.
74 Ibid., pp. 3–7.
75 These boy craftsmen were taken up in the family, but were both pupils and workers. There must have been great variation in the extent to which their masters played a fatherly, guiding role, although some parents did have it stipulated in the contract that the master was in charge of the boy's upbringing. See De Munck 2004; De Jager 1990; Dekker 2006, pp. 63, 75–76.
76 Boekholt and De Booy 1987, pp. 18–21. Lucia Helena's boarding school underwent strict inspections but was allowed to

remain in operation with no more than an occasional fine; see Abels 2010, pp. 29–35, 77–79.
77 In 1648, Lucia Helena returned home, but only for a year and half. In 1650, when she was around fifteen years old, she left for Berlaymont in Brussels, so that the nuns there could complete her education and upbringing; see Stoter 2016.
78 Bitter 2012, pp. 84, 85; Arnhem 1997, pp. 86–231; Dekker 2006, pp. 169–173. The children's ages (both on arrival and at departure) and the rules governing admission varied substantially by region and by orphanage.
79 Gijsbert, on his deathbed, had asked his sister Maria to offer a mother's care to the three children he would leave behind. Maria refused, because she children already had a mother, but she did take the girl into her home for a time. Noorman and Van der Maal 2022, pp. 34, 35, 51, 86; Van Nesse 1623–1646, fols. 41r, v.
80 For example, Joan Huydecoper Jr remained dependent on his father until the latter's death. As the eldest son, he was expected to succeed his father, but his political career could not truly begin until his father died. By that time, Joan was 36 years old and had two children of his own. See Kooijmans 2016, pp. 127–143.
81 Groenendijk 1984, pp. 157–158.

Engagement
1 Beck 1627–1628 (2014), p. 121. See also Blaak 2012, pp. 181–184, on David's amorous adventures.
2 Beck 1627–1628 (2014), p. 187 (15 September 1628).
3 Van der Heijden 1998, p. 177*ff*.
4 Voskuijl 1975, p. 50.
5 'de grote besegelde cas' and 'voor binnencamer'. See www.omropfryslan.nl/nl/nieuws/927597/belangrijke-aanwinst-hannemahuis-trouwkistje-uit-1633 (consulted 20 October 2024). The Frans Hals Museum in Haarlem holds a casket received by Tempelar's sister Elisabet from her bridegroom Johannes

Feitema, with decorations including a scene of Sarah and Tobias (inv. no. oz 65-77).

6 Leeuwarden/Kassel 2018, pp. 113–117.

7 De Mare 2003, p. 325.

8 The other images are Jacob and Rachel at the well and a wedding scene.

Marriage

1 'Myn Waerde Moey!' and 'er omtrent bij de 80 menschen syn geweest, soo wel den tweeden als den eersten dagh, bestaende meest uyt jonge luyden', Schotel 1867, pp. 308–310.

2 The emphasis on the consummation of the marriage originally came from the Catholic tradition, but it remained customary among Protestants. See Haks 1985, pp. 70–73, on virginity until marriage.

3 Thoen 2007, p. 190, asserts that household objects were sometimes presented as wedding gifts but adds that there are few sources for this claim. The only example she gives is the glasses engraved by Anna Roemers Visscher, but these glasses are part of a tradition of giving poems, possibly but not necessarily engraved in glass, and therefore cannot be considered ordinary household items.

4 The couple did give gifts to the immediate family, and a wedding was sometimes seized on as an occasion for handing down objects with sentimental value within the family. Noorman and Van der Maal 2022, pp. 81, 84; see also Van Nesse 1623–1646, fol. 23r.

5 Diercks 2024.

6 'gemaekt alleen van peerelsnoeren en diamanten'. Bridal crowns could either be worn by the bride or hung above the bride and groom; we see the latter in the painting of the wedding meal of Eraeert van Pipenpoy and Jel van Liauckema; Leeuwarden/Kassel 2018, pp. 98, 99.

7 'wort na dese kroon, de kroone van den man', Cats 1862, vol. 1, p. 418. Cats uses the metaphor of the wife as her husband's crown with some regularity in his work *Houwelick* (Marriage, 1625).

8 'Wel Bruijdegom, hoe gangt de Bruijdskroon nog, men seght in Holland als dat geschiet dat den de Bruijdt nogh maagd is', SAA, ANSA, inv. no. 3995, notary Nicolaes Brouwer, 3 September 1696, fol. 77. The groom had second thoughts about the marriage, apparently, because after nine days it still had not been consummated, and later that year the couple underwent a legal separation, known as *scheiding van tafel en bed* (separation from bed and board). The use of the phrase 'in Holland' probably has to do with Karmichel's English background.

9 'De kussens, die men, volgens gebruyk op een alcatyf in de kerk legt, waren van groen fluweel met gout, gelyck oock na proportie in de bruyts slaapkamer alles met groene stoffe was opgeschikt', Schotel 1867, pp. 308–310.

10 Leeuwarden/Kassel 2018, p. 109.

11 'ome daer mede te betuygen dat [de bruidegom] rondelijck, oprechtelijck, ende sonder eenigh bedrogh in dat heyligh Verbondt met sijn geminde was tredende', Van Leeuwen 2023, p. 55; Cats 1862, vol. 2, p. 277.

12 For an example of a ring in the form of a house, see the collection of the Jewish Cultural Quarter, Amsterdam, inv. no. M005751.

13 On these rings, see De Clercq 2016, p. 44.

Birth

1 'swellend lieve buikjen'. Pieter de la Court regularly notes the weather at the end of his letters. The eighth of February was a fine, clear day but cold and windy; following week, the weather was fine, but snow had fallen. SAA, 172, Archief van de Familie Backer en Aanverwante Families, inv. no. 465, Pieter de la Court's correspondence, 8 and 17 February 1663, fols. 71, 75.

2 SAA, 172, Archief van de Familie Backer en Aanverwante Families, inv. no. 465, Catharina van der Voort's correspondence, 20 December 1662.

3 'dat niet eene maaltijd voorbij gaat sonder te drinken op de ge-

sondheid van ons Hansken in de kelder'. SAA, 172, Archief van de Familie Backer en Aanverwante Families, inv. no. 465, Pieter de la Court's correspondence, 13 and 17 February 1663, fols. 71, 73. *Hansje in de kelder* ('Hansken' is a variation on 'Hansje'; in English 'Jack in the cellar') was a term for the unborn child, see Winschooten 1681, p. 284.

4 For the earliest description of a *hansje-in-de-kelder* with an illustration, see Le Francq van Berkhey 1772–1776, pp. 1196–1200. Pieter de la Court may have used a silver *hansje-in-de-kelder*, but he may also have proposed the toast with a conventional glass.

5 Van Beverwijck 1660, pp. 162–165.

6 Visscher 1696, pp. 260–271. Cats speaks of 'imprinting' on the foetus, see Cats 1862, vol. 1, p. 526. On this subject, see Roodenburg 1988, pp. 708–712. In Renaissance Italy, pregnant women were given terracotta or stucco baby dolls for the same reason; see J.M. Musacchio in London 2006, pp. 128–130.

7 Cats 1862, vol. 1, p. 526; Visscher 1696, p. 261; Van Beverwijck 1660, p. 163; SAA, 172, Archief van de Familie Backer en Aanverwante Families, inv. no. 465, Pieter de la Court's correspondence, 11, 14 and 25 April and 6, 8 and 17 May 1663, fols. 89–99.

8 Maternal mortality is also described in midwife Catharina Schrader's notes; see Kloosterman 1984, pp. 56–61.

9 Personal communication Marlies Stoter. Reintzen Douwedochter, Pier Sytzema's Frisian wife, stated in her will dating from 7 February 1548 that 'the time of death is uncertain' for pregnant women in particular. For a similar statement, see the will made by Hero Buirmanye's wife Frauw, also Frisian, which dates from 28 February 1543. On these two wills, see Verhoeven and Mol 1994, pp. 421–422 and 383–385 respectively. A number of wills made by pregnant women in Amsterdam likewise refer to the fragility of life; see e.g. SAA, ANSA, inv. no. 3181A, notary

Hendrik Bruijnenburgh, Herma-
nus van Aldewerelt and Tietien
Jans's will, 11 July 1663, pp. 152–
157; SAA, ANSA, inv. no. 4892,
notary Wilhelmus Sijlvius, Paulus
Bedeke and Anna van de Rijcke's
will, 20 March 1688, pp. 364–367.
Women who had just given birth
and were lying in sometimes made
wills too; see SAA, ANSA, inv. no.
2175, notary Adriaen Lock, Maria
Pronck's will, 9 June 1670, pp. 96–
102; SAA, ANSA, inv. no. 4743,
notary David Stafmaeker, Daniël
Huijsman and Geertruid Bruij-
man's will, 16 November 1683,
pp. 611–613.
10 The girl was named Sophia,
after her mother and grandmother,
but she died a year later, on 11 December 1661. See Kooijmans 2016,
p. 168.
11 HUA, 67, Familie Huydecoper, inv. no. 56, diary entry for
24 October 1660 and correspondence dating from 26 October 1660.
12 SAA, 172, Archief van de
Familie Backer en Aanverwante
Families, inv. no. 465, Pieter de
la Court's correspondence, 12 December 1661, fol. 69.
13 For 17th-century postnatal
customs, see Lunsingh-Scheurleer
1971; Pijzel-Dommisse 2000,
pp. 60–64.

Baptism
1 Ekkart 1978–1979.
2 The *doopluur* (baptismal
nappy) in the collection of the
Rijksmuseum was almost certainly
preserved as a memento of the
ceremony; see Du Mortier 2018.
3 Mennonites formed an exception, as they were not baptized
until adulthood.
4 Thoen 2007, pp. 116–121.
Similarly, Pieter Boudaen Courten
recorded the gifts in his family
chronicle; see Boudaen Courten
s.a. (2005). Some wills specified
which *pillegift* was intended for
each child; see, for example, the
will of Susanna Christoffels in
Amsterdam, the widow of Jacob
Dirxsz Sprangh (SAA, ANSA,
inv. no. 1872, notary Frans Uijten-
bogaert, 22 December 1657,
pp. 284–286). Others stipulated
that the *pillegiften* should be equally
distributed among the children; see

the will of Christiaen Bodt and
Maria Pronck (SAA, ANSA, inv. no.
2175, notary Adriaen Lock, 9 June
1670, pp. 96–102). Still other wills
stated that the difference in value
between the gifts should be compensated for with other goods
from the estate; see, for example,
the will of Constantia Victory, Jan
Ernst van Bassen's widow (SAA,
ANSA, inv. no. 6972, notary Cornelis van Loon, 15 June 1700,
fols. 27–31v). A child who had not
received a *pillegift* was sometimes
left some other valuable objects;
see the will of Stephanus Backer
and Maria Martens, 5 October 1626
(SAA, ANSA, inv. no. notary unknown). Maria van Nesse kept
careful track of her expenses on
pillegiften; see Noorman and Van
der Maal 2022, p. 85; Van Nesse
1623–1646, fols. 34v–r.
5 Hulst 2013. Some *pillegifts*
were inscribed for the occasion;
Josina van Heemskerk, the daughter
of Willem and Maria, received a
silver salt cellar with her name
engraved in it; see Ekkart 1978–
1979, p. 65. Brandy was drunk at
celebrations of births and baptisms,
see p. 279 of this publication.
6 Beck 1624 (1993), 9 August
1624, p. 148; Thoen 2007,
pp. 116–121.
7 On child mortality, see pp. 227
and 238 of this publication.
8 The first Aelke died in 1606
at the age of one; by then her
mother was already dead. Her
father Ruurd Werps Juckema remarried two more times and had
another daughter named Aelke
with each of those two wives. After
the second Aelke's mother died,
the child was renamed Barbara in
her memory, and the next daughter
could therefore again be named
Aelke. The second and third
Aelke lived to be 59 and 91 years
old, respectively.
9 It has been estimated that more
than 30 17th-century portraits of
traits have survived, but deceased
children were also frequently included in family portraits (as angels);
see J.B.M.F. Bedaux in Haarlem
2000, p. 192. Inventories often include mourning portraits of children,
which hung in the *binnenkamer*
(inner room), the *voorhuis* (front

room) and the *achterkamer* (back
room), as well as in the kitchen in
smaller households. See, for example,
the inventories of Claes Luijders
(SAA, ANSA, inv. no. 1495, notary
Gilles Borsselaer, 29 April 1671,
fol. 154r); Hendrick Christiaensz
(SAA, ANSA, inv. no. 3164, notary
Jacob Pondt, 22 June 1660, fol. 62);
and Jan Janys Moff (SAA, ANSA,
inv. no. 3164, notary Jacob Pondt,
26 April 1640, fol. 78).

Death
1 'Mijn broer salijger sijn kint,
Gijsbertus van Nesse is gestorven
… op den 17 october … 5 talf
weck na sijn vader salijger … out
wesende 2 jaren min 8 talf weck.
Ende hadden mijn broer salijger
6 weken langer geleeft, soo
hadden hij 38 jaer out gewest.'
Van Nesse 1623–1646, fol. 41r.
2 Portegies 1999, p. 51;
Hirsch 1921; Van Zalinge 2020.
3 'Den 12 jannawarie [1674] is
ons van een aenspreecker kommen
vraagen of wij ons huijs beliefden
te sluyten alsoo ons night Van Raeij
omtrent de klock 2 ueren dese
warelt ooverleden was.' Duquesnoy
and Salman 2018, p. 100.
4 Mudde 2018, p. 70.
5 Hirsch 1921, pp. 43–45. The
use of flowers and herbs was seen
as a Catholic custom and prohibited in various places in the course
of the 17th century; Mudde 2018,
pp. 70–71. During plague epidemics, placing dead bodies on
view and adorning them were
forbidden activities in many places.
6 De Vries 2007, p. 234.
7 In 1630, the local authorities
in Den Bosch banned this type of
ritual, as well as the practice of
closing windows and doors until
the funeral. In 1659, the city
leaders declared that 'leggen van
de stroyen voor die lijckhuijsen'
('laying straw in front of houses
with dead bodies') was prohibited;
see Portegies 1999, pp. 51–55.
8 Hell 2024, p. 394, from the
Jewish chronicler Abraham Idaña's
account of Christian rituals in
Amsterdam.
9 Van den Bergh-Hoogterp
and Dubbe 1997, pp. 155–162.
10 'den backer knet en backt
het (brood) gaer tot smenschen

onderhout, dees baer die is gemaekt alleen voor backers jonck
en out'. Kok 1970; Laing 2020;
Van Eeghen 2012, pp. 4–6; Stolk
2022, pp. 126–127.
11 For example, the Amsterdam
grain merchant Pieter Claesz
Listingh's list of 'Doot-Schulden'
('death debts') includes 'tien
silvere lepels' ('ten silver spoons')
for the pallbearers (SAA, ANSA,
inv. no. 3986, notary Nicolaes
Brouwer, fol. 242r).
12 Hirsch 1921, p. 126.
13 'twee hammen, een halff vat
bier, koeckjes, tarrewee broot en
witte broot, boter en kaes' and
'sarvetten, tafellaekens, kannen
en glasen'. SAA, ANSA, inv. no.
1996B, notary Jacob van Loosdrecht, 19 February 1656, p. 566.

Winter Festivals
1 In Anna (also known as
Hanna) Osorio's inventory, drawn
up after her death in 1682, 'Een
Sabbath ende Een hanuca lamp'
('A Sabbat and a Hanukkah lamp')
valued at 4 guilders are listed
under the brassware. SAA, ANSA,
inv. no. 4101, notary Dirk van
Der Groe, 25 August 1682, p. 305.
2 Anna's father was one of the
founders of the Jewish Portuguese
congregation in Amsterdam, and
her husband went so far as to
change his Portuguese name,
Fernando Dias de Britto, to the
Jewish David Abendana. See
Knotter 2024, pp. 52, 61–62.
3 Ben Israel 1645–1647. See
also Moreno-Goldschmidt 2020.
4 J. Hillegers in Haarlem 2011,
p. 118; Booy 2018, pp. 72–74. For
Sinterklaas songs see Booy 2018,
pp. 76–77, and Van Benthem 2009;
for Sinterklaas sweets see I. Day
in Cambridge 2019, pp. 69–71.
5 Wagenberg-ter Hoeven 1997,
pp. 27–58; Rotterdam 2006, pp. 46–
47; J. Hillegers in Haarlem 2011,
pp. 112–113, 122–123.
6 Nannings 1932, pp. 54–57,
72–73.
7 Bartels e.a. 2003.

At Home
1 'Ick en ede niet een zier,
zijnde luij ende alleen besig in
gedachten', Beck 1627–1628
(2014), p. 78.

2 'Oost/ West/ t'huys best',
Visscher 1614, p. 98. The literal
translation of Aesop's 'Οἶκος
φίλος οἶκος ἄριστος' is 'My home
is loved, my home is the best'.
3 Van Aken-Fehmers 2010.
4 Noorman and Van der Maal
2022, pp. 129–135.
5 Loughman and Montias
2000; Fock 2001, p. 110.
6 'daer Onse Lieve Frou in sijt
met haer lieve kint op haer schoot
die Sinte Katrijn die trouring aen
steckt', Van Nesse 1623–1646,
fol. 9r.
7 See Noorman and Van der
Maal 2022, pp. 188–194, for
Maria's life as a spiritual virgin.
8 'verbeeldende de portugees-
che Joode Kerk deser stad, sijne
geschildert door Emanuel Wit',
Kaplan 1998, pp. 149–153. See
also Van Voolen 2017, pp. 105–108.
9 Noorman 2024, p. 125.
10 Rotterdam 2006, pp. 11–16.
11 NEHA, Collectie Familie du
Tour, inv. no. 1, fol. 7v. See also
Lunsingh Scheurleer e.a. 1986–
1992, vol. 6b (1992), p. 533.
12 Fock 1997a, pp. 45–46, 50–61;
Amsterdam 2004, pp. 262–266.
13 'Wie rukt my van het Y tot in
de Grieksche Tempe?/ Hier pronkt
het bly gebloemt. daer lacht het
weelig landt./ De winter heeft geen
macht, om dit priël te dempe'./
De Lent, die 't voorjaar siert, be-
houdt hier eeuwig standt ... weeligh
leeven', Vos 1662, pp. 536–537.
14 'een Somer voor het oogh ...
verlusten ... den boogh [te] ont-
spannen', cited in Fock 2001,
p. 104.
15 For the *zaal*, see p. 58 of this
publication.
16 The inventory, drawn up after
the death of Johan Boudaen Courten in 1716, lists 'twee spiegels'
(two mirrors) and 'twee vergulde
gerridons' (two gilt gueridons) in
the *zaal*. HUA, 26, Familie Des
Tombe, inv. no. 1000, 'Inventaris
en Boedel Cedúle ...', fol. 15v.
See Amsterdam 1952, pp. 250–251,
262, on the furniture. See also
Thornton 1978, pp. 93–94, for
the rise of the 'triade' (the table,
mirror and gueridon set) in France.
See Fock 2000, p. 105, and Fock
2001, p. 108, for the earliest
examples in the Netherlands.

17 'Hortensia del Prado Moeder
van mijn Moeder Zr. Joh. Boudaen 1678', Bruijnen and Van
de Laar 2006, p. 437.
18 The note can be found
among all sorts of genealogical
notes of later date: HUA, 26,
Familie Des Tombe, inv. no. 18.
The portraits are not included in
the 1716 inventory for both the
house in Middelburg as well as
the country residence Kasteel
Popkensburg. G. Wuestman in
Amsterdam 2007, p. 249, pre-
sumes that at the time the note
was made the portraits already
hung in Popkensburg, from
where they were transferred to
the Rijksmuseum. However, it is
more likely that the list was drawn
up upon distribution of the estate,
when the mirror with the Hoeufft
coat of arms – and therefore also
the portraits – were still in the
Middelburg house.
19 For Catharina Fourmenois
see p. 89 of this publication.
20 Heyning 2010, pp. 82–84.
21 For the family history see
ibid. and Boudaen Courten *s.a.*
(2005), pp. 45–47; for the house
and Hortensia's garden, which is
laudingly described by Cats, see
De Stoppelaar 1860, pp. 42–43.
22 For Johan's family book see
also pp. 11, 89, 238 and 256 of
this publication. For the sugar
plantation that Pieter and Johan
jointly owned, see p. 214.
23 Boudaen Courten *s.a.* (2005),
p. 46; cf. also Kooijmans 2016,
pp. 14–18, 353–356. See Boudaen
Courten *s.a.* (2005) for the integral text of the family book.
24 See Ketelaar 2009, pp. 20–22,
for the international context and
a tentative overview of North
Netherlandish family books in
the 17th century.
25 'out sijnde geworden 10 weecken en 2 dagen' and 'ende den
5 januaris 1675 des avondst sijnde
drie koonige avondt in de kerck
tot holwaerdt in de kelder bij sijn
voor ouders en brouders en suster
geset'. Leeuwarden, Fries Museum,
inv. no. PL2003-314.
26 Genesis 17:7.
27 See, for instance, Keblusek
1997, pp. 147–149, for the possession of Bibles in The Hague.

28 Cats 1862, vol. 1, pp. 394, 486. For Cats, see also De Mare 2003, p. 336; for Wittewrongel see Groenendijk 1984, pp. 116–123, and Van Marle 2013, pp. 19–21; for Oomius see ibid., pp. 36–38.
29 Dekker 2001, p.19.
30 Beck 1624 (1993), pp. 36, 222 (17 December); Blaak 2009, pp. 102–103. See Spaans 2024, pp. 37–40, for the *Kalendier der Bybelen* and the popularity of lesson schedules.
31 Blaak 2009, pp. 94–95. See Van der Veen 2000 for the rise of studies in the Northern Netherlands in the 17th century.
32 The diary of Pieter Teding van Berkhout shows that he followed the much-used schedules of the Delft regent Johan van Bleiswijk in 1676, 1692–1693 and 1702–1703. Blaak 2009, pp. 150–151, 171–173. See Spaans 2024 on Van Bleiswijk.
33 See Verheggen 2024 for a discussion of Maria's devotional objects.
34 Van Nesse 1623–1646, fol. 68v.
35 See Noorman and Van der Maal 2022, p. 65, for a more extensive list of furniture and decoration in Maria's *voorkeuken*.
36 With thanks to Iris Jocker, who conducted research on the Klaeuwshofje at Museum Prinsenhof Delft. See Verheggen 2020, pp. 82–85, for the decoration of Catholic home altars and the sale of altar requisites. Compare also De Baar 2003, pp. 277–278, for the Flemish mystic Antoinette Bourignon, who as a child set up a similar altar with a crucifix in her parent's home and prayed before it for nights on end.
37 Levie Bernfeld 2012, pp. 207–210. See Moreno-Goldschmidt 2020, pp. 329–330, for a 17th-century explanation of the use of the *tallit* (prayer shawl) and its accompanying *tzitzit* (fringes or tassels) for Jews in the Dutch Republic.
38 Stolk 2022, pp. 118–122.
39 See Spaans 2024, pp. 45–52, for the rich Protestant catechizing culture.
40 Cf. J.R. Jas in Utrecht 1991, pp. 63–64.
41 Cf. Hamling 2010a. See also Hamling 2010b, pp. 255–273, in

which she goes one step further on English and Scottish households after the Reformation and suggests that religious decoration not only embodied a warning and offered comfort, but that it was also alleged to offer protection and ward off the devil.
42 Blaak 2009, p. 185.
43 For the light-hearted and humorous literature that was mainly intended for a young readership, see Dekker 2001, pp. 19–40. For the production and consumption of news, travelogues, ships' logs and maps, see Pettegree and Der Weduwen 2019, pp. 68–117.
44 For the last category, see, for instance, Schenkeveld 1991, pp. 57–75. For poetry and emblemata, see ibid., pp. 77–92.
45 For this, see Pettegree and Der Weduwen 2019, pp. 45–67, 212–216.
46 Keblusek 1997, p. 158.
47 Pijzel-Dommisse 2000, pp. 142, 288–289.
48 HUA, 26, Familie Des Tombe, inv. no. 1000, 'Inventaris en Boedel Cedúle …', fol. 15v.
49 Leesberg 2015, pp. 29–31. See Buijnsters and Buijnsters-Smets 2005, p. 89, for a historical context of the game.
50 Roberts and Groenendijk 2004, pp. 142–144. For marital problems caused by drinking or gambling see, for instance, Van der Heijden 1998, p. 221.
51 'af scheyt glaesien van danckbaaerheyt', Duquesnoy and Salman 2018, p. 120.
52 Amsterdam 2014, pp. 66–67.
53 A collection of handwritten poems by Johan Boudaen Courten entitled *Poesy* can be found in HUA, 26, Familie Des Tombe, inv. no. 1098, *Poesy*, 1668–1699. A transcription by members of the working group Paleografie in Zeeland (PaiZ) is available via www.zeeuwsarchief.nl/bronnen/transcripties-paiz/cultuur/ (consulted 9 November 2024).
54 Blaak 2009, pp. 50, 94–96; Zijlmans 1999, pp. 157–158, 173–174.
55 L.P. Grijp in The Hague/Antwerp 1994, pp. 63–80, 360–375 (for an overview of the most current instruments).

56 See Beck 1627–1628 (2014), p. 161, for the purchase of the harpsichord on 26 March 1628, and ibid., p. 165, for the purchase of paint 'tot mijn cabinet ende clavesingel' ('for my cabinet and the harpsichord') on 9 April and painting them the same day.
57 NEHA, Collectie Familie du Tour, inv. no. 1, fol. 73r; Lunsingh Scheurleer e.a. 1986–1992, vol. 6b (1992), p. 533.
58 The standard works on Dutch songs and song culture in the 17th century are Grijp 1991 and Veldhorst 2009.
59 Amsterdam 1988, vol. 2, pp. 416, 447, 453–454, with thanks to Leonore van Sloten, who directed us to the two contrafacta in Gesina's album. For the popularity of 'Amarilli mia bella' in the Dutch Republic, see https://top40vandegoudeneeuw.nl/35-amarilli-mia-bella/ (consulted 9 November 2024).
60 See, for instance, Di Stefano 2023 for this virginal.
61 See Veldhorst 2008, pp. 221–223, for the age-old notion that music is medicine and the Dutch interpretation of this in the 17th century.
62 Blaak 2009, pp. 52–53. Cf. also Keblusek 1997, p. 158, for David Beck reading for consolation. 'troostelicke hert-sterckingen', Van Marle 2013. See ibid., pp. 26–28, for Wittewrongel on psalms.
63 M. Kyrova in The Hague/Antwerp 1994, pp. 34–35.
64 Lunsingh Scheurleer 1976, pp. 85–87; Ten Hove and Swiers 2023, p. 68. During its 19th-century restoration, both the foot and the top were replaced, but the shape of the top follows the original.
65 Pijzel-Dommisse 2000, p. 288.
66 HUA, 26, Familie Des Tombe, inv. no. 1000, 'Inventaris en Boedel Cedúle …', fols. 16r, 42r.
67 SAA, ANSA, inv. no. 7532, notary Johannes van Vilekens, 28 January 1709, p. 39. Muurling 2011, p. 218.
68 Blankaart 1683, pp. 84–86. See also Hendriksen 2019, pp. 105–107.
69 Bontekoe and Blankaart 1686, p. 86.
70 Ibid., pp. 93–94.

bibliography

Archives

ATH   Archieven van de Biblioteca Thysiana, Leiden
EsH   Erfgoed (Heritage) 's-Hertogenbosch
GA   Gelders Archief, Arnhem
HCA   High Court of Admiralty, Kew, London
CO   Overijssel Collection
HUA   Het Utrechts Archief (The Utrecht Archives)
NA   Nationaal Archief, The Hague
NEHA   Nederlandsch Economisch-Historisch Archief, International Institute of Social History, Amsterdam
NHA   Noord-Hollands Archief, Haarlem
ONA   Oud Notarieel Archief
RAA   Regionaal Archief Alkmaar
RAB   Rijksarchief in België te Bergen (State Archives of Belgium in Bergen)
SAA   Stadsarchief Amsterdam (City Archives Amsterdam)
SD   Stadsarchief Delft
Tresoar   Archief Fryslân, Leeuwarden

Literature

A

Abels 2010
M.A.W.L.M. Abels, *Tussen sloer en heilige. Beeld en zelfbeeld van Haarlemse en Goudse kloppen in de zeventiende eeuw*, Amsterdam 2009

Van Aken-Fehmers 1999–2001
M.S. van Aken-Fehmers, *Delfts aardewerk. Geschiedenis van een nationaal product*, 2 vols., Zwolle 1999–2001 (vol. 1, 1999; vol. 2, 2001)

Van Aken-Fehmers 2010
M.S. van Aken-Fehmers, '"Van alle soort, gemeen en best". Delfts aardewerk in het Hollandse interieur (1600–1800)', *Desipientia. Zin & Waan* 17 (2010), no. 2, pp. 4–9

Akkerman 1987
K.M. Akkerman, 'Van haarnaald tot pereboom, van ferronnière tot stiftje. De voorhoofdssieraden van de Noordhollandse klederdracht en hun oorsprong', *Antiek* 22 (1987), no. 4, pp. 210–226

Akkerman 2017
K.M. Akkerman, ''n Kleine historie van de haarnaald. Over huwelijksmoraal, jeuk en volksgebruik', *Vind: Geschiedenis, Archeologie, Kunst en Antiek* 25 (2017), no. 7, pp. 44–49

Anonymous 1655
Anonymous, *Nutte en noodige middelen voor de pest. Ofte een bequaame maniere hoe men zich in deezen gevaarlijken tijd zal houden*, Amsterdam 1655

Anonymous 1658 (1670)
Anonymous, *Bewys dat het een predikant met sijn huys-vrouw alleen niet mogelijck en is op 500. guldens eerlijck te leven; want hy nootsakelijck 's jaers dit volgende van doen heeft*, Delft 1670 (original ed. 1658)

Anonymous 1660
Anonymous [J.C.], *De verstandige huys-houder, voor-schryvende de alderwijste wetten om profijtelick, gemackelick en vermakelik te leven, so inde stadt als op 't lant*, Amsterdam 1660

Anonymous 1753
Anonymous, *De ervarene en verstandige Hollandsche Huyshoudster. Onderwijzende alle jonge vrouwen, hoe zij zich in 't bestuuren van het huyshouden moeten gedragen*, Amsterdam 1753

Amsterdam 1952
Th.H. Lunsingh Scheurleer, *Catalogus van meubelen en betimmeringen*, cat. Amsterdam (Rijksmuseum) 1952, 3rd rev. ed. (original ed. 1907)

Amsterdam 1971
C.A. Burgers, A. van Schendel and V. Woldbye, *Geweven boeket*, exh. cat. Amsterdam (Rijksmuseum) 1971

Amsterdam 1988
A. McNeil Kettering, *Drawings from the Ter Borch Studio Estate*, 2 vols., cat. Amsterdam (Rijksmuseum) 1988 (*Catalogus van de Nederlandse tekeningen in het Rijksprentenkabinet, Rijksmuseum, Amsterdam*, vol. 5)

Amsterdam 1993
G. Luijten et al. (ed.), *Dawn of the Golden Age: Northern Netherlandish Art 1580–1620*, exh. cat. Amsterdam (Rijksmuseum) 1993

Amsterdam 1999
J.R. de Lorm, *Amsterdams goud en zilver*, cat. Amsterdam (Rijksmuseum) 1999 (*Catalogi van de verzameling kunstnijverheid van het Rijksmuseum te Amsterdam*, vol. 3)

Amsterdam 2004
E. Hartkamp-Jonxis and H. Smit, *European Tapestries in the Rijksmuseum*, cat. Amsterdam (Rijksmuseum) 2004 (*Catalogi van de verzameling kunstnijverheid van het Rijksmuseum te Amsterdam*, vol. 5)

Amsterdam 2007
J. Bikker et al., *Dutch Paintings of the Seventeenth Century in the Rijksmuseum, Amsterdam. Volume I – Artists Born between 1570 and 1600*, cat. Amsterdam (Rijksmuseum) 2007

Amsterdam 2014
A. Laméris, K. Laméris and W. Laméris, *Glasses and Their Portraits: The Kees Schoonenberg Collection*, cat. Amsterdam (Frides Laméris Glass & Antiques) 2014

Amsterdam 2018
R.J. Baarsen, *Kwab. Ornament als kunst in de eeuw van Rembrandt*, exh. cat. Amsterdam (Rijksmuseum) 2018

Amsterdam/Salem 2015
K.H. Corrigan, J. van Campen and F. Diercks (eds.), *Asia in Amsterdam: The Culture of Luxury in the Golden Age*, exh. cat. Amsterdam (Rijksmuseum)/Salem (Peabody Essex Museum) 2015

359

Antczak and Beaudry 2019
K.A. Antczak and M.C. Beaudry, 'Assemblages of Practice: A Conceptual Framework for Exploring Human–Thing Relations in Archaeology', *Archaeological Dialogues* 26 (2019), no. 2, pp. 87–110

Antwerp 1998
J. Walgrave, *Het labo van de verleiding. Geschiedenis van de make-up/The Laboratory of Seduction: History of Make-up*, exh. cat. Antwerp (Koningin Fabiolazaal) 1998

Arnhem 1997
S. Groenveld, *Wezen en boefjes. Zes eeuwen zorg in wees- en kinderhuizen*, exh. cat. Arnhem (Museum voor Moderne Kunst) 1997

Arnolli and Sloof 2004
G. Arnolli and R. Sloof, *Letter voor letter. Merklappen in de opvoeding van Friese meisjes*, Zwolle 2004

B
De Baar 2003
M. de Baar, 'Voorbij de wereld van kerken en kloosters, relieken en rozenkransen. De geestelijke zoektocht van Antoinette Bourignon (1616–1680)', in A.L. Molendijk, *Materieel christendom. Religie en materiële cultuur in West-Europa*, Hilversum 2003, pp. 273–294

Bakker 2020
J.K. Bakker, 'Eetgewoonten op Vlooienburg. Wat voedselresten ons vertellen', in K. van Kempen and H. Berg (eds.), *Waterlooplein. De buurt binnenstebuiten*, Zutphen 2020, pp. 44–50

Bakker et al. 2006
P.C.M. Bakker, J.M.A. Noordman and M. Rietveld-van Wingerden, *Vijf eeuwen opvoeden in Nederland. Idee en praktijk 1500–2000*, Assen 2006

Barlösius 1991
E. Barlösius, 'Köchin und Koch. Familial-häusliche Essenszubereitung und berufliches Kochen', in T. Ehlert (ed.), *Haushalt und Familie in Mittelalter und früher Neuzeit*, Wiesbaden 1991, pp. 207–218

Bartels 2009
M.H. Bartels, 'Early Medieval Glass Linen Smoothers from the Emporium of Deventer: A Comparative Study of the Context and Use of Glass Linen Smoothers in Deventer, the Low Countries and North-Western Europe (AD 700–1200)', in H. Clevis (ed.), *Medieval Material Culture: Studies in Honour of Jan Thijssen*, Zwolle 2009, pp. 95–113

Bartels 2021
S. Bartels, 'Kaaskoppen en butterboxes', in A. Jager and M. Osnabrugge (eds.), *Op bezoek in de Republiek. Reisverslagen uit de zeventiende en achttiende eeuw*, Zwolle 2021, pp. 34–36

Bartels et al. 2003
M.H. Bartels, W. von Ende and D. Schütte, 'Broodversiering uit de Koekstad. Achttiende-eeuwse patacons uit een kuil aan de Polstraat te Deventer', *Westerheem. Tijdschrift voor de Nederlandse archeologie* 52 (2003), no. 3, pp. 95–107

Beck 1624 (1993)
D. Beck, *Spiegel van mijn leven. Een Haags dagboek uit 1624* (ed. E. Veldhuijzen), Hilversum 1993 (original manuscript 1624) (*Egodocumenten*, vol. 3)

Beck 1627–1628 (2014)
D. Beck, *Mijn voornaamste daden en ontmoetingen. Dagboek van David Beck Arnhem 1627–1628* (ed. J. Blaak), Hilversum 2014 (*Egodocumenten*, vol. 31)

Bedaux 1990
J.B. Bedaux, *The Reality of Symbols: Studies in the Iconology of Netherlandish Art 1400–1800*, The Hague/Maarssen 1990

Ben Israel 1645–1647
M. ben Israel, *Thesouro dos Dinim*, 5 vols., Amsterdam 1645–1647

Van Benthem 2009
H. van Benthem, *Sint-Nicolaasliederen. Oorspronkelijke teksten en melodieën*, Leidschendam 2009

Van den Bergh-Hoogterp and Dubbe 1997
L.E. van den Bergh-Hoogterp and B. Dubbe, *Edele en onedele metalen. De verzamelingen van het Centraal Museum Utrecht*, vol. 4, Utrecht 1997

Den Besten and Den Besten-den Burger 1983
G.J. den Besten and L.S.J. den Besten-den Burger, *Strijken, streek, gestreken. Over de geschiedenis, het gebruik, de stijl, de herkomst, enz. van strijkbouten, plooitangen (...)*, Zutphen 1983

Van Beverwijck 1636
J. van Beverwijck, *Schat der gesontheyt. Met verssen verçiert door heer Jacob Cats*, Dordrecht 1636

Van Beverwijck 1637
J. van Beverwijck, *Steen-Stuck, Aenwijsende den oorspronck, teyckenen, 'tvoor-komen ende ghenesen van Steen ende Graveel*, Dordrecht 1637

Van Beverwijck 1642
J. van Beverwijck, *Schat der ongesontheyt, ofte geneeskonste van de sieckten. met Historyen ende Kopere platen als oock met Verssen van Heer Jacob Cats; Ridder, Raedt-Pensionaris van Hollant*, Dordrecht 1642

Van Beverwijck 1651
J. van Beverwijck, *Inleydinge tot de Hollandtsche Genees-middelen. Ofte kort bericht, dat elck Landt ghenoegh heeft, tot onderhoudt van het Leven, ende de Gesontheyt der Inwoonders*, Amsterdam 1651

Van Beverwijck 1660
J. van Beverwijck, *Alle de wercken, zo in de medicyne als chirurgie*, Amsterdam 1660

Bitter 2009
P. Bitter, 'Toying with Miniatures: Finds of "Doll's-house Items" from Alkmaar', in H. Clevis (ed.), *Medieval Material Culture: Studies in Honour of Jan Thijssen*, Zwolle 2009, pp. 47–65

Bitter 2011
P. Bitter, 'Into the Pit? Waste Management and Cesspit Finds in Alkmaar', in H. Clevis (ed.), *Assembled Articles 4. Symposium on Medieval and Post-medieval Ceramics, Zwolle 16 and 17 September 2010*, Zwolle 2011, pp. 35–36

Bitter 2012
P. Bitter, 'Young in Old Alkmaar: Some Observations on Childhood and Adolescence in Alkmaar', in C. Kimminus-Schneider, M. Schneider and D. Oltersdorf (eds.), *Lübecker Kolloquium zur Stadtarchäologie im Hanseraum VIII: Kindheit und Jugend, Ausbildung und Friezeit*, Lübeck 2012, pp. 81–96

Bitter 2016
P. Bitter, *Schaven aan Alkmaar: 25 jaar archeologisch onderzoek in beeld*, Alkmaar 2016

Bitter 2022
P. Bitter (ed.), *Zeven eeuwen wonen, werken en winkelen in de Langestraat van Alkmaar*, vol. 2, Vondstmateriaal, Rapport Archeologie en Monumenten Alkmaar (RAMA) 25, Alkmaar 2022

Blaak 2004
J. Blaak, *Literacy in Everyday Life: Reading and Writing in Early Modern Dutch Diaries*, Hilversum 2009 (*Egodocuments and History Series*, vol. 2)

Blaak 2012
J. Blaak, 'Een schoolmeester in Arnhem. Het Journael ofte Dagboeckje van David Beck, 1626–1628', *aHt* 4 (2012), pp. 168–185

Blankaart 1683
S. Blankaart, *De borgerlyke tafel, om lang gesond sonder ziekten te leven. Waar in van yder spijse in 't besonder gehandelt werd. Mitsgaders een beknopte manier van de spijsen voor te snijden, en een onderrechting der schikkelijke wijsen, die men aan de tafel moet houden. Nevens De Schola Salernitana*, Amsterdam 1683

Blankaart 1684
S. Blankaart, *Verhandelinge van de opvoedinge en ziekten der kinderen*, Amsterdam 1684

Blijleven 2022
R. Blijleven, *Wijn in Nederland. Een wondermiddel voor economie & gezondheid*, Zutphen 2022

Blom et al. 1999
F.R.E. Blom, H.G. Bruin and K. Ottenheym, *Domus. Het huis van Constantijn Huygens in Den Haag*, Zutphen 1999

Boekholt and De Booy 1987
P.T.F.M. Boekholt and E.P. de Booy, *Geschiedenis van de school in Nederland vanaf de middeleeuwen tot aan de huidige tijd*, Assen 1987

Bontekoe and Blankaart 1686
C. Bontekoe and S. Blankaart, *Gebruik en Mis-bruik van de Thee, Mitsgaders een Verhandelinge wegens de Deugden en Kragten van de Tabak (...)*, The Hague/Amsterdam 1686

De Booy 1977
E.P. de Booy, 'Het "basisonderwijs" in de zeventiende en achttiende eeuw – De Stichtse dorpsscholen', *Bijdragen en Mededelingen betreffende de Geschiedenis der Nederlanden* 92 (1977), pp. 208–222

Booy 2018
F. Booy, '"Sinter-Klaes, ô Heil'ge Man, hoort mijn bidden en mijn smeken!" Het sinterklaasfeest in zeventiende-eeuwse teksten', *Boekenwereld* 34 (2018), no. 4, pp. 72–77

Bos 1998
S. Bos, '*Uyt liefde tot malcander'. Onderlinge hulpverlening binnen de Noord-Nederlandse gilden in internationaal perspectief (1570–1820)*, Amsterdam 1998 (*IISG Studies + Essays*, vol. 27)

Boston 2015
R. Baer et al., *Class Distinctions: Dutch Painting in the Age of Rembrandt and Vermeer*, exh. cat. Boston (Museum of Fine Arts) 2015

Boudaen Courten s.a. (2005)
P. Boudaen Courten, 'Familjie boeckje van dheer Pieter Boudaen Courten en sijn huijsvrouw Catharina Fourmenois' (transcr. G. Wuestman), *Bulletin van het Rijksmuseum* 53 (2005), no. 1, pp. 52–61

Brouwer 2014
J. Brouwer, *Levenstekens. Gekaapte brieven uit het rampjaar 1672*, Hilversum 2014

Bruijnen 2002
Y. Bruijnen, 'Over de Twelf Maendekens en de Vier Tyden 's iaers. De maanden en de jaargetijden in de kunst van de Nederlanden circa 1500 tot 1750', in Y. Bruijnen and P. Huys Janssen (eds.), *De vier jaargetijden in de kunst van de Nederlanden 1500–1750*, exh. cat. Den Bosch (Het Noordbrabants Museum)/Leuven (Stedelijk Museum Vander Kelen-Mertens) 2002, pp. 51–71

Bruijnen and Van de Laar 2006
Y. Bruijnen and M. van de Laar, 'Geschreven, gestempeld of geplakt. Verscholen informatie op de keerzijde van schilderijen', *Bulletin van het Rijksmuseum* 54 (2006), no. 4, pp. 428–449

Buijnsters and Buijnsters-Smets 2005
P.J. Buijnsters and L. Buijnsters-Smets, *Papertoys. Speelprenten en papieren speelgoed in Nederland (1640–1920)*, Zwolle 2005

Buijsen 2010
E. Buijsen, *De jonge Vermeer*, Zwolle 2010

Buisman 1996
J. Buisman, *Duizend jaar weer, wind en water in de Lage Landen. Deel 4: 1575–1675*, Franeker 1996

Burgers 1960
C.A. Burgers, 'De Friese wapens tussen andere wapeninwevingen in Haarlemse linnen tafeldamasten uit de 17de eeuw', *De Vrije Fries* 44 (1960), pp. 123–148

Van Burkom 2001
F. van Burkom (ed.), *Leven in toen. Vier eeuwen Nederlands interieur in beeld*, Zwolle 2001

Buursma 2009
A. Buursma, '*Dese bekommerlijke tijden'. Armenzorg, armen en armoede in de stad Groningen 1594–1795*, Assen 2009 (*Groninger Historische Reeks*, vol. 37)

C

Cambridge 2019
V.J. Avery and M.T. Calaresu (eds.), *Feast & Fast: The Art of Food in Europe, 1500–1800*, exh. cat. Cambridge (Fitzwilliam Museum) 2019

Carlson 1993
M. Carlson, *Domestic Service in a Changing City Economy: Rotterdam, 1680–1780*, Madison 1993 (thesis University of Wisconsin)

Casimiro and Newstead 2019
T.M. Casimiro and S. Newstead, '400 Years of Water Consumption: Early Modern Pottery Cups in Portugal', *Ophiussa: Revista do centro de arqueologia da universidade de Lisboa* 3 (2019), pp. 145–153

Caspers 2003
C. Caspers, 'Tegen de pest en tegen de ketters. Amuletten en hun werking volgens de Brabantse norbertijn Augustinus Wichmans in zijn Apotheca spiritualium pharmacorum (1626), in A.L. Molendijk (ed.), *Materieel christendom. Religie en materiële cultuur in West-Europa*, Hilversum 2003, pp. 249–272

Cats 1862
J. Cats, *Alle de wercken* (ed. J. van Vloten), 2 vols., Zwolle 1862

Chomel and De Chalmot 1778–1793
N. Chomel and J.A. de Chalmot, *Algemeen huishoudelijk-, natuur-, zedekundig- en konst-woordenboek (...)*, 7 vols., 1778–1793

Christen and Christen 2003
A.G. Christen and J.A. Christen, 'A Historical Glimpse of Toothpick Use: Etiquette, Oral and Medical Conditions', *Journal of the History of Dentistry* 51 (2003), no. 2, pp. 61–69

De Clercq 2016
D. de Clercq, 'De huwelijksring van Michiel Block en Aeltje Anslo. Doperse rijkdom in de Gouden Eeuw', *Gen.magazine* 22 (2016), no. 3, pp. 44–47

Clevis 2001
H. Clevis, *Zwolle ondergronds. Zeven blikvangers van archeologische vondsten in Zwolle*, Zwolle 2001

Colenbrander 2013
S. Colenbrander, *When Weaving Flourished: The Silk Industry in Amsterdam and Haarlem 1585-1750*, Leiden 2013

Corbeau 1993
M. Corbeau, 'Pronken en koken. Beeld en realiteit van keukens in het vroegmoderne Hollandse binnenhuis', *Volkskundig Bulletin* 19 (1993), pp. 354–379

Crawford 1981
P. Crawford, 'Attitudes to Menstruation in Seventeenth-Century England', *Past & Present* 91 (1981), no. 1, pp. 47–73

D

Daleman 2021
M. Daleman, 'Portable Antiquities of the Netherlands (PAN). Ontwikkelingen en vondsten uit het afgelopen jaar belicht', *De Vrije Fries* 101 (2021), pp. 176–179

Van Dekken 2009
M. van Dekken, *Brouwen, branden en bedienen. Werkende vrouwen in de Nederlandse dranknijverheid, 1500-1800*, Utrecht 2009 (diss. Utrecht University)

Dekker 1979
R.M. Dekker, *Oproeren in Holland gezien door tijdgenoten. Ooggetuigenverslagen van oproeren in de provincie Holland ten tijde van de Republiek (1690–1750)*, Assen 1979

Dekker 1994
R.M. Dekker, 'Moeders en kinderen in de zeventiende eeuw. Opvattingen over moederschap in de autobiografie van Hermannus Verbeecq', in A.J. Gelderblom and H. Hendrix (eds.), *De vrouw in de Renaissance*, Amsterdam 1994, pp. 58–73

Dekker 1995
R.M. Dekker, *Uit de schaduw in 't grote licht. Kinderen in egodocumenten van de Gouden Eeuw tot de Romantiek*, Amsterdam 1995

Dekker 2001
R.M. Dekker, *Humour in Dutch Culture of the Golden Age*, London 2001

Dekker 2006
J.J.H. Dekker, *Het verlangen naar opvoeden. Over de groei van de pedagogische ruimte in Nederland sinds de Gouden Eeuw tot omstreeks 1900*, Amsterdam 2006

Den Bosch 2000
P. Huys Janssen (ed.), *Meesters van het zuiden. Barokschilders rondom Rubens*, exh. cat. Den Bosch (Noordbrabants Museum) 2000

The Hague 2005
H.H. Pijzel-Dommisse, *Haags goud en zilver. Edelsmeedkunst uit de Hofstad*, exh. cat. The Hague (Gemeentemuseum The Hague) 2005

The Hague 2015
H.H. Pijzel-Dommisse (ed.), *Nederland dineert. Vier eeuwen tafelcultuur*, exh. cat. The Hague (Gemeentemuseum The Hague) 2015

The Hague/Antwerp 1994
E. Buijsen and L.P. Grijp (eds.), *The Hoogsteder Exhibition of Music and Painting in the Golden Age*, exh. cat. The Hague (Hoogsteder & Hoogsteder)/ Antwerp (Hessenhuis) 1994

Denver/Newark 2001
M. Westermann, *Art & Home: Dutch Interiors in the Age of Rembrandt*, exh. cat. Denver (Denver Art Museum)/Newark (Newark Museum) 2001

Descola 2013
P. Descola, *Beyond Nature and Culture* (trans. J. Lloyd), Chicago/ London 2013 (original ed. *Par-dela nature et culture*, Paris 2005)

Van Deursen 1991
A.Th. van Deursen, *Mensen van klein vermogen. Het kopergeld van de Gouden Eeuw*, Amsterdam 1991

Van Deursen 1994
A.Th. van Deursen, *Een dorp in de polder. Graft in de zeventiende eeuw*, Amsterdam 1994

Dibbits 2001
H.C. Dibbits, *Vertrouwd bezit. Materiële cultuur in Doesburg en Maassluis 1650–1800*, Nijmegen 2001

Diercks 2024
F. Diercks, 'Goudbestek', *Ons Amsterdam* 76 (2024), no. 10, https://onsamsterdam.nl/ artikelen/goudbestek

Van Dijk 1999
L. van Dijk, *Glans langs de IJssel. Zilver uit Zutphen, Deventer, Zwolle en Kampen*, Zwolle 1999

Dodonaeus 1644
R. Dodonaeus, *Herbarius oft Cruydt-Boeck*, Antwerp 1644

Van Domselaer 1665
T. van Domselaer, *Beschrijvinge van Amsterdam*, Amsterdam 1665

Van Doorninck and Kuijpers 1993
M. van Doorninck and E. Kuijpers, *De geschoolde stad. Onderwijs in Amsterdam in de Gouden Eeuw*, Amsterdam 1993

Duijn et al. 2018
D.M. Duijn, C.P. Schrickx, L. Kuijvenhoven-Groeneweg and M.H. Bartels, *Een huwelijk aan diggelen. Het turbulente leven van een Enkhuizer echtpaar in de Gouden Eeuw*, Edam 2018

Duquesnoy and Salman 2018
L. Duquesnoy and J.L. Salman, *De handelsgeest van Isaac Pool. Dagboek van een Amsterdammer in de Gouden Eeuw*, Hilversum 2018

E
Van Eeghen 1960
I.H. van Eeghen, 'Het Deutzen Hofje', *Jaarboek van het Genootschap Amstelodamum* 52 (1960), pp. 97–123

Van Eeghen 2012
I.H. van Eeghen (trans. J. Hillegers), 'The Amsterdam Guild of Saint Luke in the 17th Century', *Journal of Historians of Netherlandish Art* 4 (2012), no. 2, DOI: 10.5092/Jhna.2012.4.2.4

Eibach 2011
J. Eibach, 'Das offene Haus. Kommunikative Praxis im sozialen Nahraum der europäischen Frühen Neuzeit', *Zeitschrift für Historische Forschung* 38 (2011), no. 4, pp. 621–664

Ekkart 1978–1979
R.E.O. Ekkart, 'Familiekroniek Van Heemskerck en Van Swanenburg', *Jaarboek van het Centraal Bureau voor Genealogie* 32 (1978), pp. 41–70, and 33 (1979), pp. 44–75

Van Elburg 2022
W. van Elburg, *Met de deur in huis. Historische woonhuisplattegronden in Nederland. De typologie van de entreeruimte ca. 1550–1950*, Amsterdam 2022

Enschede 2018
R.E.O. Ekkart and C. van den Donk, *Lief & leed. Realisme en fantasie in Nederlandse familiegroepen uit de zeventiende en achttiende eeuw*, exh. cat. Enschede (Rijksmuseum Twenthe) 2018

Erasmus 1530 (1693)
D. Erasmus, *Van de borgerlyke wellevendheid der kinderlyke zeden* (trans. M. Komans), Amsterdam 1693 (original ed. 1530)

Exalto 2023
J. Exalto, 'Catechism Primers in the Netherlands', in B. Juska-Bacher et al. (ed.), *Learning to Read, Learning Religion: Europe from the 16th to the 19th Centuries*, Amsterdam 2023, pp. 204–217

F
De Fijne 1694
P. de Fijne, *Het leeven en eenige bysondere voorvallen van Passchier de Fyne*, Vrederijk-Stad 1694

Fock 1982
C.W. Fock, 'Het eerste huwelijk van Pieter de la Court in 1657', *Jaarboekje voor geschiedenis en oudheidkunde van Leiden en omstreken* 74 (1982), pp. 72–85

Fock 1997a
C.W. Fock, '"Kleet den wand van 't graft pallais in tapijt: ontzie geen kosten". Tapijten in het burgerinterieur ten tijde van de Republiek', *Textielhistorische Bijdragen* 37 (1997), pp. 41–76

Fock 1997b
C.W. Fock, 'Verwarmd door de bijbel. De ijzeren kachel in het zeventiende-eeuwse Nederlandse interieur', *Antiek* 31 (1997), pp. 462–483

Fock 1998
C.W. Fock, 'Werkelijkheid of schijn. Het beeld van het Hollandse interieur in de zeventiende-eeuwse genreschilderkunst', *Oud Holland* 112 (1998), no. 4, pp. 187–246

Fock 2000
C.W. Fock, 'The décor of domestic entertaining at the time of the Dutch Republic', in J. de Jong et al. (ed.), *Wooncultuur in de Nederlanden/The Art of Home in the Netherlands 1500–1800*, Zwolle 2000 (*Nederlands Kunsthistorisch Jaarboek/Netherlands Yearbook For History of Art*, vol. 51), pp. 103–135

Fock 2001
C.W. Fock (ed.), *Het Nederlandse interieur in beeld, 1600–1900*, Zwolle 2001

Fokkens 1662
M. Fokkens, *Beschrijvinge der wijdtvermaarde koop-stadt Amstelredam*, Amsterdam 1662

Le Francq van Berkhey 1772–1776
J. Le Francq van Berkhey, *Natuurlyke historie van Holland*, vol. 3, Amsterdam 1772–1776

Franits 1986
W. Franits, 'The Family Saying Grace: A Theme in Dutch Art of the Seventeenth Century', *Simiolus. Netherlands Quarterly for the History of Art* 16 (1986), no. 1, pp. 36–49

Franits 1993
W. Franits, *Paragons of Virtue: Women and Domesticity in Seventeenth-Century Dutch Art*, Cambridge 1993

Frijhoff and Spies 1999
W.Th.M. Frijhoff and M. Spies, *1650. Bevochten eendracht*, The Hague 1999

G
Gawronski and Jayasena 2007
J. Gawronski and R. Jayasena, 'Opgraving van een mikwe in de Nieuwe Synagoge', *Amsterdamse Archeologische Rapporten (AAR)* 8 (2007), pp. 1–44

Gentilcore 2016
D. Gentilcore, *Food and Health in Early Modern Europe: Diet, Medicine and Society, 1450–1800*, London 2016

Goedings 1998
T. Goedings, 'Een bijzonder rederijkersmanuscript. Het *Ghedenckboeck* van de schilder Jan Sieuwertsz Kolm (1590–1637)', *Amstelodamum* 85 (1998), pp. 194–209

Goeree 1681
W. Goeree, *D'Algemeene Bouw-kunde Volgens d'Antyke en heden-daagse Manier*, Amsterdam 1681

Grijp 1991
L.P. Grijp, *Het Nederlandse lied in de Gouden Eeuw. Het mechanisme van de contrafactuur*. *Amsterdam*, Utrecht 1991 (diss. Utrecht University)

Groenendijk 1984
L.F. Groenendijk, *De nadere Reformatie van het gezin. De visie van Petrus Wittewrongel op de christelijke huishouding*, Dordrecht 1984

Groenendijk 2004
L.F. Groenendijk, 'Jeugd en deugd. Een onderzoek van preken en andere stichtelijke literatuur uit de zeventiende en achttiende eeuw', in L.F. Groenendijk and B.B. Roberts (eds.), *Losbandige jeugd. Jongeren en moraal in de Nederlanden tijdens de late Middel-eeuwen en de Vroegmoderne Tijd*, Hilversum 2004

Grooss 2001
K. Grooss, 'Spoelen met zeepwater voorkwam zwangerschappen in de 17de eeuw', *de Volkskrant*, 26 juni 2001

H
De Haan 2005
J.B.H. de Haan, *'Hier ziet men uit paleizen'. Het Groninger interieur in de zeventiende en achttiende eeuw*, Assen 2005 (*Groninger Historische Reeks*, vol. 31) (diss. University of Groningen)

Haarlem 1986
E.S. de Jongh, *Portretten van echt en trouw. Huwelijk en gezin in de Nederlandse kunst van de zeventiende eeuw*, exh. cat. Haarlem (Frans Halsmuseum) 1986

Haarlem 2000
J.B.M.F. Bedaux and R.E.O. Ekkart (eds.), *Pride and Joy: Children's Portraits in the Netherlands, 1500–1700*, exh. cat. Haarlem (Frans Hals Museum) 2000

Haarlem 2011
A. Tummers (ed.), *De Gouden Eeuw viert feest*, exh. cat. Haarlem (Frans Hals Museum) 2011

Van der Hagen 1699
P. van der Hagen, *De Heydelbergh-sche catechismus, verklaert in twee-en-vijftigh predicatien, met vier Inleudinghs predicatien*, Amsterdam 1699

Haks 1985
D. Haks, *Huwelijk en gezin in Holland in de 17de en 18de eeuw*, Utrecht 1985 (2de ed.)

Van der Ham 2010
G. van der Ham, 'The Clergyman and his Grandson: The Story of a Family', *The Rijksmuseum Bulletin* 58 (2010), no. 4, pp. 366–388

Hamling 2010a
T. Hamling, 'Reconciling Image and Object: Religious Imagery in Protestant Interior Decoration', in T. Hamling and C. Richardson (eds.), *Everyday Objects: Medieval and Early Modern Material Culture and its Meanings*, Farnham 2010, pp. 321–334

Hamling 2010b
T. Hamling, *Decorating the 'Godly' Household: Religious Art in Post-Reformation Britain*, New Haven 2010

Van der Heijden 1998
M.P.C. van der Heijden, *Huwelijk in Holland. Stedelijke rechtspraak en kerkelijke tucht 1550–1700*, Amsterdam 1998

Hell 2014
M. Hell, 'Bancken, Margaretha van', *Digitaal Vrouwenlexicon van Nederland* (2014), https://resources.huygens.knaw.nl/vrouwenlexicon/lemmata/data/Bancken

Hell 2024
M. Hell, *Verloren wereld in de Amstelbocht. Leven op Vlooien-burg, 1600–1815*, Zutphen 2024

Hell and Meijer 2019
M. Hell and F. Meijer, 'Uit eten in Amsterdam', in S. Bosmans and M. Klein (eds.), *De smaak van Am-sterdam. 700 jaar stedelijke eetcul-tuur*, Amsterdam 2019, pp. 38–71, 195–199 (*Jaarboek van het Genoot-schap Amstelodamum*, vol. 111)

Hendriksen 2019
M. Hendriksen, 'Blankaart en Bontekoe. Smaak, geneeskunde en gezondheid in de Lage Landen rond 1700', *Tijdschrift voor Gezondheidszorg en Ethiek* 29 (2019), no. 4, pp. 104–109

Heurneman 2002
W.A. Heurneman, 'Pillengift, papegaai en patrijzenjacht. Huiselijk leven en vrijetijds-besteding', *Erfgenamen aan het Janskerkhof. De familie Martens in Utrecht, 1628–1972*, Utrecht 2002 (*Jaarboek Oud-Utrecht 2002*), pp. 111–150

Van den Heuvel 2018
D.W.A.G. van den Heuvel, 'A Mar-ket Economy', in H.J. Helmers and G.H. Janssen (eds.), *The Cambridge Companion to the Dutch Golden Age*, Cambridge 2018 (*Cambridge Companions to Culture*), pp. 149–165

Van den Heuvel (forthcoming)
D.W.A.G. van den Heuvel, *Gender and Urban Space in the Global City: Amsterdam, Batavia, and Edo (1600–1850)* (forthcoming)

Heyning 2010
C.E. Heyning, 'Een kostbare aanwinst. Een tazza van de familie Courten', *Zeeland. Tijdschrift van het Koninklijk Zeeuwsch Genoot-schap der Wetenschappen* 19 (2010), no. 3, pp. 82–87

Hirsch 1921
R.J. Hirsch, *Doodenritueel in de Nederlanden vóór 1700*, Amster-dam 1921 (diss. University of Amsterdam)

Hirsch 2023
A. Hirsch, *The History of Women in 101 Objects. A Walk through Female History*, Edinburgh 2023

L'Honoré Naber 1930
S.P. L'Honoré Naber, *Walvisch-vaarten, overwinteringen en jacht-bedrijven in het hooge Noorden 1633–1635*, Utrecht 1930

Hoorn 2016
E. Blanken (ed.), *Jan Albertsz Rotius. Meesterschilder van Hoorn*, exh. cat. Hoorn (Westfries Museum) 2016

Houtzager and Verschuyl 2001
H.L. Houtzager and M.E. Verschuyl, 'De behandeling van blaasstenen in het verleden: Willem Boenaert, steensnijder te Zierikzee', *Tijdschrift voor Geneeskunde* 57 (2001), no. 19, pp. 1371–1374

Ten Hove and Swiers 2023
J. ten Hove and S. Swiers, *Het vrouwenhuis van Aleida Greve. Hofje vol historie*, Zwolle 2023

Hulst 2013
M. Hulst, 'Een bijzondere kelderfles uit de beerput. Een vroeg 17de-eeuwse gegraveerde gelegenheidsfles, opgegraven in Amsterdam', *De Oude Flesch* 133 (2013), pp. 13–15

Huygens s.a. (2003)
C. Huygens, *Mijn leven verteld aan mijn kinderen in twee boeken* (trans. and ed. F.R.E. Blom), 2 vols., Amsterdam 2003

I
IJzereef 1987
G. IJzereef, 'De vleesconsumptie op Vlooyenburg in de zeventiende eeuw', in R. Kistemaker and T. Levie Bernfeld (eds.), *Éxodo. Portugezen in Amsterdam, 1600–1680*, Amsterdam 1987, pp. 25–31

J
Jacobs 1626
H. Jacobs, *Den schat der armen oft een medecijn-boecxken*, Antwerp 1626

De Jager 1990
R. de Jager, 'Meester, leerjongen, leertijd. Een analyse van zeventiende-eeuwse Noord-Nederlandse leerlingcontracten van kunstschilders, goud- en zilversmeden', *Oud Holland* 104 (1990), pp. 69–111

Janssen 2017
G.H. Janssen, 'The Republic of the Refugees: Early Modern Migrations and the Dutch Experience', *The Historical Journal* 60 (2017), no. 1, pp. 233–252

Jobse-van Putten 1996
J.J. Jobse-van Putten, *Eenvoudig maar voedzaam. Cultuurgeschiedenis van de dagelijkse maaltijd in Nederland*, Nijmegen/Amsterdam 1996 (2nd rev. ed.)

De Jonge and Ottenheym 2007
K. de Jonge and K. Ottenheym (eds.), *Unity and Discontinuity: Architectural Relationships between the Southern and Northern Low Countries 1530–1700*, Turnhout 2007

De Jongh 2014
E.S. de Jongh, 'Aan de maaltijd. Voeden en opvoeden aan de vroegmoderne eettafel', *Kunstschrift* 58 (2014), no. 4, pp. 18–25

K
Kaplan 1998
Y. Kaplan, 'For Whom did Emanuel de Witte Paint his Three Pictures of the Sephardic Synagogue in Amsterdam?', *Studia Rosenthaliana* 32 (1998), no. 2, pp. 133–154

Keblusek 1997
M. Keblusek, *Boeken in de hofstad. Haagse boekcultuur in de Gouden Eeuw*, Hilversum 1997 (*Hollandse studiën*, vol. 33)

Keijser et al. 2021
H. Keijser, M. Knotter and L. Meiboom (eds.), *Rammelaars en rinkelbellen. De collectie van Heinz Keijser*, Zutphen 2021

Ketelaar 2009
E. Ketelaar, 'The Genealogical Gaze: Family Identities and Family Archives in the Fourteenth to Seventeenth Centuries', *Libraries & the Cultural Record* 44 (2009), no. 1 (*Personal Papers in History: Papers from the Third International Conference on the History of Records and Archives*), pp. 9–28

Der Kinderen-Besier 1950
J.H. der Kinderen-Besier, *Spelevaart der Mode. De kledij onzer voorouders in de zeventiende eeuw*, Amsterdam 1950

Kloek 2009
E. Kloek, *Vrouw des huizes. Een cultuurgeschiedenis van de Hollandse huisvrouw*, Amsterdam 2009

Kloosterman 1984
G.J. Kloosterman, 'Verloskundige kanttekeningen bij vrouw Schraders "Memoryboeck"', in C. Schrader, *Memoryboeck van een Friese vroedvrouw 1693–1745*, Amsterdam 1984, pp. 47–79

Knoeff 2017
R. Knoeff (ed.), *Gelukkig gezond! Histories of Healthy Ageing*, exh. cat. Groningen (University Museum, University of Groningen) 2017

Knoester and Graafhuis 1970
H. Knoester and A. Graafhuis, 'Het kasboek van Mr. Carel Martens 1602–1649', *Jaarboek Oud-Utrecht* (1970), pp. 154–210

Knotter 2024
M. Knotter, 'Rembrandt and His (Jewish) Neighbors: A Stroll Through the Neighborhood', in M. Knotter and G. Schwartz (eds.), *Rembrandt Seen Through Jewish Eyes: The Artist's Meaning to Jews from His Time to Ours*, Amsterdam 2024, pp. 45–69

Koelman 1679
J. Koelman, *De pligten der ouders, in kinderen voor Godt op te voeden. Nevens dryderley catechismus, als mede twintig exempelen, van godtzalige en vroeg stervende jonge kinderen*, Amsterdam 1679

Kok 1970
H.L. Kok, *De geschiedenis van de laatste eer in Nederland*, Lochem 1970

Koldeweij 2001
E.F. Koldeweij, 'Goudleren behangsels in Hoorn', in C. Boschma-Aarnoudse, *Het Statenlogement in Hoorn. Dit logiment der Heeren Gecommitteerde Raden van 't Noorderquartier eertijds het klooster der Jeronijmiters*, Hoorn 2001, pp. 185–196 (*Bouwhistorische Reeks Hoorn*, vol. 10)

Kooijmans 2004
L. Kooijmans, *De doodskunstenaar. De anatomische lessen van Frederik Ruysch*, Amsterdam 2004

Kooijmans 2016
L. Kooijmans, *Vriendschap en de kunst van het overleven in de zeventiende en achttiende eeuw*, Amsterdam 2016, 2nd rev. ed. (original ed. 1997)

Kooijmans 2023
L. Kooijmans, *Melancholie in de Gouden Eeuw*, Amsterdam 2023

Koorn 2013
F. Koorn, *Elisabeth Strouven*, in E. Kloek (ed.), *1001 vrouwen uit de Nederlandse geschiedenis*, Nijmegen 2013, pp. 323–325

Koorn 2021
F.W.J. Koorn, 'Strouven, Elisabeth', *Digitaal Vrouwenlexicon van Nederland* (2021), https://resources. huygens.knaw.nl/vrouwenlexicon/ lemmata/data/Strouven,%20 Elisabeth

De Kreyger 2011
F. de Kreyger, *Strijkglazen in de Lage Landen. Status quaestionis, inventarisatie en analyse voor Nederland en Vlaanderen*, Ghent 2011 (unpub. diss. Ghent University)

Kuijpers 2005
E. Kuijpers, *Migrantenstad. Immigranten en sociale verhoudingen in 17e-eeuws Amsterdam*, Hilversum 2005

Kuijpers and Prak 2002
E. Kuijpers and M. Prak, 'Burger, ingezetene, vreemdeling: burgerschap in Amsterdam in de 17e en 18e eeuw', in J.J. Kloek and C.P.H.M. Tilmans, *Burger. Een geschiedenis van het begrip 'burger' in de Nederlanden van de Middeleeuwen tot de 21ste eeuw*, Amsterdam 2002, pp. 113–132

Kuus 1994
S. Kuus, 'Rokkekinderen in de Nederlanden 1560–1660. Een onderzoek naar het verschil in kleding tussen meisjes en jongens in rokken', *Kostuum. Jaaruitgave van de Nederlandse kostuumvereniging voor mode en streekdracht* (1994), pp. 6–13

L
Laing 2000
R.A. Laing, 'Commemorative Family Medals during the DEIC Period', *Historia* 45 (2000), no. 2, pp. 438–450

Landwehr 1995
J. Landwehr, *Het Nederlandse kookboek 1510–1945. Een bibliografisch overzicht*, 't Goy-Houten 1995

Lange 2017
S. Lange, *Uit het juiste hout gesneden. Houten gebruiksvoorwerpen uit archeologische context tot 1300 n.Chr.*, Amersfoort 2017 (*Nederlandsche Archeologische Rapporten*, vol. 54)

Leesberg 2015
M. Leesberg, '*El Juego Real de Cupido*: A Spanish Board Game Published in Antwerp, c. 1620', *Delineavit et Sculpsit* 39 (2015), pp. 23–43

Leeuwarden/Kassel 2018
M.E. Stoter (ed.), *Rembrandt & Saskia. Liefde in de Gouden Eeuw*, exh. cat. Leeuwarden (Fries Museum)/Kassel (Museumlandschaft Hessen Kassel, Gemäldegalerie Alte Meister) 2018

Van Leeuwen 2023
S. van Leeuwen, '"Met Diamanten Omset": Hoop Rings in the Northern Netherlands (1600–1700)', *The Rijksmuseum Bulletin* 71 (2023), no. 1, pp. 42–61

Lenarduzzi 2019
C. Lenarduzzi, *Katholiek in de Republiek. De belevingswereld van een religieuze minderheid 1570–1750*, Nijmegen 2019

Lesger 2013
C.I. Lesger, *Het winkellandschap van Amsterdam. Stedelijke structuur en winkelbedrijf in de vroegmoderne en moderne tijd, 1550–2000*, Hilversum 2013

Lesger 2024
C.I. Lesger, *Power and Urban Space in Pre-Modern Holland: Arenas of Appropriation in the Netherlands, 1500–1850*, London 2024

Levie Bernfeld 2012
T. Levie Bernfeld, 'Matters Matter: Material Culture of Dutch Sephardim (1600–1750)', *Studia Rosenthaliana* 44 (2012), pp. 191–216

Levie Bernfeld 2020
T. Levie Bernfeld, 'Masters, Maids, and Mistresses: Aspects of Domestic Life among the Portuguese Jews in the Seventeenth-Century Dutch Republic', in S. Rauschenbach (ed.), *Sefardische Perspektiven/Sephardic Perspectives*, Leipzig 2020, pp. 11–40

London 2006
M. Ajmar-Wollheim and F. Dennis (eds.), *At Home in Renaissance Italy*, exh. cat. London (Victoria and Albert Museum) 2006

Longman 2002
C. Longman, 'Joodse menstruatieriten: symbool van vrouwenonderdrukking of vrouwelijke identiteit?', *Tijdschrift voor Seksuologie* 26 (2002), pp. 146–152

Loughman and Montias 2000
J. Loughman and J.M. Montias, *Public and Private Spaces: Works of Art in Seventeenth-Century Dutch Houses*, Zwolle 2000 (*Studies in Netherlandish Art and Cultural History*, vol. 3)

Lugtigheid 2021
D.O.R. Lugtigheid, *Van aardse stof tot hemels lof. De transitie van achttiende-eeuwse Noord-Nederlandse damesjapon van modeartikel tot kerkelijk gewaad in de katholieke eredienst*, Amsterdam 2021 (diss. University of Amsterdam)

Lunsingh Scheurleer 1971
Th.H. Lunsingh Scheurleer, 'Enkele oude Nederlandse kraamgebruiken', *Antiek* 6 (1971), pp. 297–332

Lunsingh Scheurleer 1976
Th.H. Lunsingh Scheurleer, 'The Dutch at the Tea Table', *The Connoisseur* 193 (1976), pp. 85–93

Lunsingh Scheurleer et al. 1986–1992
Th.H. Lunsingh Scheurleer, C.W. Fock and A.J. van Dissel, *Het Rapenburg. Geschiedenis van een Leidse gracht*, 6 vols., Leiden 1986–1992

M
Magalotti 1945
L. Magalotti, *Lettere sopra i buccheri, con l'aggiunta di lettere contro l'ateismo, scientifiche ed erudite, e di relazioni varie* (ed. M. Praz), Florence 1945

De Mare 2001
H. de Mare, 'Het huis, de natuur en het vroegmoderne architectonisch kennissysteem van Simon Stevin', in J. de Jong et al. (eds.), *Wooncultuur in de Nederlanden 1500–1800/The Art of Home in the Netherlands 1500–1800*, Zwolle 2001 (*Nederlands Kunsthistorisch Jaarboek/Netherlands Yearbook for History of Art*, vol. 51), pp. 34–59

De Mare 2003
H. de Mare, *Het huis en de regels van het denken. Een cultuurhistorisch onderzoek naar het werk van Simon Stevin, Jacob Cats en Pieter de Hoogh*, Amsterdam 2003 (diss. Vrije Universiteit Amsterdam)

Van Marle 2013
H.J. van Marle, *Huisgodsdienst, het eerste middel tot nadere reformatie. Een onderzoek naar de visie van Petrus Wittewrongel en Simon Oomius op de huisgodsdienst en de invloed van Willem Teellinck op hen*, Utrecht 2013 (unpub. thesis Utrecht University)

Matthews Grieco 1991
S.F. Matthews Grieco, 'Breast-feeding, Wet Nursing and Infant Mortality in Europe (1400–1800)', in S.F. Matthews Grieco and C.A. Corsini, *Historical Perspectives on Breastfeeding*, Florence 1991, pp. 16–26

Meischke et al. 1993–2000
R. Meischke, H.J. Zantkuijl and P.T.E.F. Rosenberg, *Huizen in Nederland. Architectuur-historische verkenningen aan de hand van het bezit van de Vereniging Hendrick de Keyser*, 4 vols., Zwolle 1993–2000

Minderhoud 2017
P.J. Minderhoud, *Van de goudsmid. De historie en de ontwikkeling van Zeeuwse en andere streeksieraden*, Enschede 2017

De Moederloose 1695
I. de Moederloose, *Vrede Tractaet, Gegeven van den Hemel door Vrouwen Zaet. Beschreven door Isabella, de Moederloose Weduwe van Domini Laurentius Hoogentoren. In zijn leven Predikant in Zuit-Beverland*, 3 vols., Amsterdam 1695

Moerman 2021
D. Moerman, '"Och wod het toch een lutie regenen". Droogte en waterschaarste in laatmiddeleeuws en vroegmodern Europa, een geschiedenis van klimaatverandering en sociale veerkracht', *Leidschrift* 36 (2021), no. 1, pp. 53–78

Moesker (forthcoming)
T.P. Moesker, *Brouwerij de Dubbele Arent en omliggende percelen. Opgraving Vijfhoeklaan te Purmerend*, Amersfoort (forthcoming)

Molhuysen and Blok 1912
P.C. Molhuysen and P.J. Blok (eds.), *Nieuw Nederlandsch Biografisch Woordenboek*, vol. 2, Leiden 1912, p. 85

De Mooij 1999
C.C.M. de Mooij, 'Op bezoek bij de familie Copes. Een rondgang door de woning van een Bosch regentengezin', in C.C.M. de Mooij and A. Vos (eds.), *'s-Hertogenbosch binnenskamers. Aspecten van stedelijke woon- en leefculturen 1650–1850*, exh. cat. Den Bosch (Het Noordbrabants Museum) 1999, pp. 78–100

Moreno-Goldschmidt 2020
A. Moreno-Goldschmidt, 'Menasseh ben Israel's *Thesouro dos Dinim*: Reeducating the New Jews', *Jewish History* 33 (2020), no. 3/4, pp. 325–350

Du Mortier 1986
B.M. du Mortier, 'Het kledingbeeld op Amsterdamse portretten in de 16de eeuw', in R. Kistemaker and M. Jonker (eds.), *De smaak van de élite. Amsterdam in de eeuw van de beeldenstorm*, exh. cat. Amsterdam (Amsterdams Historisch Museum) 1986, pp. 40–60

Du Mortier 2010
B.M. du Mortier, 'Costume in Gabriel Metsu's Paintings: Mode and Manners in the Mid-Seventeenth Century', in A.E. Waiboer (ed.), *Gabriel Metsu*, exh.cat. Dublin (National Gallery of Ireland)/Amsterdam (Rijksmuseum)/Washington (National Gallery of Art), pp. 127–153

Du Mortier 2012
B.M. du Mortier, 'Features of Fashion in the Netherlands in the 17th century', in J. Pietsch and A. Jolly (eds.), *Netherlandish Fashion in the Seventeenth Century*, Riggisberg 2012 (*Riggisberger Berichte*, vol. 19), pp. 17–40

Du Mortier 2018
B. du Mortier, 'Recent Acquisitions – Doopluier or Padded Cover', *The Rijksmuseum Bulletin* 66 (2018), no. 3, pp. 282–283

Du Mortier 2023
B.M. du Mortier, 'De plooikraag ondersteund', in J. Gawronski (ed.), *Onder de Amstel. Stadsvertellingen over Amsterdam met archeologische vondsten van de Noord/Zuidlijn uit Damrak en Rokin*, Amsterdam 2023, pp. 204–208

Mourits 2016
E. Mourits, *Een kamer gevuld met de mooiste boeken. De bibliotheek van Johannes Thysius (1622–1653)*, Nijmegen 2016

Mourits 2017
E. Mourits, 'Wie was Johannes Thysius?', in W. van Anrooij and P. Hoftijzer (eds.), *Vijftien strekkende meter. Nieuwe onderzoeksmogelijkheden in het archief van de Bibliotheca Thysiana*, Hilversum 2017, pp. 77–90

Mudde 2018
C.J. Mudde, *Rouwen in de marge. De materiële rouwcultuur van de katholieke geloofsgemeenschap in vroegmodern Nederland*, Utrecht 2018 (diss. Utrecht University)

Muinck 1965
B.E. de Muinck, *Een regentenhuishouding omstreeks 1700. Gegevens uit de privé-boekhouding van Mr. Cornelis de Jonge van Ellemeet, Ontvanger-Generaal der Verenigde Nederlanden (1646–1721)*, The Hague 1965

De Munck 2004
B. De Munck, 'In loco parentis? De disciplinering van leerlingen onder het dak van Antwerpse ambachtsmeesters (1579–1680)', *Tijdschrift voor sociale en economische geschiedenis* 1 (2004), no. 3, pp. 3–30

Muurling 2011
S.T.D. Muurling, 'Een schatkamer in Europa. Koffie, thee en porselein in de Hollandse materiële cultuur', *Holland. Historisch Tijdschrift* 43 (2011), no. 3, pp. 212–222

Muusers 2013
C. Muusers, 'Proef het stilleven. Comfits, letterkoeken en marmelade in Nederlandse kookboeken uit de achttiende eeuw', *Jaarboek De Gulden Roos* 73 (2013), pp. 123–142

Muusers 2015
C. Muusers, 'Meid, meester, cuisinier. Een driehoeksverhouding?', *De Boekenwereld* 31 (2015), no. 3, pp. 50–55

Muusers and Willebrands 2020
C. Muusers and M. Willebrands, *Het excellente kookboek van doctor Carolus Battus uit 1593. Proef de smaak van de 16de eeuw*, Gorredijk 2020

N

Naaktgeboren 1987
C. Naaktgeboren, 'Wonder en realiteit in verleden en heden; een verkenning van de gedachten over zwangerschap en baring bij onze voorouders', in H.M. Dupuis et al., *Een kind onder het hart. Verloskunde, volksgeloof, gezin, seksualiteit en moraal vroeger en nu*, Amsterdam 1987, pp. 57–84

Nannings 1932
J.H. Nannings, *Brood- en gebakvormen en hunne beteekenis in de folklore*, Scheveningen 1932

Van Nederveen Meerkerk 2007
E.J.V. van Nederveen Meerkerk, *De draad in eigen handen. Vrouwen en loonarbeid in de Nederlandse textielnijverheid, 1581–1810*, Amsterdam 2007 (diss. Vrije Universiteit Amsterdam)

Van Nederveen Meerkerk and Schmidt 2006
E.J.V. van Nederveen Meerkerk and A. Schmidt, 'Tussen arbeid en beroep. Jongens en meisjes in de stedelijke nijverheid, ca. 1600–1800', *TSEG – The Low Countries Journal of Social and Economic History* 3 (2006), no. 1, pp. 24–50

Van Nesse 1623–1646
M. van Nesse, *Memorieboek*, Alkmaar 1623–1646 (manuscript), www.regionaalarchiefalkmaar.nl/images/Documenten/Transcriptie_memorieboek_Maria_van_Nesse.pdf

Van Nierop 1930
L. van Nierop, 'De zijdenijverheid van Amsterdam historisch geschetst', *Tijdschrift voor Geschiedenis* 45 (1930), pp. 18–40, 151–172

Nijboer 2007
H.T. Nijboer, *De fatsoenering van het bestaan. Consumptie in Leeuwarden tijdens de Gouden Eeuw*, Groningen 2007 (diss. University of Groningen)

Noordegraaf 1995
L. Noordegraaf, 'De arme', in H.M. Beliën, A.Th. van Deursen and G.J. Setten (eds.), *Gestalten van de Gouden Eeuw. Een Hollands groepsportret*, Amsterdam 1995, pp. 315–347

Noordegraaf and Valk 2020
L. Noordegraaf and G. Valk, *De gave Gods. De pest in Holland vanaf de late Middeleeuwen*, Amsterdam 2020 (3rd rev. ed.)

Noorman 2024
J. Noorman, 'Household Heroines: Maria van Nesse's Memory-book and the Interplay between the Art Market and Household Consumption', in E.A. Honig, J. Noorman and Th. Weststeijn (eds.), *Women: Female Roles in Art and Society of the Netherlands, 1500–1950*, Leiden 2024 (*Nederlands Kunsthistorisch Jaarboek/Netherlands Yearbook For History of Art*, vol. 74), pp. 106–133

Noorman and Van der Maal 2022
J. Noorman and R.J. van der Maal, *Het unieke memorieboek van Maria van Nesse (1588-1650). Nieuwe perspectieven op huishoudelijke consumptie*, Amsterdam 2022

North 2020
S. North, *Sweet & Clean? Bodies & Clothes in Early Modern England*, Oxford 2020

Nylandt 1669
P. Nylandt, *Den ervaren huyshouder, zijnde het III. deel van het Vermakelyck landt-leven (...)*, Amsterdam 1669

Nylandt 1670
P. Nylandt, *De Nederlandtse Herbarius of Kruydt-Boeck*, Amsterdam 1670

O

Obladen 2012
M. Obladen, 'Guttus, Tiralatte and Téterelle: A History of Breast Pumps', *Journal of Perinatal Medicine* 40 (2012), no. 6, pp. 669–675

Oddens 2020
J. Oddens, 'You Can Leave your Hat on: Men's Portraits, Power, and Identity in the Seventeenth-Century Dutch Republic', *The Seventeenth Century* 36 (2020), no. 5, pp. 797–853

Van Oosten 2015
R.M.R. van Oosten, *De stad, het vuil en de beerput. De opkomst, verbreiding en neergang van de beerput in stedelijke context*, Leiden 2015

Van Oosten et al. 2017
R.M.R. van Oosten, Y. Meijer, C.R. Brandenburgh and A.C.L. van Noort, 'Leidse weuershuizen in seriebouw. Een materiele getuigenis van "projectontwikkeling" in de Gouden Eeuw', *Archeologie in Nederland* 1 (2017), no. 3, pp. 36–45

Orlers 1614
J.J. Orlers, *Beschrijvinge der stad Leyden*, Leiden 1614

Ostkamp 2003
S. Ostkamp, 'Faience uit de werkplaats van Quirijn Aldertsz en zijn vrouw Engeltje Kleijnoven (1655–1693). Vondsten uit een beerput op het voormalige bedrijfsterrein van "De Porceleyne Fles" in Delft', *Assembled Articles: Symposium on Medieval and Post-medieval Ceramics*, vol. 3, Zwolle 2003, pp. 185–242

Otten 2019
J. Otten, 'Sibbeli, matres, houdster van een kleine kinderschool, 1643', *Vergeten Harlingers* (2019), www.vergetenharlingers.nl

Ottenheym 1989
K. Ottenheym, *Philips Vingboons (1607–1678), architect*, Zutphen 1989

Ottenheym and Terwen 1993
K. Ottenheym and J. Terwen, *Pieter Post (1608–1669)*, Zutphen 1993

P

Paré 1655
A. Paré, *De chirurgie, ende opera van alle de wercken, van Mr. Ambrosius Paré*, Amsterdam 1655

Peelen 1908
I. Peelen, 'Mangelplanken', *Het Huis. Oud & Nieuw* 6 (1908), pp. 51–59

Pettegree and Der Weduwen 2019
A. Pettegree and A. der Weduwen, *The Bookshop of the World: Making and Trading Books in The Dutch Golden Age*, New Haven/London 2019

Piemontese 1602
A. Piemontese, *De sekreten vanden eerweerdigen Heere Alexis Piemontois: inhoudende de seer excellente ende wel gheapprobeerde remedien, teghen veelderhande crancheden, wonden, ende andere accidenten: met de manier van te distilleren, parfumeren, confitueren maken, te verwen, coleuren, ende gieten*, Amsterdam 1602

Pierik 2022
B.T. Pierik, *Urban Life on the Move: Gender and Mobility in Early Modern Amsterdam*, Amsterdam 2022 (diss. University of Amsterdam)

Pierik 2023
B.T. Pierik, 'Shifting Attitudes to Drinking Common Water in Dutch Medicine, 1630–1750', *European Journal for the History of Medicine and Health* 80 (2023), no. 2, pp. 283–312

Pijzel-Dommisse 1987
H.H. Pijzel-Dommisse, *Het poppenhuis van Petronella de la Court*, Utrecht 1987

Pijzel-Dommisse 2000
H.H. Pijzel-Dommisse, *Het Hollandse pronkpoppenhuis. Interieur en huishouden in de 17de en 18de eeuw*, Amsterdam/Zwolle 2000

Platteschorre-Weurman 2008
C.J. Platteschorre-Weurman, 'De peignoir', *Kostuum. Jaaruitgave van de Nederlandse Vereniging voor Kostuum, Kant, Mode en Streekdracht* (2008), pp. 17–28

Poelwijk 2003
A.H. Poelwijk, *'In dienste vant suyckerenbacken.' De Amsterdamse suikernijverheid en haar ondernemers, 1580–1630*, Hilversum 2003 (diss. University of Amsterdam)

Ponte 2018
M. Ponte, '"Al de swarten die hier ter stede comen." Een Afro-Atlantische gemeenschap in zeventiende-eeuws Amsterdam', *Tijdschrift voor Sociale en Economische Geschiedenis* 15 (2018), no. 4, pp. 33–62

Ponte 2022
M. Ponte, 'Zwarte vrouwen in het midden van de zeventiende eeuw', in M. Hell (ed.), *Alle Amsterdamse Akten. Ruzie, rouw en roddels bij de notaris, 1578–191*, Amsterdam 2022 (*Jaarboek van het Genootschap Amstelodamum*, vol. 114), pp. 130–143

Portegies 1999
M. Portegies, *Dood en begraven in 's-Hertogenbosch. Het Sint-Janskerkhof 1629–1858*, Utrecht 1999

Prak 1998
M. Prak, 'Armenzorg 1500–1800', in J.L.J.M. van Gerwen and M.H.D. van Leeuwen (eds.), *Studies over zekerheidsarrangementen. Risico's, risicobestrijding en verzekeringen in Nederland vanaf de Middeleeuwen*, Amsterdam/The Hague 1998, pp. 49–90

Praz 1982
M. Praz, *An Illustrated History of Interior Decoration: From Pompeii to Art Nouveau*, London 1982

R

Raimond-Waarts 2014
L.L. Raimond-Waarts, *Badkamers voor pausen en prelaten. Leven en welzijn aan het Vaticaanse hof in de Renaissance*, Groningen 2014 (diss. University of Groningen)

Regtdoorzee Greup-Roldanus 1936
S.C. Regtdoorzee Greup-Roldanus, *Geschiedenis der Haarlemmer bleekerijen*, The Hague 1936, pp. 98–100

De Rijk 2015
J.H. de Rijk, *Vogels en mensen in Nederland 1500–1920*, Amsterdam 2015 (diss. Vrije Universiteit Amsterdam)

Roberts 1998
B.B. Roberts, *Through the Keyhole: Dutch Child-rearing Practices in the 17th and 18th Century: Three Urban Elite Families*, Hilversum 1998

Roberts 2012
B.B. Roberts, *Sex and Drugs before Rock 'n' Roll: Youth Culture and Masculinity during Holland's Golden Age*, Amsterdam 2012

Roberts and Groenendijk 2004
B.B. Roberts and L.F. Groenendijk, '"Wearing out a Pair of Fool's Shoes": Sexual Advice for Youth in Holland's Golden Age', *Journal of the History of Sexuality* 13 (2004), no. 2, pp. 139–156

Roodenburg 1983
H.W. Roodenburg, 'De autobiografie van Isabella de Moerloose. Seks, opvoeding en volksgeloof in de zeventiende eeuw', *Tijdschrift voor Sociale Geschiedenis* 9 (1983), pp. 311–342

Roodenburg 1988
H.W. Roodenburg, 'The Maternal Imagination: The Fears of Pregnant Women in Seventeenth-Century Holland', *Journal of Social History* 21 (1988), no. 4, pp. 701–716

Rösslin 1650
E. Rösslin, *Het Kleyn Vroetwijfsboeck: ofte vermeerderden Roosengaert: Van de bevruchte vrouwen, en hare secreten, ontfanginge, baringe, vrouwen en mannen raedt te gheven die onvruchtbaer zijn (...)*, Amsterdam 1650

Rotterdam 1983
J.R. ter Molen (ed.), *Brood. De geschiedenis van het brood en het broodgebruik in Nederland*, exh. cat. Rotterdam (Museum Boymans-van Beuningen) 1983

Rotterdam 2006
M. Schapelhouman et al. (ed.), *Prenten in de Gouden Eeuw. Van kunst tot kastpapier*, exh. cat. Rotterdam (Museum Boijmans Van Beuningen) 2006

Rueff 1591
Jacob Rueff, *T'Boeck vande vroetwijfs. Int welcke men mach leeren alle heymelicheden vande vrouwen, ende in wat ghestalte de mensche in zijn moeders lichaem ontfanghen, groeyt, ende ghebooren wort (...)*, Amsterdam 1591

Rybczynski 1986
W. Rybczynski, *Home: A Short History of an Idea*, New York 1986

S

Saelens 2020
W. Saelens, 'Energie en materiële cultuur. Huishoudelijke verwarming en verlichting in de vroegmoderne stad', *Groniek. Gronings Historisch Tijdschrift* 52 (2020), no. 222, pp. 43–56

Salman 1999
J.L. Salman, *Populair drukwerk in de Gouden Eeuw. De almanak als lectuur en handelswaar,* Zutphen 1999

Sarti 2002
R. Sarti, *Europe at Home: Family and Material Culture, 1500–1800,* New Haven 2002

Schama 1987
S. Schama, *The Embarrassment of Riches: An Interpretation of Dutch Culture in the Golden Age,* London 1987

Schenkeveld 1991
M.A. Schenkeveld, *Dutch Literature in the Age of Rembrandt: Themes and Ideas,* Amsterdam 1991

Schmidt 2001
A. Schmidt, *Overleven na de dood. Weduwen in Leiden in de Gouden Eeuw,* Amsterdam 2001

Schmidt and Van der Heijden 2016
A. Schmidt and M.P.C. van der Heijden, 'Women Alone in Early Modern Dutch Towns: Opportunities and Strategies to Survive', *Journal of Urban History* 42 (2016), no. 1, pp. 21–38

Schmidt and Van Nederveen Meerkerk 2012
A. Schmidt and E. van Nederveen Meerkerk, 'Reconsidering The "First Male-Breadwinner Economy": Women's Labor Force Participation in the Netherlands, 1600–1900', *Feminist Economics* 18 (2012), no. 4, pp. 69–96

Schotel 1867
G. Schotel, *Het Oud-Hollandsch huisgezin der zeventiende eeuw,* Haarlem 1867

Schrevelius 1750
T. Schrevelius, *Harlemias of Eerste stichting der stad Haarlem,* Haarlem 1750

Schrickx 2025 (forthcoming)
C.P. Schrickx, *De beerput van Sonck en Coninck. De vondsten uit een beerput van een opgraving aan het Nieuwe Noord in Hoorn,* Hoorn 2025 (forthcoming) (*West-Friese Archeologische Rapporten*)

Schrickx and Stellingwerf 2020
C.P. Schrickx and W. Stellingwerf, *De brouwerij in de Hoek. Archeologisch onderzoek op het perceel van het voormalige veilinggebouw van Bloemenlust aan de Admiraliteitsweg in Enkhuizen,* Hoorn 2020 (*West-Friese Archeologische Rapporten,* vol. 151)

Scultetus 1657
J. Scultetus, *Magazyn ofte wapenhuys van D. Johannes Scultetus, eertijds seer geluckich natuyrkender, en chirurgyn tot Ulm,* Amsterdam 1657

Sennert 1656
D. Sennert, *The Institutions or Fundamentals of the whole Art, both of Physick and Chirurgery,* London 1656

Smits-Veldt 1991
M.B. Smits-Veldt, 'De nalatenschap van Jan Sijwertsz Kolm (1589–1637). Het gezicht van een Amsterdamse rederijker', *Literatuur* 8 (1991), pp. 93–102

Soetens 2001
J. Soetens, *In glas verpakt/Packaged in Glass: European Bottles, Their History and Production,* Amsterdam 2001

Songer and Van Lottum 2007
S. Sogner and J. van Lottum, 'An Immigrant Community? Norwegian Sailors and their Wives in 17th-century Amsterdam', *The History of the Family* 12 (2007), no. 3, pp. 153–168

Sorber 1988
F. Sorber, 'Textiel in het huiselijk milieu 16de–18de eeuw', in P. Maclot and W. Pottier (eds.), *'n Propere tijd!? (On)leefbaar Antwerpen thuis en op straat (1500–1800),* Antwerp 1988, pp. 111–120

Spaans 2024
J. Spaans, 'Een Beréer in Delft. Johan Cornelis van Bleiswijk en zijn alledaagse omgang met de Bijbel', *Jaarboek De Zeventiende Eeuw. Cultuur in de Nederlanden in interdisciplinair perspectief* (2024), pp. 37–52

Steenmeijer 2005
G. Steenmeijer, *Tot cieraet ende aensien deser stede. Arent van 's-Gravesande (ca. 1610–1662), architect en ingenieur,* Leiden 2005

Di Stefano 2023
G.P. di Stefano, 'Een virginaal uit de tijd van Vermeer', *Tijdschrift Oude Muziek* 1 (2023), pp. 10–11

Stolk 2020
M. Stolk, 'Rattles, Toys and Miniature Artefacts: Archaeological Insights into Childhood and Children's Identities at Vlooienburg', *Kleos – Amsterdam Bulletin of Ancient Studies and Archeology* (2020), no. 3, pp. 64–81

Stolk 2022
M. Stolk, *The Archaeology of Vlooienburg: Materiality and Daily Life in Multicultural Amsterdam, 1600–1800,* Amsterdam 2022 (diss. University of Amsterdam)

Stone-Ferrier 2022
L. Stone-Ferrier, *The Little Street: The Neighborhood in Seventeenth-Century Dutch Art and Culture,* New Haven 2022

De Stoppelaar 1860
J.H. de Stoppelaar, *Jacob Cats te Middelburg, 1603–1623, en zijn huis aldaar, ook in betrekking tot de vroegere en latere bewoners,* Middelburg 1860

Stoter 2014
M.E. Stoter, 'Reliekdoosje', in J.R. ter Molen (ed.), *Fries goud en zilver,* vol. 3, Gorredijk, pp. 358–359

Stoter 2016
M.E. Stoter, 'The lady of the manor. Het aantekenboek van Andriese Lucia van Bronkhorst', in H. Oly and G. de Vries (eds.), *Leeuwarden in de Gouden Eeuw,* Hilversum 2016 (*Leeuwarder Historische Reeks,* vol. 12), pp. 53–82

Strouven 1638–1649 (2020)
E. Strouven, *De moeder van de Kommel. De autobiografie van Elisabeth Strouven* (ed. A.Th.M. van Iterson), Amsterdam 2020 (original manuscript 1638–1649)

Van Suchtelen 2021
A. van Suchtelen (ed.), *Vervlogen. Geuren in kleuren,* exh. cat. The Hague (Mauritshuis) 2021

De Swaef 1621 (1740)
J. de Swaef, *De geestelycke queeckerye van de jonge planten des Heeren, opdatse mochten werden boomen der gerechtigheydt, ten pryse des alderhoofsten, cieraad van syne voorhoven, ende der planten behoudinge: ofte Tractaet van de christelycke opvoedinghe der kinderen, uyt den woorde Godes ter nedergestelt*, Middelburg 1740 (original ed. 1621)

T
Teske 2011
J. Teske, 'Embroidery for Ambassadors', *The Rijksmuseum Bulletin* 59 (2011), no. 1, pp. 58–73

Teunissen and Stolk 2024
M. Teunissen and M. Stolk, *Textiel uit Hollandse bodem. Archeologisch textiel uit de 17de en 18de eeuw*, Oegstgeest 2024

Thoen 2007
I. Thoen, *Strategic Affection? Gift Exchange in Seventeenth-Century Holland*, Amsterdam 2007

Thornton 1978
P. Thornton, *Seventeenth-Century Interior Decoration in England, France and Holland*, New Haven 1978

Van Toorn and Spies 1990
A. van Toorn and M. Spies, 'Christen Jeugd, leerd Konst en Deugd. De zeventiende eeuw', in W. van Toorn et al. (ed.), *De hele Bibelebontse berg. De geschiedenis van het kinderboek in Nederland & Vlaanderen van de middeleeuwen tot heden*, Amsterdam 1990, pp. 105–167

Treffers 2009
P.E. Treffers, 'Geboortedaling eind 19e en eerste helft 20e eeuw. Coïtus interruptus belangrijkste vorm van anticonceptie', *Nederlands Tijdschrift voor Geneeskunde* 153 (2009), no. 5, pp. 201–205

Van Tussenbroek 2023
G. van Tussenbroek, *De houten eeuw van Amsterdam. Bouwen, werken en wonen in de middeleeuwse stad (1275–1578)*, Amsterdam 2023

U
Unger 2001
R.W. Unger, *A History of Brewing in Holland, 900–1900: Economy, Technology and the State*, Leiden 2001

Utrecht 1991
T. Kootte, *De bijbel in huis. Bijbelse verhalen op huisraad in de zeventiende en achttiende eeuw*, exh. cat. Utrecht (Rijksmuseum Het Catharijneconvent) 1991

Utrecht 2004
L.M. Helmus (ed.), *Vis. Stillevens van Hollandse en Vlaamse meesters 1550–1700*, exh. cat. Utrecht (Centraal Museum) 2004

V
Valcooch 1591 (1875)
D.A. Valcooch, *Den reghel der Duytsche schoolmeesters* (ed. G.D.J. Schotel), The Hague 1875 (original ed. 1591)

Van der Veen 2000
J. van der Veen, 'Eenvoudig en stil. Studeerkamers in zeventiende-eeuwse woningen, voornamelijk te Amsterdam, Deventer en Leiden', in J. de Jong et al. (eds.), *Wooncultuur in de Nederlanden/ The Art of Home in the Netherlands 1500–1800*, Zwolle 2000 (*Nederlands Kunsthistorisch Jaarboek/ Netherlands Yearbook For History of Art*, vol. 51), pp. 137–171

Veerkamp 2021
J. Veerkamp, *Zeepziederij De Clock, Stadsontwikkeling tussen Keizerrijk en Wijdesteeg (1525–1950), Archeologische Opgraving Spuistraat, Keizerrijk, Wijdesteeg Amsterdam (2015–2017)*, Amsterdam 2021 (*Amsterdamse Archeologische Rapporten*, vol. 129)

Veldhorst 2008
N. Veldhorst, 'Pharmacy for the Body and Soul: Dutch Songbooks in the Seventeenth Century', *Early Music History: Studies in Medieval and Early Modern Music* 27 (2008), pp. 217–286

Veldhorst 2009
N. Veldhorst, *Zingend door het leven. Het Nederlandse liedboek in de Gouden Eeuw*, Amsterdam 2009

Venette 1687
N. Venette, *Venus Minsieke Gasthuis*, Amsterdam 1687

Verbeeck s.a. (1999)
H. Verbeeck, *Memoriaal ofte mijn levens-raijsinghe* (ed. J. Blaak), Hilversum 1999

Verheggen 2020
E.M.F. Verheggen, 'Flowerpower in de Contrareformatie. Bloemen en planten in de katholieke verbeelding van deugdzaamheid', *Jaarboek De Zeventiende Eeuw. Cultuur in de Nederlanden in interdisciplinair perspectief* (2020), pp. 67–86

Verheggen 2024
E.M.F. Verheggen, 'De santenkraam van Maria van Nesse. Nieuwe inzichten over devotieprenten en devotionalia in de Republiek', *Jaarboek De Zeventiende Eeuw. Cultuur in de Nederlanden in interdisciplinair perspectief* (2024), pp. 53–70

Verhoeven and Mol 1994
G. Verhoeven and J.A. Mol (eds.), *Friese testamenten tot 1550*, Leeuwarden 1994

Verwaal 2023
R. Verwaal, *Bloed, zweet en tranen. Een geschiedenis van de vloeibare mens*, Amsterdam 2023

Vigarello 1988
G. Vigarello, *Concepts of Cleanliness: Changing Attitudes in France since the Middle Ages* (trans. J. Birrell), Cambridge 1988

Vincent 2018
S.J. Vincent, *Hair: An Illustrated History*, London 2018

Visscher 1614
Roemer Visscher, *Sinnepoppen*, Amsterdam 1614

Visscher 1696
T. Visscher, *Heelkonstige Aanmerkingen (…) Beneevens een genees- en licchaamkundige verhandeling van de kracht der moederlijke inbeelding op de vrucht, wiskunstiger wijze voorgesteld*, Amsterdam 1696

Van der Vlis 2001
I. van der Vlis, *Leven in armoede. Delftse bedeelden in de zeventiende eeuw*, Amsterdam 2001 (*Cultuurgeschiedenis van de Republiek in de 17de eeuw*)

Van Voolen 2017
E. van Voolen, 'De gezichten in de Portugese synagoge', in G. Wuestman (ed.), *Emanuel de Witte 1616/ 17–1691/92. Meester van het licht*, exh. cat. Alkmaar (Stedelijk Museum Alkmaar) 2017, pp. 100–109

Vos 1662
J. Vos, *Alle de gedichten van den poëet Jan Vos* (ed. J. Lescaille), Amsterdam 1662

Voskuijl 1975
J.J. Voskuijl, 'Van onderpand tot teken. De geschiedenis van de trouwring als voorbeeld van functieverschuiving', *Volkskundig Bulletin* 1 (1975), pp. 47–79

Voskuil 1983
J.J. Voskuil, 'De weg naar Luilekkerland', *Bijdragen en mededelingen betreffende de geschiedenis der Nederlanden* 98 (1983), no. 3, pp. 460–482

De Vries 1990
L. de Vries, 'Portraits of People at Work', in J. Locher and J. van Jong (eds.), *Werk. Opstellen voor Hans Locher*, Groningen 1990, pp. 52–59

De Vries 2007
A. de Vries, 'De boedelinventaris van Arent van Oostwaert alias de bakker van Jan Steen', *The Rijksmuseum Bulletin* 2007) 55), nos. 2/3, pp. 218–241

De Vries 2019
J. de Vries, *The Price of Bread: Regulating the Market in the Dutch Republic*, New York 2019

De Vries and Van der Woude 1997
J. de Vries and A. van der Woude, *The First Modern Economy: Success, Failure, and Perseverance of the Dutch Economy, 1500–1815*, Cambridge 1997

Vrouwaart 1699
F. Vrouwaart, *D'Openhertige Juffrouw, Of D'Ontdekte Geveinsdheid*, Amsterdam 1699

W
Wagenaar 1765
J. Wagenaar, *Amsterdam in zyne opkomst, aanwas, geschiedenissen, voorregten, koophandel (…)*, vol. 2, Amsterdam 1765

Wagenberg-ter Hoeven 1997
A.A. van Wagenberg-ter Hoeven, *Het Driekoningenfeest. De uitbeelding van een populair thema in de beeldende kunst van de zeventiende eeuw*, Amsterdam 1997 (*Publicaties van het P.J. Meertens-Instituut*, vol. 28)

Walle 2005
K. Walle, *Buurthouden. De geschiedenis van burengebruiken en buurtorganisaties in Leiden (14e–19e eeuw)*, Leiden 2005 (*Leidse Historische Studies*, vol. 3)

Welch 2011
E.S. Welch, 'Scented Buttons and Perfumed Gloves: Smelling Things in Renaissance Italy', in B. Mirabella (ed.), *Ornamentalism: The Art of Renaissance Accessoires*, Ann Arbor 2011

Weterings 2011
T. Weterings, 'Zeeuws Suriname, 1667–1683', *OSO. Tijdschrift voor Surinaamse taalkunde, letterkunde en geschiedenis* 30 (2011), pp. 338–355

Van Wijngaarden 2000
H. van Wijngaarden, *Zorg voor de kost. Armenzorg, arbeid en onderlinge hulp in Zwolle 1650–1700*, Amsterdam 2000 (*Cultuurgeschiedenis van de Republiek in de 17de eeuw*)

Willebrands 2023
M. Willebrands, 'De arts in de laatmiddeleeuwse keuken. Gezondheidsregels en zestiende-eeuwse keukenrecepten voor de zieke of verzwakte mens', *De Boekenwereld* 39 (2023), no. 4, pp. 14–19

Willebrands et al. 2022
M. Willebrands, A. van Dongen and M. Henzen, *De verstandige kock. Proef de smaak van de 17de eeuw*, Gorredijk 2022

Willemse 2003
J.M.F. Willemsen, '"Poppe-goed in anders niet". Speelgoed in Holland in de 16de en 17de eeuw', *Holland* 35 (2003), no. 2, pp. 80–91

Winschooten 1681
W. à Winschooten, *Seeman: behelsende een grondige uitlegging van de Nederlandse Konst, en spreekwoorden, voor soo veel die uit de seevaart sijn ontleend, en bij de beste schrijvers deeser eeuw gevonden werden*, Leiden 1681

Van Winter 2016
J.M. van Winter, '"De kok is de beste arts". Planten voor voeding en gezondheid: recepten en voorschriften', in C.A. Chavannes-Mazel and L. IJpelaar (eds.), *De groene Middeleeuwen. Duizend jaar gebruik van planten (600– 1600)*, Eindhoven 2016

Witgeest 1684
S. Witgeest [W. Goeree], *Het Natuurlyk Tover-Boek, Of't Nieuw Speel-Toneel Der Konsten*, Amsterdam 1684

Witteveen 1992
J. Witteveen, 'Kookboeken over kookgerei. Het kookgerei van de middeleeuwen tot de twintigste eeuw', in E. de Schipper (ed.), *Quintessens. Wetenswaardigheden over acht eeuwen kookgerei*, cat. Rotterdam (Museum Boymans-van Beuningen) 1992, pp. 14–32

Wittewrongel 1661
P. Wittewrongel, *Oeconomia christiana, ofte christelicke huyshoudinge: vervat in twee boecken: ter bevoordering der oeffeninge der ware godtsaligheydt in de bysondere huys-ghesinnen*, Amsterdam 1661

Wuestman 2005
G. Wuestman, 'Het familjie boeckje van Pieter Boudaen Courten (1594–1668). Memoires van een geportretteerde', *Bulletin van het Rijksmuseum* 53 (2005), no. 1, pp. 41–51

Y
Van Ysselsteyn 1946
G.T. van Ysselsteyn, *Van linnen en linnenkasten*, Amsterdam 1946 (*Patria – Vaderlandse cultuurgeschiedenis in monografieën*, vol. 38)

Z
Van Zalinge 2020
A. van Zalinge, *Burenplicht en rozemarijn. Begrafenisrituelen in Haarlem tot de 18e eeuw*, Haarlem 2020, www.archeologischmuseum haarlem.nl/wp-content/uploads/ 2021/01/erfgoed-haarlem-2-Begraven.pdf

Zijlmans 1999
J.M. Zijlmans, *Vriendenkringen in de zeventiende eeuw. Verenigingsvormen van het informele culturele leven te Rotterdam*, The Hague 1999

list of images

People and Possessions

p. 8 Detail of the kitchen in Petronella Oortman's doll's house (fig. 7)

1 Page from the account book of Sara L'Empereur, 1660–1663. Amsterdam, International Institute of Social History, NEHA, Collectie Familie Du Tour, inv. no. 1, fols. 5v–6r

2 Warming pan, Northern Netherlands, 1602, inscription around the rim: *Dees pan is bequaem voor vrouwen die [be] geeren in een werm bedt ghaen en nimant en hebben om hen te verwermen soo moet si haer bedt viren [vuren] met de pan als si niet en hebben eenen man die hen de voeten verwermen kan anno 1602.* Brass, l. 104.1 cm. London, Victoria and Albert Museum, inv. no. 4214-1855; © Victoria and Albert Museum, London

3 Wedding glass, possibly for Zacheus de Jager and Margaretha van Berensteyn, Netherlands (engraving: Northern Netherlands), c. 1625–1675. Glass, h. c. 18 cm. Hoorn, Archeologie West-Friesland, inv. no. ENK-748-49-G12

4 Theodoor van Thulden, *Allegorical Portrait of Josina Schade van Westrum with Five of her Children*, 1651. Oil on canvas, 195 × 253 cm. Den Bosch, Het Noordbrabants Museum, inv. no. 09740.1. Photo: Peter Cox

5 Doll's house of Petronella de la Court, Amsterdam, c. 1668–1690. Various materials, h. 206.5 × w. 182 × d. 74.5 cm. Utrecht, Centraal Museum, inv. no. 5000. Photo: Adriaan van Dam

6 Doll's house of Petronella Dunois, Amsterdam, c. 1676. Various materials, h. 200 × w. 150.5 × d. 56 cm. Amsterdam, Rijksmuseum, inv. no. BK-14656; gift of A.S.M. van Tienhoven-Hacke

7 Doll's house of Petronella Oortman, Amsterdam, c. 1686–1710. Various materials, 255 × 190 × 78 cm. Amsterdam, Rijksmuseum, inv. no. BK-NM-1010

8 Ceiling of the art room in Petronella de la Court's doll's house (fig. 5). Photo: Adriaan van Dam

House

p. 28 Detail of the tapestry room in Petronella Oortman's doll's house (fig. 7)

9 Gravesteen neighbourhood regulations kept by L. Elsevier, 1607–1617. Ink on parchment, 745 × 570 mm. Leiden, Museum De Lakenhal, inv. no. 30

10 Anonymous, *View of the Vismarkt in Leiden*, c. 1600. Oil on panel, 48.5 × 102.5 cm. Leiden, Museum De Lakenhal, inv. no. S268; gift from the heirs of P. Blaauw, lord of the 'Meersmansteeg'(?) neighbourhood, 1871

11 Door and door frame of a house in Ouderkerk aan de IJssel, Northern Netherlands, 1655. Wood, glass, metal, 233 × 118 cm. Amsterdam, Rijksmuseum, inv. no. BK-BFR-205

12 Goblet, Netherlands (engraving: Willem Jacobsz van Heemskerk), 1684, inscription on bowl: *Liefde Bind Volkomen*; under the base: *Houwelijks Huysraed. Voor den Hr. Lucas van Rijp en Margareta Flamen, wettelijk vereenigt op den 25en January Anno 1684.* Glass, 18 × 9.7 cm. Leiden, Museum De Lakenhal, inv. no. 2066

13 Laurens Scherm, *The Looting of Burgomaster Boreel's House During the Aansprekersoproer (Undertaker's Riot) of 1696*, c. 1702/1725–1733. Engraving, 135 × 83 mm. Amsterdam, Rijksmuseum, inv. no. RP-P-OB-60.543

14 A. van 's-Gravensande, Design for houses in Hoefstraat and Vestwal, 1643. Leiden, Erfgoed Leiden en Omstreken, inv. no. PV_PV30824.1b

15 Gerrit Grasdorp, *Broerentrans in Zwolle*, c. 1700. Brush, brown ink. Zwolle, Collectie Vereeniging tot beoefening van Overijsselsch Regt en Geschiedenis (VORG), inv. no. 01492

16 *Annetie with the small head*, c. 1698–1750, inscription: *Annetie met het klijn hooftie genaampt Annetie Visser. Gebooren 1600, gestorven 1698. Sij riep altijt sonder verveelen Godt die sijt gij moet niet steelen.* Pen, brush in colour. Amsterdam City Archives, image no. 010097007723

17 The estate inventory of Tomes Hendricks, 14 October 1673: '14 October 1673/ the estate of Tomes Hendricks in Trans/ A bed and pillow/ Two cushions/ A clean white blanket/ A green blanket/ 10 sheets, another sheet and smock/ 14 smocks, for [...] and clothing/ 21 silver buttons/ 14 *batsen* [?]/ 6 pillow tickings/ A brass bed warmer/ A brass pot/ A brass kettle/ A grate/ A pot hook and tongs/ And a pan/ A caltrop [a type of weapon]/ Three ceramic cups/ 8 coloured dishes/ 11 pewter spoons'. Zwolle, Collectie Overijssel, 0741, Stadsarmenkamer te Zwolle, inv. no. 246

18 Daniel van Breen, The interior layout of a house on Anjeliersgracht (now Westerstraat 130) in Amsterdam, property of Theodore (Dirck) Blevet, drawn by his brother-in-law, 3 March 1634. Amsterdam City Archives, image no. 010056914692

19 Egbert van Heemskerck, *Portrait of Jacob Fransz Hercules and his Family in the Surgeon's Shop*, 1669. Oil on canvas, 70 × 59 cm. Amsterdam Museum, inv. no. SA 2121

20 *Voorkamer* with *hangkamer* in Huis Bonck, Binnenluiendijk 3, Hoorn, built in 1624, property of Vereniging Hendrik de Keyser, Amsterdam. Photo: Arjan Bronkhorst

21 Panelling with built-in fireplace and box bed and a child's bed in a similar style, Northern Netherlands, 1617. Various types of wood, h. 248 cm. Amsterdam, Rijksmuseum, inv. nos. BK-NM-3931-A, BK-KOG-1810

22 Jan van der Heyden, *Cross-section of a Burning House with Firefighters*, c. 1690. Brown ink, black chalk, 340 × 461 mm. Amsterdam City Archives, image no. JVDH00007000001

23 Anthony van Velzen, Floor plan of Rapenburg 48, 1719. The Hague, National Archives of the Netherlands, inv. no. PV_PV31351.10

24 Pieter Post, Design for the façade of De Onbeschaamde, Wijnstraat 123, Dordrecht, from J.J. Terwen and K.A. Ottenheym, *Pieter Post (1608–1669). Architect,*

Zutphen 1993. Amsterdam, Rijksmuseum Research Library, 426 H 23
25 Pieter Post, The interior layout of the ground floor of De Onbeschaamde, Wijnstraat 123, Dordrecht, 1650. Regionaal Archief Dordrecht, inv. no. 552_230184
26 Philip Vinckboons (designer) and Joachim von Sandrart (painter), Chimney piece from Joan Huydecoper's house, Singel 548, Amsterdam, c. 1639. Various materials, h. 435 × w. 310 × d. 115 cm. Amsterdam, Rijksmuseum, inv. no. BK-NM-10269; gift of D. Franken, Le Vésinet
27 Gabriel Metsu, *Portrait of Jan Jacobsz Hinlopen, Leonora Huydecoper, their Children and a Wet Nurse*, 1662/1663. Oil on canvas, 77 × 82.6 cm. Berlin, Staatliche Museen zu Berlin – Gemäldegalerie, inv. no. 792. Photo: Staatliche Museen zu Berlin – Gemäldegalerie/Jörg P. Anders

Body
p. 66 Detail of the tapestry room in Petronella Oortman's doll's house (fig. 7)
28 De Porceleyne Schotel (made by Gerrit Kam), Shaving basin decorations with shaving equipment, c. 1690–1710, inscription: *MYN IAER IS OM*. Tin-glazed earthenware, diam. 29 cm. Museum Rotterdam, inv. no. 61757
29 Attributed to Jan de Vos IV, *Portrait of Johannes Thysius*, c. 1658. Oil on canvas. Leiden, Bibliotheca Thysiana – Universiteit Leiden
30 Chamber pot, Northern Netherlands, 1696, inscription: *[?] tijt soete lief koomt te bedt*. Red earthenware with decorations in white slip, h. 16.7 cm. Rotterdam, Museum Boijmans Van Beuningen, inv. no. F 9509 (KN&V); on loan from Stichting het Nederlandse Gebruiksvoorwerp, 2006. Photo: Tom Haartsen
31 Kitchen with privy in Petronella Dunois's doll's house (fig. 6)
32 Men's smock, Northern Netherlands, c. 1690–1710. Linen, 132 × 100 cm. Leeuwarden, Fries Museum, inv. no. T1997-024
33 Stays and busk, Northern Netherlands, c. 1660–1680. Silk, linen, baleen, centre back length:

c. 48 cm. London, Victoria and Albert Museum, inv. no. T.14-1951; given by Miss C.E. Gallini © Victoria and Albert Museum, London
34 Baby jacket, Northern Netherlands, c. 1690–1720. Silk, linen, l. 30 cm. Amsterdam, Rijksmuseum, inv. no. BK-2018-79; purchased with the support of the Jessy & Betty Blumenthal Fonds/ Rijksmuseum Fonds
35 Bodkin, Northern Netherlands, c. 1620, inscription: *SARA*. Blue glass, brass, l. 12.5 cm. Zeeland, private collection
36 Wenceslaus Hollar, *Woman with ruff, coif and bodkin*, 1645. Etching, 103 × 95 mm. Amsterdam, Rijksmuseum, inv. no. RP-P-OB-116.291
37 Ruff, Northern Netherlands, c. 1615–1635. Linen, silk, 1950 × 13 cm. Amsterdam, Rijksmuseum, inv. no. BK-NM-13112; on loan from the heirs of H.G. Rahusen
38 Supportasse, Northern Netherlands, c. 1615. Silver-plated copper, diam. 21.5 cm. Amersfoort, Rijksdienst voor het Cultureel Erfgoed, inv. no. [MA]OB71-317
39 Book mirror, pincushion, two brushes, a comb bag, and a cloth for the table, Northern Netherlands, c. 1675–1725. Various materials. Leeuwarden, Fries Museum, inv. nos. T01182–T01188; Koninklijk Fries Genootschap Collection
40a–i Ointment jars, Northern Netherlands, 17th century. Red and yellow earthenware, h. c. 4–6.5 cm. Amsterdam, Rijksmuseum, inv. nos. BK-KOG-1708-3, -1708-5 to -1708-9, -1706-39, -1706-40, -418-B; on loan from the Koninklijk Oudheidkundig Genootschap
41 Ear spoon and toothpick in the shape of a mermaid, Northern Netherlands, c. 1600–1625. Bronze, l. 7.8 cm. Archeologie Rotterdam, Achterhaven (VOC/AKZO), inv. no. 12-57
42 Lice comb, Northern Netherlands, c. 1550–1573. Wood, 10.5 × 7.5 cm. Alkmaar, Archeologische dienst, inv. no. 91WOR61-RAT
43 *Kamdoek*, Northern Netherlands, c. 1620–1650. Linen, 60 × 97 × 38 cm. Amsterdam, Rijksmuseum, inv. no. BK 1980-786; gift of the Stichting Twickel

44 Pomander, possibly Amsterdam, c. 1600–1625. Various materials, h. 4.2 cm. Amsterdam, Rijksmuseum, inv. no. BK-1960-1
45 Catharina Fourmenois's bladder stone, 5 cm in length, surgically removed in 1647. Delft, Michel Arnold Verschuyl Collection
46 Vaginal syringe in the shape of a phallus, Northern Netherlands, 17th century. Boxwood, l. 22.5 cm. Municipality of Zwolle
47 Pessaries or suppositories, woodcut from Ambroise Paré, *De chirurgie, ende opera van alle de wercken*, 1655, p. 754. Amsterdam, Allard Pierson, University of Amsterdam, KF 62-166
48 Hans Christiaens, Reliquary of Aelke van Juckema, 1628, inscription lid: *ALEGONDE VAN IUCKEMA ANNO 1628*; side of the box: *S. LUCIA*; *S. BREGITTA*; *S. CATHARINA*. Silver, h. 6 cm. Leeuwarden, Fries Museum, inv. no. Z2003-006; on loan from Stichting Herbert Duintjer Fonds

Mealtime
p. 100 Detail of the kitchen in Petronella Oortman's doll's house (fig. 7)
49 Market bucket, Mechelen, c. 1625–1675. Brass, h. 41 cm. Amsterdam, Rijksmuseum, inv. no. BK-18766
50 Food cupboard with ventilation grilles, Northern Netherlands, c. 1610–1630. Wood, metal, paint, h. 100 × w. 80 × d. 42 cm. Arnhem, Dutch Open Air Museum, inv. no. NOM.17788-53
51 Cellar in Petronella Oortman's doll's house (fig. 7)
52 Spouted jug with lid, Northern Netherlands, c. 1650–1675. Pewter, h. 25.8 cm. Terra Verde Collection, inv. no. TVC 4109. Photo: Rijksmuseum, Amsterdam
53 Jug with lid, possibly Delft, 17th century. Pewter, h. 14.4 cm. Amsterdam, Rijksmuseum, inv. no. BK-16511
54 Rummer, Germany or Netherlands (engraving: Northern Netherlands), 1640, inscription on bowl: *Dit is stomachael*. Glass, h. 22.8 cm. Private collection, inv. no. P 154
– PvdM

55 Jan Albertsz Rotius, *Portrait of Meindert Sonck, Agatha van Neck and their Childeren*, 1662. Oil on canvas, 148.3 × 173.3 cm. Antwerp, Museum Mayer van den Bergh, inv. no. mmB.0138. Photo: Bart Hysmans and Michel Wuyts
56a–f Food remains from the cesspit of the Sonck family. Hoorn, Archeologie West-Friesland. Photos: Rijksmuseum, Amsterdam
57a–l Cooking utensils from the cesspit of the Sonck family, Northern Netherlands, 17th century. Lead-glazed red and yellow earthenware, diam. 12.5–36 cm, h. 7–24.5 cm. Hoorn, Archeologie West-Friesland, inv. nos. HOO-498-108-C54, -C56, -C71, -C74, -C78, -C100, -C117, -C118, -C120, -C134, C-136, -C146
58 Reynier Covyn, *Kitchen Interior* (detail), c. 1665–1670. Oil on panel, 36.3 × 41 cm. Dordrecht, Dordrechts Museum, inv. no. DM/930/120; purchase 1930
59a–g Dinnerware from the cesspit of the Sonck family, Delft, Liguria and Jingdezhen, c. 1600–1675. Tin-glazed earthenware, porcelain, diam. 14–24 cm. Hoorn, Archeologie West-Friesland, inv. nos. HOO-498-108-C01, -C02, -C13, -C14, -C15, -C30, -C31
60a–d Waffle beaker and three berkemeyers from the cesspit of the Sonck family, Germany or Netherlands, 17th century. Glass, h. 9–16 cm. Hoorn, Archeologie West-Friesland, inv. nos. HOO-498-108-G18, -G29, -G30, G-35
61a–d Spoons from the cesspit of the Sonck family, Engeland, c. 1610–1630. Copper alloy, l. c. 17.5 cm. Hoorn, Archeologie West-Friesland, inv. nos. HOO-498-108-M04, -M06, -M10, M05
62 Table carpet with the four elements and a strewn floral pattern, Northern Netherlands, c. 1650. Wool, silk, linen, 156 × 206 cm. Amsterdam, Rijksmuseum, inv. no. BK-1975-75; purchased with the support of the Stichting tot Bevordering van de Belangen van het Rijksmuseum
63 Napkin with scenes of three of the four seasons, Northern Netherlands, c. 1650–1675. Linen damask, 101 × 81 cm. Amsterdam, Rijksmuseum, inv. no. BK-2007-19; gift of the museum TwentseWelle

64 Martinus van den Heuvel, Gilt leather panel with Bacchus and Ceres, c. 1670. Gilt leather, 86 × 69 cm. London, Victoria and Albert Museum, inv. no. W.67-1911; © Victoria and Albert Museum, London
65 Anonymous, *Portrait of a Family Saying Grace*, 1627. Oil on panel, 122 × 191 cm. Amsterdam, Rijksmuseum, inv. no. SK-A-4469
66 Dish, Northern Netherlands, c. 1615–1630, inscription: *Eert God*. Lead- and tin-glazed earthenware, diam. 32.9 cm. Amsterdam, Rijksmuseum, inv. no. BK-NM-11715
67 Dish with Madonna and child, Northern Netherlands, c. 1590–1620. Lead- and tin-glazed earthenware, diam. 22 cm. Amsterdam, Rijksmuseum, inv. no. BK-1956-20
68a–g Cooking vessels and drinking cups, Portugal, 17th century. Earthenware, various dimensions. City of Amsterdam, Collectie Monumenten en Archeologie, inv. nos. WLO-116-21, WLO-114-6, WLO-280-3, WLO-110-6, WLO-274-1
69 Regents' room in the Deutzenhofje, Prinsengracht 857, Amsterdam, c. 1695–1700. Photo: Rijksdienst voor het Cultureel Erfgoed, Amersfoort/Kris Roderburg
70a, b Andries Grill, Ewer and basin with Gerard Meerman's family crest, 1649. Silver, h. 27 cm (ewer), diam. 59 cm (basin). Amsterdam, Rijksmuseum, inv. nos. BK-NM-13270-A, -B; on loan from the Regenten van het Deutzenhofje
71a–d Johannes Grill (top left) and Willem Brugman (other three), Four silver candlesticks in the auricular style, 1652. Silver, h. 33 cm. Amsterdam, Rijksmuseum, inv. nos. BK-NM-13269, BK-NM-13268-A to -C; on loan from the Regenten van het Deutzenhofje
72 Attributed to Jan Gerritsz Oosterlingh, Spice box with the coats of arms of Frans Meerman and Maria Ysbrandtsdr De Bije, holding five loose containers, 1616. Silver, h. 7.9 × w. 21.4 × d. 13.4 cm. Amsterdam, Rijksmuseum, inv. no. BK-NM-13271; on loan from the Regenten van het Deutzenhofje
73 Several dishes with miniature fruits from Petronella Oortman's doll's house, c. 1690–1710. Glass,

wax, resp. 0.2–0.9 cm. Amsterdam, Rijksmuseum, inv. nos. BK-NM-1010-353 (fruits) op -207, -342, -347-A, -B, 350-A to -C (dishes)

Housekeeping
p. 148 Detail of the lying-in chamber in Petronella Oortman's doll's house (fig. 7)
74 Map with parcels of land on and near Rapenburg, 1652. Pen in brown, brush in colour, 505 × 640 mm. Leiden, Erfgoed Leiden en Omstreken, inv. no. PV_ PV1012.13
75 Thomas Muntinck, Lolle Jeltes and Berent Alberts, Belt with cutlery case, c. 1614–1651. Silver, l. 99 cm. Schoonhoven, Dutch Silver Museum, inv. no. 10197.01=05. Photo: Eileen van Arkel, Create Studio
76 Joachim Wtewael, *Portrait of Eva Wtewael*, 1628. Oil on panel, 54.7 × 40.5 cm. Utrecht, Centraal Museum, inv. no. 18022
77 Draw-leaf table of Joachim Wtewael, possibly Utrecht, c. 1620–1628. Oak, bog oak, ebony, h. 88 × l. 202.5 × w. 88 cm. Utrecht, Centraal Museum, inv. no. 8465. Photo: Ernst Moritz
78 Linen cupboard of Joachim Wtewael, possibly Utrecht, c. 1620–1630 Oak, ebony, walnut, pear wood, h. 255 × w. 215 × d. 82 cm. Utrecht, Centraal Museum, inv. no. 8441. Photo: Adriaan van Dam
79 Jacobus Vrel, *Woman at the Hearth*, c. 1654–1662. Oil on panel, 36 × 27.5 cm. Amsterdam, Rijksmuseum, inv. no. SK-A-3127; purchased with the support of the Commissie voor Fotoverkoop
80 Fire curfew depicting the explorers searching for the Promised Land, Northern Netherlands, 1637. Red earthenware with decorations in white slip, h. 55 cm. Arnhem, Dutch Open Air Museum, inv. no. N.7978
81 Steven Huygens, Longcase clock, c. 1690–1695. Walnut burr, oak, brass, glass, h. 228.5 × w. 56.5 × d. 32 cm. Amsterdam, Rijksmuseum, inv. no. BK-16479
82 Linen cupboard from Petronella Dunois's doll's house, Northern Netherlands, c. 1676.

Oak, cedar, olive, ebony, iron, gilt, linen, h. 20.5 × w. 19.2 × d. 8.8 cm. Amsterdam, Rijksmuseum, inv. no. BK-14656-175; gift of A.S.M. van Tienhoven-Hacke
83 Sewing pillow, Northern Netherlands, c. 1580–1620. Wood, leather, brass, silk, velvet, l. 22 cm. Amsterdam, Rijksmuseum, inv. no. BK-NM-3582
84 Basket of peat from Petronella Dunois's doll's house, Northern Netherlands, c. 1676. Osier, peat, h. 8.9 cm. Amsterdam, Rijksmuseum, inv. no. BK-14656-198; gift of A.S.M. van Tienhoven-Hacke
85 Peat attic in Petronella Dunois's doll's house (fig. 6)
86 *Field of seventy tiles with animals and herdsmen* (detail), Northern Netherlands, c. 1625–1650. Tinglazed earthenware, 133 × 93 cm. Amsterdam, Rijksmuseum, inv. no. BK-1955-233; gift of the heirs of A. Isaac, Amsterdam
87 Fireback with allegory of the Peace of Münster, Germany, c. 1648–1675, inscription: *PAX/ Ao 1648 24OC*. Metal, 112 × 81 cm. Amsterdam, Rijksmuseum, inv. no. BK-BFR-297
88a, b Attributed to Tobias and David Schaep, Valance and table cloth with the coats of arms of Anna Spiegel and Anthony Oetgens van Waveren, c. 1642–1644. Linen, wool, silk, 26.5 × 183 cm (valance), 190 × 306 cm (table cloth). Amsterdam, Rijksmuseum, inv. nos. BK-16495-A, -B
89 Oil lamp, Northern Netherlands, c. 1650. Lead-glazed yellow earthenware, brass, h. 15.2 cm. Rotterdam, Museum Boijmans Van Beuningen, inv. no. F 5292 a-b (KN&V); gift Coll. Van Beuningen-de Vriese. Photo: Tom Haartsen
90a–c Whisk broom, broom, and scrubber from Petronella Oortman's doll's house, Northern Netherlands, c. 1690–1710. Wood, l. 4.4–18 cm. Amsterdam, Rijksmuseum, inv. nos. BK-NM-1010-301, 300-A, -299
91 Heather whisk, Northern Netherlands, ca.1600–1625. Wood, l. 18 cm. Archeologie Rotterdam, inv. no. 05-54 849 1
92 Attic laundry room from Petronella de la Court's doll's house (fig. 5)

93 Laundry list from Petronella de la Court's doll's house, Northern Netherlands, c. 1680. Poplar, paper, 9.3 × 5.7 cm. Utrecht, Centraal Museum, inv. no. 5000/376
94 Table cloth with Frisian coats of arms and Orpheus surrounded by animals (detail), Haarlem, 1642. Linen, 514 × 212.5 cm. Amsterdam, Rijksmuseum, inv. no. BK-NM-12028-35-B; H. Gluysteen-van Ommeren Bequest, Amsterdam
95 Linen press, Northern Netherlands, c. 1600–1640. Oak, 72 × 44 × 43 cm. Amsterdam, Rijksmuseum, inv. no. BK-1960-27
96 Linen cupboard depicting biblical scenes of Susanna and the elders, Northern Netherlands, c. 1630–1650. Oak, ebony, 212.5 × 159 × 78.5 cm. Amsterdam, Rijksmuseum, inv. no. BK-NM-11448; purchased with the support of the Vereniging Rembrandt
97 Mangle board, Northern Netherlands, 1665, inscription: *WITE×GHE×WOS/ CKEN×EN ×NET×/ IN×DIE×VOV×DAT×/ IS×EEN×SIERAET×V/ OOR×EE× SCHOONN/ E×VROV×1665×*. Wood, l. 85 cm. Delft, Sanny de Zoete, Antiek & Design Linnengoed Collection. Photo: Patrick Nagtegaal
98 Two charcoal irons with stands from Petronella Oortman's doll's house, Northern Netherlands, c. 1690–1710. Rosewood, wrought iron, brass. Amsterdam, Rijksmuseum, inv. nos. BK-NM-1010-260-A, -B, -261-A, -B

Work
p. 192 Detail of the library in Petronella Oortman's doll's house (fig. 7)
99 Anthonie Beerstraten, *The Spaarne River near the De Drie Klaveren Brewery and the Eendjes or Leidse Waterpoort in Haarlem*, 1660. Pencil, brush, 222 × 391 mm. Haarlem, Noord-Hollands Archief, inv. no. 43220
100 Excavated fire place of a brewery – later soapmaking business – in Spuistraat, Amsterdam, 2016. City of Amsterdam, Collectie Monumenten en Archeologie
101 Cornelis Henricxz Duyndam, Floor plan of the De Windhond brewery at the corner of Bakenes-

sergracht and Kokstraat, 1648. Pen, 333 × 458 mm. Haarlem, Noord-Hollands Archief, inv. no. 52059
102 De Porceleyne Fles, Plate, 1637, inscription: *Engeltie Kleijnoven*. Tin-glazed earthenware, diam. 24.5 cm. Aad Schapers Collection, inv. no. 1139
103 De Porceleyne Fles, Plate with bookkeeping notes, 1660–1680. Unglazed earthenware (biscuit), diam. 21 cm. Aad Schapers Collection, inv. no. 1100
104 Jan de Braij, *Portrait of the Married Couple Abraham Casteleyn and Margarieta van Bancken* (detail), 1663. Oil on canvas, 83 × 106.5 cm. Amsterdam, Rijksmuseum, inv. no. SK-A-3280
105 Anonymous, *Portrait of Elisabeth Strouven*, possibly 17th century, pasted into an 18th-century copy of her autobiography. Maastricht, Regionaal Historisch Centrum Limburg, inv. no. 507
106 Bread token, Northern Netherlands, 1677. Brass, diam. 5.9 cm. Utrecht, Museum Catharijneconvent, inv. no. SPKK m14. Photo: Ruben de Heer
107 Frans van Mieris (I), *Saying Grace* (detail), c. 1650–1655. Oil on panel, 34.3 × 40 cm. Washington D.C., National Gallery of Art, inv. no. 2014.136.31; Corcoran Collection (William A. Clark Collection)
108 Whorls, Northern Netherlands, 17th century. Stoneware, earthenware, engobe, diam. 1.5–3.5 cm. Amsterdam, Rijksmuseum, inv. no. BK-NM-5336
109 Tally stick, Northern Netherlands, 1717, inscription: *1717 den 111 Mij. Vrou Volkman. Den 22 Mij het laatste broot gehalt*. Wood, l. 28 cm. Den Bosch, Brabants Historisch Informatie Centrum. Photo: Ben Nienhuis
110 Jan Havicksz Steen, *Portrait of the Baker Couple Arent van Oostwaert and Catharina van Keijserswaert*, 1658. Oil on panel, 37.7 × 31.5 cm. Amsterdam, Rijksmuseum, inv. no. SK-A-390
111 Page from Isaac Pool's diary, 1663. The Hague, Koninklijke Bibliotheek, inv. no. 122 D 4
112 Writing desk, possibly Amsterdam, c. 1670–1685. Oak,

walnut burr, olive, h. 134.5 ×
w. 132 × d. 65 cm. Amsterdam,
Rijksmuseum, inv. no. BK-1985-
20; purchased with the support
of the Belport Familienstiftung
113 Stove decorated with scenes
of the Battle of Gibeon and King
David, Germany, 1660. Cast iron,
h. 76 (without legs) × w. 95 ×
d. 45.5 cm. Amsterdam, Rijksmuseum, inv. no. BK-NM-10256
114 Letter bag, Algiers, c. 1676,
inscription: *De Edele Heer Tomas
Hees Ambassadeur van Staate
Generael der Vereenige Needer-
landen 1676.* Leather, velvet, gold
thread, 16.7 × 28.3 cm. Amsterdam, Rijksmuseum, inv. no. SK-
C-1216; on loan from the Koninklijk Kabinet van Schilderijen
Mauritshuis
115 Michiel van Musscher, *Portrait of Thomas Hees and his Servant
Thomas and Nephews Jan and
Andries Hees*, 1687. Oil on canvas,
76 × 63 cm. Amsterdam, inv. no.
SK-C-1215; on loan from the
Koninklijk Kabinet van Schilderijen Mauritshuis
116 Cornelis Janssens van Ceulen
(II), *Portrait of Johan Boudaen
Courten*, 1668. Oil on canvas,
116 × 94 cm. Amsterdam, Rijks-
museum, inv. no. SK-A-921;
Jonkheer J. de Witte van Citters
Bequest, The Hague
117 Funnel and jars, Northern
Netherlands, c. 1575–1700. Red
earthenware, various dimensions.
City of Amsterdam, Collectie
Monumenten en Archeologie, inv.
nos. TU15-1, SST-20-3, -6, -8, -10

Parenting
p. 224 Detail of the lying-in
chamber in Petronella Oortman's
doll's house (fig. 7)
118 Beaker, Netherlands
(engraving: N. Stampioen), 1656.
Glass, h. 15.4 cm. Amsterdam
Museum, inv. no. KA 5199
119 Layette with the circumcision
of Jesus, Delft, c. 1670–1690. Tin-
glazed earthenware, w. 37.5 cm.
Amsterdam, Rijksmuseum, inv. no.
BK-NM-9504
120 Layette cupboard, Northern
Netherlands, c. 1660–1670.
Oak, walnut, h. 171.5 × w. 118 ×
d. 55.3 cm. Private collection.
Photo: Rijksmuseum

121 Cradle and cradle cover from
Petronella Dunois's doll's house,
Northern Netherlands, c. 1676.
Osier, baleen, wire, glass, silk,
gold thread, l. 10 cm (cradle), 18 ×
18 cm (cradle cover). Amsterdam,
Rijksmuseum, inv. nos. BK-
14656-207, -208; gift of
A.S.M. van Tienhoven-Hacke
122 Cover for cradle or child's bed,
Northern Netherlands, c. 1675–
1700. Silk, wool, 105 × 86 cm.
Amsterdam, Rijksmuseum,
inv. no. BK-2017-18; purchased
with the support of the BankGiro
Lottery and J.W. Edwin vom
Rath Fonds/Rijksmuseum Fonds
123 *Bakermat* from Petronella
Oortman's doll's house, possibly
Halle, c. 1690–1710. Osier, l. 18 cm.
Amsterdam, Rijksmuseum, inv.
no. BK-NM-1010-220
124 Willem van de Passe, *Woman
Cleaning a Child* (detail), 1624.
Engraving, 77 × 111 mm. Amster-
dam, Rijksmuseum, inv. no. RP-P-
1938-1427; F.G. Waller Bequest,
Amsterdam
125 Breast pump, Germany or
Netherlands, c. 1600–1800. Glass,
l. 18.7 cm. Rotterdam, Museum
Boijmans Van Beuningen, inv. no.
F 10117 (KN&V); gift of H.E.
Henkes, 1994. Photo: Tom Haartsen
126 Frans Hals, *Portrait of Catharina Hooft with her Nurse*, 1619–
1620. Oil on canvas, 91.8 × 68.3 cm.
Berlijn, Staatliche Museen zu
Berlin – Gemäldegalerie, inv. no.
801G; purchased from the
collection of Barthold Suermondt,
Aachen, 1874. Photo: Christoph
Schmidt
127 Rattle, possibly Northern
Netherlands, c. 1685–1700. Quartz,
gold, l. 13.4 cm. Amsterdam, Rijksmuseum, inv. no. BK-NM-8994
128 Abraham van den Tempel,
*Portrait of David Leeuw and Cor-
nelia Hooft with their Children*,
1671. Oil on canvas, 190 × 200 cm.
Amsterdam, Rijksmuseum, inv. no.
SK-A-1972; gift of J.H. Willink
van Bennebroek, Oegstgeest
129 *Voorhuis* in Petronella de la
Court's doll's house (fig. 5).
Photo: Adriaan van Dam
130 Johannes Cornelisz Verspronck,
Trompe-l'oeil with a child in a potty
chair, 1654. Oil on panel, 97.4 ×
67 cm. Den Bosch, Noordbrabants

Museum; long-term loan JK Art
Foundation. Photo: Peter Cox
131a–d Jan Kolm, *Portraits of
Hansje, Sieuwert and Anna Kolm
and their Mother Fijtje Lindemans*,
from *Ghedenckboeck*, 1618–1630.
Amsterdam City Archives, inv. no.
15030/77884
132a–f Various *poppengoed*: fire
curfew, saucepan, cooking pot,
tripod vessel, chamber pot and
candlestick, Northern Netherlands,
resp. 1600–1800. Tin-glazed red
and yellow earthenware, pipe
clay, metal, h. 5.3–17.4 cm. City
of Amsterdam, Collectie Monumenten en Archeologie, inv. nos.
TAAN-4-2, LEG2-49, KG17-6,
NZK5-206-15, WEY-28-4, WLO-
17-36, WLO-273-23, WLO-
HAH1-1, WLO-312-3
133 Emanuel de Witte, *Portrait of
Adriana van Heusden and Daughter
at the Fishmarket* (detail), c. 1662.
Oil on canvas, 57.1 × 64.1 cm.
London, The National Gallery,
inv. no. NG3682
134 Child's sword, Northern
Netherlands, 1639. Iron, brass,
l. 75 cm. Loosdrecht, Kasteel-
Museum Sypesteyn. Photo:
Graham Pascoe
135a, b Two letters from Annetje
Jochems to her father Jochem
Jansen, May 1672. Kew, The
National Archives, inv. nos. HCA
30/1062/2/35, HCA 30/1062/2/
32bii. Photos: Huygens Institute,
Amsterdam/ National Archives
of the Netherlands, The Hague
136 J. Heuvelman and W. van der
Laech, *Stichtich ABC tot nut der
jeucht geschreven*, 1659. Haarlem,
Noord-Hollands Archief, Library,
185 H 11
137 Anonymous, *Susanna and the
Elders*, 1781–1800. Engraving,
314 × 386 mm. Amsterdam, Rijksmuseum, inv. no. KOG-ZG-1-
19A-181; on loan from the
Koninklijk Oudheidkundig
Genootschap
138a Medal given by Isaac
Pontanus to his grandson on his
eighth birthday, Northern Netherlands, 1688, inscription (translated from Latin): G*row up, child,
in virtue before God, in love for
your mother, dear to your family
through affection, to good people
through righteousness, harming no*

one, nourished by honest study, in your fearless character equal to good fortune or ill, righteous as long as you live and blessed after death. May long-suffering God hear these fervent prayers! Be always the best and stand out above the rest. Gold, diam. 9 cm. Amsterdam, Rijksmuseum, inv. no. NG-2008-41-B; gift from the Vereniging Rembrandt, with support from TEFAF and the Remonstrants Church Rotterdam

138b Michiel van Musscher, *Double Portrait of Isaac Pontanus and Hendrik van Beek*, 1689. Oil on silver-plated brass, diam. 9 cm. Amsterdam, Rijksmuseum, inv. no. NG-2008-40; gift from the Vereniging Rembrandt, with support from TEFAF and the Remonstrants Church Rotterdam

139 Sampler, Friesland, 1677. Linen, 32 × 62.5 cm. Amsterdam, Rijksmuseum, inv. no. BK-1967-88; gift of J. Haga-André de la Porte, Amsterdam

Engagement

140 Wedding casket of Frans Reyniers Tempelar and Yfke Tjesma, Northern Netherlands, 1633, inscription: *Blijft hoop, geloof, En liefd' ons bij:/ Soo houdt ons Godt van tweedracht vrij.; Waer trou falieert: ist heel verkeert: Bemint: daer ghy trou in vindt./ Als Jacob Rachel vindt. Soo drinckt hijt' vee met lust:/En gaet bij Laban t'huijs en neemt aldaer sijn rust./ Geen heyl int houlyck grooter dan/ D'eenstemmichheyt van vrou en man.* Silver, h. 10 cm. Harlingen, Gemeentemuseum Het Hannemahuis, inv. no. 5933. Photo: Albertine Dijkema

Marriage

141 Salom Italia (decorative frame), Ketubah for the marriage of Isaac de Pinto and Rachel Rovigo, 1654. Amsterdam, Joods Museum, inv. no. CV0916; Ets Haim – Livraria Montezinos Collection

142 Cutlery set of Anna Roelofs de Vrij, possibly Amsterdam, c. 1607–1608. Enamelled gold, damascened iron, l. 19.2 cm (knife), 18.5 cm (fork). Amsterdam, Rijksmuseum, inv. no. BK-2024-7; purchased with the

support of the VriendenLoterij and H.B. van der Ven, The Hague

143 Bridal crown, Northern Netherlands, 1667. Gold and silver thread, glass, h. 6 cm. Amsterdam Museum, inv. no. KB 1001; on loan from Backer Stichting. Photo: Rijksmuseum

144 Wedding ring of Michiel Block and Aeltjen Ansloo, Northern Netherlands, 1658, inscription: *Aeltien Anslo/ Michiel Block/ getrouwt 13 October/ Anno 1658.* Gold, enamel, diam. 16 mm. London, Paula Weideger Collection. Photo: Sonia Butler, S.J. Phillips Ltd

145 Bowl covered with symbols of matrimony, Bergen op Zoom, 1609, inscription: *GODT IS ONS TROU GHEWIS IN ROU 1609.* Red earthenware with decorations in white slip, w. 25.1 cm. Amsterdam, Rijksmuseum, inv. no. BK-KOG-580; on loan from the Koninklijk Oudheidkundig Genootschap

Birth

146 Gerrit Stoffels, Jack in the cellar, c. 1600–1650. Silver, h. 14.5 cm. Amsterdam, Rijksmuseum, inv. no. BK-NM-591

147 Adriaen van de Venne, in Jacob Cats, *Houwelyck, dat is de gansche gelegentheyt des echtenstaets*, 1625, n.p. Amsterdam, Rijksmuseum Research Library, 327 J 23

148 Lying-in chamber in Petronella Oortman's doll's house (fig. 7)

149 Rummer, Germany or Netherlands (engraving: Northern Netherlands), c. 1675–1700, inscription on bowl: *De Gesontheijt van de Kraamvrouw.* Glass, h. 26 cm. The Hague, Kunstmuseum Den Haag, inv. no. OGL-1954-0031

Baptism

150 *Doopluur*, Northern Netherlands, c. 1675–1700. Silk, wool, h. 116 cm. Amsterdam, Rijksmuseum, inv. no. BK-2017-17; purchased with the support of the BankGiro Lottery and J.W. Edwin Vom Rath Fonds/Rijksmuseum Fonds

151 Engraved square bottle, Northern Netherlands, 1601. Glass, h. 11.4 cm. City of Amsterdam,

Collectie Monumenten en Archeologie, inv. no. KON-34-35

152 Anonymous, *Mourning Portrait of Aelke van Juckema*, 1607. Oil on panel, 55.5 × 73 cm. Franeker, Museum Martena; on loan from Stichting Eysinga-Harinxma

Death

153 Gesina ter Borch, 'Minnaersklacht', *Poëzie-album*, c. 1654, fol. 67r. Ink, watercolour, 313 × 204 cm. Amsterdam, Rijksmuseum, inv. no. BI-1890-1952-67; purchased with the support of the Vereniging Rembrandt

154 Bier for a bakers' guild, Friesland, 1666, inscription: *D'backers-baer. Proeft, eedt. anno 1666./ als adam door den fal voor godt stondt naekt en bloodt/ sin hij en wij te saem gewesen tot der doot/ maer lof sij jesu christ ghij twede adam groodt/ die door u bietter doot ons bringht in abrams schoot. Rom. 5/ het korn twelck uit der aerden spruit tot foedtsel van de menschen moet doet het malen fijn den backer na sijn wens/ den backer knet en backt het gaer tot smenschen onderhout/ dees baer die is gemaekt alleen voor backers jonck en out.* Wood, l. 434 cm. Hindeloopen, Museum Hindeloopen/Workum, St Gertrudis Church, Workum. Photo: Els de Bok

155 Funeral medal of the carpenters' guild, Northern Netherlands, 1682. Tinned copper, diam. 2.5 cm. Nieuw-Dordrecht, Museum Collectie Brands

Winter Festivals

156 *Hanukkiah*, Northern Netherlands, c. 1700. Brass, h. 32.8 cm. Amsterdam, Jewish Museum, inv. no. M000206

157 Experiens Sillemans, *Le jeu des hauts-crieurs du Roy boit/ 't Vermakelyck drie Coningen spel*, c. 1645–1701. Engraving, 258 × 322 mm. Amsterdam, Rijksmuseum, inv. no. RP-P-1908-1934; gift of H.P. Gerritsen, The Hague

158 Epiphany crown, Northern Netherlands, 17th century. Woodcut, 156 × 366 mm. Amsterdam, Rijksmuseum, inv. no. RP-P-2024-248; purchased with the support

of the F.G. Waller-Fonds
159 Jan Havicksz Steen, *The Feast of St Nicolas*, 1665–1668. Oil on canvas, 82 × 70.5 cm. Amsterdam, Rijksmuseum, inv. no. SK-A-385
160 Decorative discs, Northern Netherlands, c. 1675–1725. Pipe clay, resp. c. 12 × 15 cm. Deventer, Provinciaal Depot voor Bodemvondsten Overijssel. Photo: Archeologie Deventer

At Home
p. 294 The entrance hall in Petronella Oortman's doll's house (fig. 7)
161 Claes Jansz Visscher, *T'huys best*, etching from Roemer Visscher, *Sinnepoppen*, 1614, p. 98. Amsterdam, Rijksmuseum Research Library, 325 G 12
162 Dish painted blue with chinoiserie decoration, Delft, c. 1650–1675. Tin-glazed earthenware, diam. 33 cm. Amsterdam, Rijksmuseum, inv. no. BK-1972-78
163 Emanuel de Witte, *Interior of the Portuguese Synagogue in Amsterdam*, 1680. Oil on canvas, 110 × 99 cm. Amsterdam, Rijksmuseum, inv. no. SK-A-3738
164 The *zaal* in Petronella Oortman's doll's house (fig. 7)
165 Adriaen Pietersz van de Venne, *Interior of a Room*, c. 1620. Chalk, ink, 196 × 324 mm. Amsterdam, Rijksmuseum, inv. no. RP-T-1891-A-2471
166a, b François Coppens, *Park Landscape with a Horseman and an Elegant Company* and *Park Landscape with Seated Couple and Resting Hunters*, c. 1685–1740. Wool, silk, linen, resp. 356 × 497 and 351 × 558 cm. Amsterdam, Rijksmuseum, inv. nos. BK-16440-A, -B
167a, b Philip van Dijk after Caspar Netscher, *Portraits of Johan Boudaen Courten and Anna Maria Hoeufft*, c. 1690–1753. Oil on canvas, 49 × 40 cm. Amsterdam, Rijksmuseum, inv. nos. SK-A-901, -902; Jonkheer J. de Witte van Citters Bequest, The Hague
168a–d Set of two mirrors and two gueridons with the coats of arms of Johan Boudaen Courten and Anna Maria Hoeufft, Northern Netherlands, c. 1680–1700.

Mirrors: gilded lime wood, glass, resp. 150 × 115 and 145 × 110 cm. Middelburg, Zeeuws Museum, inv. no. G2224 (Boudaen's mirror); Amsterdam, Rijksmuseum, inv. no. BK-NM-11729; A.A. des Tombe Bequest, The Hague (Hoeufft's mirror). Gueridons: gilded and polychromed lime wood, h. 115 cm. Amsterdam, Rijksmuseum, inv. nos. BK-NM-3277, -3278; Jonkheer J. de Witte van Citters Bequest, The Hague. Photomontage: Rijksmuseum
169a–i Anonymous, *Portraits of Guillaume Courten* (1575, oil on panel, 45.1 × 33.4) and *Margarita Cassier* (1616, oil on panel, 130.7 × 95.3 cm) Attributed to Salomon Mesdach, *Portraits of Margarita Courten* (1625, oil on panel, 102.8 × 74.4 cm), *Pieter Courten* (1630, oil on panel, 71.3 × 58 cm), *Hortensia del Prado* (ca. 1625, oil on panel, 72.5 × 58.6 cm), *Pieter Boudaen Courten* (1619, oil on panel, 104.5 × 73.5 cm), *Catharina Fourmenois* (1619, oil on panel, 104.7 × 72.9 cm), *Jacob Pergens* (1619, oil on panel, 94.7 × 69.1 cm) and *Anna Boudaen Courten* (1619, oil on panel, 94.6 × 68.9 cm). Amsterdam, Rijksmuseum, inv. nos. SK-A-904, -905, -2073, -2074, -910, -2068, -2069, -918, -919; Jonkheer J. de Witte van Citters Bequest, The Hague
170 Attributed to Salomon Mesdach, *Portrait of Peter Courten*, 1617. Oil on canvas, 192 × 106.5 cm. Amsterdam, Rijksmuseum, inv. no. SK-A-913; Jonkheer J. de Witte van Citters Bequest, The Hague
171 Tazza with the imprisonment of Guillaume Courten, London?, c. 1568–1597, inscription: *Den 2 Marcy in meenen 1567 dacht duc dalve Guillaume Courten te beroven Sijn leven Maar godt heeft den 29 Marty 1567 door sijn huysvroue Marghuerite victorie ghegheven*. Silver, h. 16 cm × diam. 15 cm. Amsterdam, Rijksmuseum, inv. no. BK-NM-3220; Jonkheer J. de Witte van Citters Bequest, The Hague
172 *Statenbijbel* (the earliest Dutch-language Bible translation) from 1660 with genealogical notes made by the Van Aylva family,

1665–1752. Brass, leather, paper, ink, 31 × 46 cm. Leeuwarden, Fries Museum, inv. no. PL2003-314
173 Andreas Hyperius, *Kalendier der Bybelen* (trans. Johannes Gerobulus), Amsterdam 1628. Amsterdam, Allard Pierson, University of Amsterdam, inv. no. O 63-6024 (5)
174a, b Attributed to De Klaauw, Two altar vases, 1667, inscriptions: *IHS* (front)/*1667* (back); *MAR* (front)/*1667* (back). Tin-glazed earthenware, h. resp. 22.5 and 22.8 cm. Delft, Museum Prinsenhof, inv. nos. B 49-19, -20; on loan via Stichting Kerkelijk Erfgoed Delft. Photo: Tom Haartsen
175 Tokens, Northern Netherlands, 17th century. Earthenware, various dimensions. City of Amsterdam, Collectie Monumenten en Archeologie, inv. nos. NZR2.00635BWM001, NZR2.00664BWM001, NZR2.00269BWM001, NZD1.00049BWM003, NZD1.00168BWM002, NZD1.00087BWM004, NZD1.00097BWM002
176 Game board from Petronella Oortman's doll's house, Northern Netherlands, c. 1690–1710. Walnut, olive, ebony, palm wood, bone, 5.8 × 5.8 cm. Amsterdam, Rijksmuseum, inv. no. BK-NM-1010-276
177 Anonymous, Game of the Goose with the rules of the game, c. 1625–1650. Engraving, 419 × 476 mm. Amsterdam, Rijksmuseum, inv. no. RP-P-1893-A-18144
178 Welcome glass, Netherlands (engraving: Willem Mooleyser), c. 1675–1700, inscription on bowl: *De Wellekomst van de Vriende*. Glass, h. 14.8 cm. Private collection, inv. no. P 379 – PvdM
179 Gesina ter Borch, 'Rosamonde mijn beminde', *Poëziealbum*, c. 1654, fol. 54r. Pen in brown, brush in black and colour, 313 × 204 mm. Amsterdam, Rijksmuseum, inv. no. BI-1890-1952-54; purchased with the support of the Vereniging Rembrandt
180 Attributed to Johannes Ruckers, Virginal, 1640, inscription: *MUSICA LABORUM/ DULCE LEVAMEN*. Poplar, spruce, oak, bone, paper, metal,

leather, 106 × 42.5 × 78 cm.
Amsterdam, Rijksmuseum, inv. no.
BK-KOG-595; on loan from the
Koninklijk Oudheidkundig
Genootschap
181 Cornelia van Marle, *The Tea
Party*, 1689. Oil on canvas, 63 ×
51 cm. Zwolle, Stichting het
Vrouwenhuis, inv. no. 67
182 Tea table from Petronella
Oortman's doll's house (painting
attributed to Willem Hendrik
Wilhelmus van Royen), c. 1690.
Softwood, h. 13 cm. Amsterdam,
Rijksmuseum, inv. no. BK-NM-
1010-27

index

The numbers in **bold** refer to photographs; others are page numbers

lenders

Alkmaar, Municipality of Alkmaar,
Archeologisch Centrum
Amsterdam, Collectie Monu-
menten en Archeologie
Amsterdam, Deutzenhofje
Amsterdam, Jewish Museum
Collection
Amsterdam, Six Collection
Antwerp, Museum Mayer
van den Bergh
Arnhem, Dutch Open Air
Museum
Benthuizen, Terra Verde
Collection
Castricum, Province of North
Holland, Huis van Hilde
Delft, Sanny de Zoete, Antiek &
Design Linnengoed
Delft, Michel Arnold Verschuyl
Den Bosch, Brabants Historisch
Informatie Centrum (BHIC)
Den Bosch, Het Noordbrabants
Museum
Den Bosch, JK Art Foundation
The Hague, KB, national library
of the Netherlands
The Hague, Kunstmuseum
Den Haag
Harlingen, Gemeentemuseum
Het Hannemahuis
Hindeloopen, Museum
Hindeloopen
Hoorn, Municipality of Hoorn,
Archeologie West-Friesland
Leeuwarden, Fries Museum
London, Victoria and Albert
Museum
Middelburg, Zeeuws Museum
Private collection – PvdM
Richmond, The National Archives
Rotterdam, Archeologie
Rotterdam
Rotterdam, Museum Boijmans
Van Beuningen
Rotterdam, Museum Rotterdam
Schoonhoven, Dutch Silver
Museum
Utrecht, Centraal Museum
Workum, St Gertrudiskerk
Zwolle, Municipality of Zwolle

And all private lenders who
wish to remain anonymous

acknowledgements

We would like to thank our reading committee – Thijs Boers, Danielle van den Heuvel, Marika Keblusek and Marlies Stoter – for their critical eye and their guidance at crucial moments, as well as for their enthusiasm and faith in this project. We are grateful to the Vereniging Hendrick de Keyser and Isja Finaly for offering us the finest meeting place imaginable at Huis van Brienen in Amsterdam.

The Strategic Partnership Programme between the Victoria and Albert Museum and the Rijksmuseum, initiated in part by Tristram Hunt, has led to a lively and ongoing exchange with Jenny Saunt and many of her colleagues.

We could always rely on the extensive knowledge of our former colleagues Reinier Baarsen and Bianca du Mortier, even after their retirement. Our intern Marieke Sanders showed great enthusiasm and made a substantial contribution to our research and our network.

Although Willemijn Fock, emeritus professor of decorative arts at Leiden University, did not live to experience the making of this book, her fundamental research on domestic culture remains a major source of inspiration.

Many others have also assisted us: the institutions that offered us access to their expertise and collections, the speakers and participants in the afternoon seminars we organized in cooperation with the Leiden University Centre for the Arts in Society (LUCAS), the specialists who opened our eyes to their disciplines, the individuals who welcomed us into their homes, and numerous colleagues. Our thanks to Alex Anselmgeest, Hugo ter Avest, the board of the Backer Stichting, Michiel Bartels, Jessica van den Berg, Dirk Jan Biemond, Naomi Bisping, Peter Bitter, Irma Boom, Manon Borst, Judith Brouwer, Denise Campbell, Aernout van Citters, Jacques Dane, Alexandra van Dongen, Natalie Dubois, Wouter van Elburg, Elif Ergün, Elke Finkh, Menno Fitski, Karen Gamester, Ad Geerdink, Esther van Gelder, Judith van Gent, Anne Gerritsen, Leen Groen, Julie de Groot, Jasmijn ter Haar, Mieneke te Hennepe, Katie Heyning, Eveline Holsappel, Maria Holtrop, Merit Hondelink, Jacco Hooikammer, Olivia Horsfall Turner, Tim Huisman, Michel Hulst, Ranjith Jayasena, Vanessa Jones, Marieke de Jong, Prosper de Jong, Nancy de Jong-Lambregts, Marthe Kes, Egge Knol, Eloy Koldeweij, Barbera van Kooij, Saskia Kuus, Suzanne Lambooy, Kitty and Anna Laméris, Friso Lammertse, Katell Laveant, Nora Leijen, Clé Lesger, Tirtsah Levie Bernfeld, David McKay, Suzan Meijer and the object and painting conservation teams, Piet van der Meulen, Tijmen Moesker, Esther Mourits, Christianne Muusers, Judith Noorman, Oda Nuijs, Jeanine Otten, Koen Ottenheym, Angus Patterson, Frans Pegt, Pascale Pere, Frederik Pesch, Hans Piena, Josse Pietersma, Jet Pijzel-Dommisse, Benjamin Roberts, Pieter Roelofs, Laura Roscam Abbing and her colleagues, Amy van Saane, Caroline van Santen, Aad and Rob Schapers, Eddy Schavemaker, Anne Schenkels, Rutger Schimmelpenninck and the board of the Deutzenhofje, Inge Schippers, Erik Schmitz, Renate Schoon, Ben Schräder, Christiaan Schrickx, Anne-Marie Segeren, Bas Six, Ellen Slob, Leonore van Sloten, Tim Smeets, Kim Snapper, Jo Spaans, Jacco Spil, Giovanni Paolo Di Stefano, Larry Steigrad, James Symonds, Luke Syson, Lucinda Timmermans, Ron Tousain, Jørgen Veerkamp, Ruben Verwaal, Karin Vingerhoets, Pieter Vlaardingerbroek, Irma de Vries, Anniek Vrij, Laurien van der Werff, Tim Zeedijk, Sanny de Zoete, and Saskia Zwiers.

Finally, in a book about home, we would like to thank all the members of our own households, large and small, who supported us through this book's many drafts.